Michael Schmaus

THE ESSENCE OF CHRISTIANITY

MICHAEL SCHMAUS

Professor of Dogmatic Theology
at the University of Munich

THE ESSENCE

of

CHRISTIANITY

Foreword by Kevin McNamara

SCEPTER

CHICAGO-DUBLIN-LONDON

THIS EDITION PRINTED BY
THE KERRYMAN LTD., TRALEE, IRELAND
FOR SCEPTER PUBLISHERS LIMITED
144 LOWER BAGGOT STREET . DUBLIN
AND SCEPTER PRESS
5544 WOODLAWN AVENUE . CHICAGO

First Published 1961

NIHIL OBSTAT: THOMAS F. O'REILLY,
VIC. GEN., CENSOR LIBRORUM.

IMPRIMI POTEST: ✠ JOANNES CAROLUS,
ARCHIEP. DUBLINEN.,
HIBERNIAE PRIMAS,
DUBLINI DIE 15 NOV. 1960.

TRANSLATION BY J. HOLLAND SMITH

CONTENTS

FOREWORD

Monsignor Michael Schmaus, the author of the work here presented
in English translation, is perhaps the best-known German theologian
of the present day. A member of the Roman Pontifical Theological
Academy, he has been Professor of Dogmatics at the University of
Munich since the war. He came to Munich from the University of
Münster in Westphalia, where he had held the Chair of Dogmatics
since 1933. His massive, five-volume *Katholische Dogmatik*[1], the
fifth edition of which was completed in 1959, has been enthusiast-
ically received both in Germany and abroad, and is at present being
translated into various languages. Despite the magnitude of the
task, it can be only a matter of time until an English translation of
the *Dogmatik* is made available. Meanwhile English readers are
fortunate in having an excellent introduction to his thought in this
translation of *Vom Wesen des Christentums*, the first work by Schmaus
to appear in English. More than an introduction, it presents in
summary form much that is developed at length and scientifically
elaborated in the voluminous pages of the *Dogmatik*.

Monsignor Schmaus has made it his life-task to present the
truths of the Gospel in all their fulness and saving power to the
minds and hearts of his contemporaries. To this purpose all his
academic work is directly or indirectly subservient: his lectures to
large audiences in the University of Munich, his original research
in medieval theology, his work as director of the Grabmann
Institute, founded by him at Munich for the study and publication
of medieval theological and philosophical texts, his prominent role
in the Catholic-Protestant theological discussions sponsored by
the *Una Sancta* movement in Germany, his numerous writings
culminating in the comprehensive *Dogmatik*. For Monsignor

[1] M. Schmaus, *Katholische Dogmatik*, Munich, 1954-59 (Fifth Edition).

Schmaus is keenly conscious that theology, however faithful it be to its intellectual task of analyzing and organizing the faith, is failing in an essential function if it does not at the same time serve the needs of contemporary life. His own theological writings are vibrant with the force and urgency of the Gospel message. To read them is to come into contact with a personality possessed by a powerful vision of the truth and absolutely convinced of the relevance of that vision to the human race in the present moment of its history.

Recently a group of scholars drawn from among Professor Schmaus' many friends and admirers in Germany and elsewhere and including several of his former pupils presented him with an imposing *Festschrift* to mark the celebration of his sixtieth birthday. The volume, whose varied contents were an eloquent tribute to the Professor's contribution to many diverse branches of theological science, was named *Theology in History and in Our Time*[1], a title which underlines the twofold programme he has constantly kept before him: an exact and deep study of the sources of Christian theology with a view to placing the great heritage of the past as fully as possible at the service of present-day Christians. This programme is indeed no more than the essential pre-requisite of a genuine and fruitful theology at any time, and if the twentieth century has witnessed a true renewal of theology, this is due to the energetic and loyal pursuit of precisely this programme in many centres of Catholic scholarship. Few contemporary theologians, however, have laboured so successfully as Monsignor Schmaus. A rare gift of synthesis, a penetrating and original theological insight, a readiness to accept every genuine advance in knowledge, irrespective of its source—qualities such as these combined with a vast erudition and an unwearying devotion to the task of theology have led to an impressive, indeed spectacular, yet wholly solid achievement.

For the general educated public, for whom the greater part of his writings are intended, Schmaus' works have the added advantage of being written in contemporary idiom, which gives them direct access to the mind of the modern reader. The style of exposition

[1] *Theologie in Geschichte und Gegenwart.* Edited by Johann Auer and Herman Volk, Munich, 1957.

too is leisurely and full, the movement of thought unhurried, giving the reader time to assimilate each new idea as it comes. Hence the great success of Schmaus' writings not only among the clergy but among the serious Catholic—and non-Catholic—reading public, for whom the technical language and compressed style of much theological writing, even in the vernacular, is a considerable obstacle.

In recent years the desire for an English translation of the works of Professor Schmaus has been frequently expressed. It is good that a beginning has now been made. Scepter Publishers, who have already shown praiseworthy enterprise in publishing translations of important Catholic works from the Continent, have done English readers a valuable service in introducing them to the thought of this most modern of Catholic thinkers. Already the influence of Schmaus is vast and extends far beyond Germany. One senses a genuine spirit of discipleship in the response which contact with his thought and with his dynamic personality has evoked in students of many nationalities. Many of these have attended his lectures in Munich or taken part in the popular discussions and study-circles which are held in the Professor's house in the Munich *Universitätsplatz*. Here the Professor stimulates and guides discussion on a wide range of topics, showing his students how the Christian revelation may be used to illuminate every human problem and harmonized with even the most revolutionary discoveries of the natural sciences.

In the work which now lies before us in English translation the author reveals the inner core of the Christian message, setting it forth eloquently and with compelling power. Putting aside as inadequate and ultimately misleading some rather commonly held theories on what constitutes the essence of Christianity, he offers us the following concise statement of the position which he elaborates throughout the book: 'In its inmost essence Christianity is the living Christ who is present in the Church continually until the last day'. This theme is brought into ever sharper focus as the author turns his attention to successive Christian mysteries, which are brilliantly expounded in a harmonious blend of traditional teaching with the insights of modern thought. Special emphasis is laid on the significance of these mysteries for man's personal fulfilment and security, the anguished search for which in the modern world is mocked by so many false hopes and illusory promises. Throughout these pages the reader will find himself constantly in the presence of those major themes which are the central pre-occupation of so much contemporary literature: the sovereign value and dignity of human personality, the fateful significance of human freedom, the ultimate meaning of history, the enigmas of suffering and death, the absolute necessity of love and of vigorous personal decision in favour of goodness and truth. Sympathy and understanding characterize the author's approach to these grave problems, which lie at the heart of the present crisis of humanity. With clarity and vigour he presents the Christian answer to man's difficulties and shows how it alone makes due allowance for the complex demands of human nature. In sharp contrast to all human philosophies and to the many pale and shrunken 'gospels' which today pass for the Christian message, Professor Schmaus presents the divine plan of salvation in all its supernatural power and radiance, from its origins in the eternal designs of the Blessed Trinity to its final consummation in the life of glory. He shows that only by giving itself to God in the love of Christ can the human personality reach fulfilment, as it makes its way through successive crises to the final catastrophe of death, the necessary condition of man's entry into final blessedness.

Here, powerfully stated, is a theology of 'transcendence', in which the transience of the present world is constantly stressed and we are bidden direct our eyes to the future time for the realization of our deepest longings and the final solution to the many enigmas of history. Nevertheless, this theology is far from making light of the world or turning man away from the tasks of civilization and progress, from the problems of social, economic and political life. The author rather shows that it is man's God-given duty to build an ordered society and to master the forces and secrets of nature, thus sanctifying the world together with himself. There is here, then, inspiration in abundance for a programme of Christian humanism, which will be a true humanism precisely because it is Christian. For as such it will escape being deluded by the mirage of an earthly paradise or by the intoxicating myth of man's constant progress in knowledge, dignity and power;

and it will be safe too from the chilling pessimism that would despair of finding any meaning in human history or would counsel complete withdrawal from the life of the world. For it will be guided by the twofold vision of Christ's Cross and His glorious Resurrection, which alone set the universe and human history in proper perspective.

Kevin McNamara.

St. Patrick's College,
Maynooth.

PREFACE

The following pages are a slightly enlarged recapitulation of lectures read by Professor Schmaus before an audience drawn from all faculties of the University of Munich in the winter semester of 1945/46, the first semester after the collapse of Nazi Germany. In them the Faculty of Theology of the University of Munich spoke to a wider public for the first time after a silence of seven years. The gravity of the part theology has to play in the framework of a university is such that it has a special responsibility towards everyone. Hence immediately it was free to speak again, the Faculty of Theology felt bound to look out beyond the walls of its lecture halls and turn to all those who were expecting and demanding enlightenment from Christian theology in the profound darkness of those days. The lectures were read in one of the few remaining lecture halls of the university. Their background was heaps of rubble that had once been the University of Munich. The ruined waste that had once been Munich's Ludwigstrasse and the mountains of rubble throughout Germany gave rise to the question: 'What has remained of all that used to be?' It became clear that there is nothing in this world that is not exposed to the danger of destruction. Everything born of the earth is menaced by death. Death and destruction are built into the strongest walls. Every earthly foundation is shaky, and nothing stands firm. Everyone who stood in the midst of this desert of destruction was tormented by the question: 'What has survived? Has anything? Where is the foundation on which we can stand fast and hold out?' After the re-opening of the University of Munich, Professor Schmaus believed it his duty to answer such questions as these for the widest audience possible. He looked for the answers in giving an account of what we understand by Christianity.

The primary purpose of this account of Christianity is the establishment of a spiritual outlook, in which we can begin to live again. It therefore renounces the help of the customary devices of scholars. The author was able to rely on many previous studies for help: he would especially like to mention his predecessors Karl Adam and Romano Guardini. The lectures are also an attempt to come to terms positively with Protestant enquiries into the nature of Christianity, accepting from them what the lecturer thought right in them, and passing over in silence what seemed wrong. He feels himself especially indebted with regard to work done on the theology of the New Testament.

Academic demonstration of much that is said here is to be given in a work on the last things to be published shortly at Regensburg, or is to be found in the author's work on dogmatic theology.

CHAPTER ONE

AN OUTLINE

At the end of the war, we were under the impression that nothing man had made would survive the whirlpool that was sucking everything down into itself. Today, however, we see that many things have survived, and the question now is whether among them is that reality we can call God. In former times we used to believe that if everything vanished, he, the only saviour, would remain. But this does not seem quite so certain today. Indeed, our primary question—and it is a difficult and very important one—is whether the God, who was manifested in Christ and has been immanent in every age since, still lives today. Did he not die in many hearts during the war, and has he not died in many since then, in as much as he has lost his power over them?

As early as two generations ago, Nietzsche believed it possible to prove God had died. Perhaps at that time the certificate of death was issued prematurely. But would it not be to a large degree true today? Was not God also sucked down by the vortex that destroyed everything? Did not God's promises, and Christianity which lives on them, receive a mortal wound like everything else? For has not Christianity too broken down? In the final reckoning only nothingness may be left. Then we should be living in a nihilistic world. What then is Christianity? What does it want? What does it do?

It may surprise us to realize that Christianity has never hitherto given a final and conclusive account of itself. To the question as to what it is, Christians and non-Christians give answers of the most varied kind, sometimes mutually contradictory.

The reason for this variety and disparity is not any lack of clarity and precision in what we call Christianity, but the fulness and variety of its essence and outward appearance. It is hardly possible

15

for the human mind to comprehend the totality of what constitutes Christianity. As a result of its inadequacy, it is exposed to the temptation to seize on this or that characteristic from the fulness of Christianity and forget that it was only part of an interrelated whole. In this way it may come to partial and erroneous conceptions of the essence of Christianity. Often there is still in them, however, a grain of truth in so far as they are built up on one of Christianity's essential characteristics. The error lies in that the validity of such a characteristic is dependent on its position relative to the whole. A few characteristics, true, but from which derive incomplete and therefore biased answers are considered below.

Thus it was once claimed that Christianity is truth, the light needed by the soul. And so, indeed, it is. Christianity throws light on life and the world, and so furnishes the illumination whereby mankind is enabled to pass through life and history without being forced into despair.

The significance of this function of Christianity becomes clear if we take into account the scale of the calamity that brought about the revolt from truth. Annihilation of truth implies the extinction of light. If a man shuns the truth, he plunges into darkness. The eclipse of the mind to which the denial of truth leads is the mother of destruction, because it violates the mind's true being. The creator of catastrophe is the lie.

The role played by Christianity in human history is therefore far-reaching and beneficial, for it kindles and tends the light of truth, in the world of darkness and lies. But Christianity has not come into the world merely to be the truth, for truth alone would not be enough for men. When truth exists alone, the heart remains cold and solitary. If it existed alone, men would have to step out into an icy world in which they could not breathe. Truth is indispensable for the redemption of men, but it alone cannot redeem. In fact, Christianity is more than, and other than, the sum total of all truths, although it is also this and although, as history shows, truth—ultimate and essential truth—is lost wherever it is not guarded by the might of Christianity.

From another point of view Christianity may appear to the attentive observer to be a particular system of morals. It sets up a programme indispensable to mankind if it is to have a way of life

16

truly worthy of men. By continually telling us: 'Thou shalt', it confirms the dignity of humanity and the ordering of human society. Without its programme, both the individual and society would sink into chaos. Revolt against its imperatives is the beginning of those byroads and sideturnings at the ends of which are piled up the ruins and rubbish-heaps of the world.

But although the Christian imperatives are so essential and indispensable, Christianity does not consist in them either. Nor, if it were merely a moral code, could it help men in any real way in the realization of those aspirations which arise continually in their hearts, for it could then lead only to correctness, to legal rectitude, which would force a man to carry on a narrow and harassing existence, for which he had received instructions on all questions of conduct. That would mean the end of all life, and would lead to the state of things Rainer Maria Rilke has called the ready-made Church: tidy, shut and disillusioning as a Post Office on Sunday.

A third attempt to define the essence of Christianity is to be found in the view that Christianity is love. Love is, of course, a feature characteristic of Christianity. To say that Christianity is love may, indeed, lead to the heart of the matter. The scope and importance of this essential characteristic shine out brightly from the darker background of human history. Wherever hate speaks the first word, death rules. History shows hate to be the murderer of human happiness and of the social order. Where it arises, a gateway is opened for invasion by demons. It is the great destroyer of the world. It changes the world into hell. Where it is organized into a social system, it makes the district it rules into a great concentration camp. The significance of love now becomes obvious: it is able to make the world fair and bright.

In his work *Das Reich der Dämonen*, Frank Thiess says that three things are necessary for a fully human life: beauty, order and love. Beauty, the radiance of truth was, he says, given to the world by the Greeks. The creators of order, the expression of law, were the Romans. Christianity brought forth the third force, love, without which human history could not reach its consummation because without it the heart of man pines away.

Love is indeed the heart of Christianity. But this definition is still too indefinite and indistinct. Is it, in fact, a correct definition at all? Does not the same amount of hate, lies and calumny seem to rule under Christians as under non-Christians? We still need a more exact definition.

What then is the nature of that love in which the whole essence of Christianity is contained? If we say casually that Christianity is 'the religion of love', it is to be feared that we hold the word love all too cheap. To define Christianity as the religion of love causes great misunderstanding. It might entice us into thinking that Christianity is concerned only with the treatment of hearts in this world, that its essence resides in crying aloud: Embrace, O millions! It could also lead to the error of thinking that Christianity is identical with a particular social order, born of love.

Such interpretations miss the heart of the matter. They understand love—in which they see the innermost secret of Christianity—altogether too much from the human point of view. They see it as an emotion by which hearts are drawn to one another, from which a particular social order is born. And in fact this is true. But love, which is the core of Christianity, is more than this. Love seen only as an emotion between heart and heart could also be produced and nourished by the powers of the world. In a certain, though distorted, way we can also speak of it where kin and country are regarded as driving forces in human history. It shares in the weakness and infirmity of all temporal things, and in the fickleness of human hearts. It is permeated by the selfishness and autocratic attitude of those who experience it.

The common definition of Christianity as the religion of love cannot confer an unequivocal and distinct character on Christianity. It would burden Christianity with that element of the doubtful which is found in everything human. The question is therefore, what kind of love is it that should be seen as the inmost secret of Christianity? On this point it may be said that it is love, not of the human but of the divine kind. Its origin lies not in this world but in heaven, and therefore, its form is no earthly form, but a heavenly form. The kind of love meant comes from the realms of God. Its home is in the uncreated splendour of the divine life and it has come from there and entered human history. In the world of men, it has shone forth from a human face, the face

18

of Jesus Christ. The form of love, therefore, that we are referring to here is that of the incarnate Son of God.

This complex of ideas becomes clearer when we recall that answers of a most diverse kind may be given to the question: What is God? Philosophical and theological systems through the centuries and millennia have attempted to answer this fundamental question in many ways. The Apostle John tells us that 'God is love'. And our world springs from love, which is God. Its inmost nature is determined by this origin. Love, therefore, is the very heart of the world.

In their revolt against God, men have revolted against love, from which they themselves and the world in which they live are sprung. Flight from God is therefore flight from the realms of love. In that way events and the world are delivered over to hate, and hate has therefore become a power in history. It bears the responsibility for the fact that the paths of human history are soaked in blood, and that there is to be heard in them the groans and cries of the numberless victims of the story of man. Human history is made up of a tumultuous throng of human hates. Men exhaust themselves in their hatred of God and their fellows.

In the midst of the uproar of hate, however, the voice of divine love is never quite stilled. Time after time God has uttered words of peace and consolation, grace and promise. His activities as a peace-maker reached their culmination at that moment when he personally entered men's history. In the incarnation of the Son of God, Love made its appearance in the world of hate. All previous history was directed towards this act of God. Whatever God had done had been guided by his future coming into human history. So, by the incarnation of God, love became the core of human affairs. It did not appear merely as an emotion in minds and hearts, but as an incarnate person. Every man who has eyes to see and an open mind can discern God and love in the coming of Christ. Now, in the midst of the darkness of hate, man can grasp the hand of love. In the historical setting within which his laborious and sorrowful life takes place, he can look love in the face. In Christ, it stretches out its hand to him from the darkness of hate and pain. It turns its face to him in the confusion and chaos of existence.

To mankind, this is a fact of saving significance, for love has the power to save, and its mission is one of salvation: it is an *evangel*.

In the Hellenistic world the word *evangelion* was used to denote the announcement made of special events in the life of the emperor: for example, the news that the emperor was to honour a city with a visit. The ruler's arrival was seen as a guarantee of good fortune. The temporal meaning of the word *evangelion* found its fulfilment in the coming of God, of love, into this world.

The coming of love into human history brought a new state of affairs into being in the world. Since then the universe—creation—has been characterized by the presence of the love of God. The world's new character constitutes the fundamental historical factor in the lives of all generations living after the advent of the love of God. The entry of God into the world was the beginning of a great movement which will reach its fulfilment only at the end of history. It is like a stone that is thrown into the water and sets it all in motion, till the ripples lap against the banks. The universal motion begun by Christ will find its consummation when the waves of time beat upon the shores of eternity and become forever still.

If the love of God which came into the world has become the most intimate mystery of Christianity, then Christianity is grounded on a person: it is not a philosophical or theological system, but something personal. And this fact cannot be characterized more exactly by any different definition concerned with other details of its nature. As a result the name Christianity runs the risk of being misunderstood, for this word suggests an abstract thing, a system, an impersonal phenomenon. Such a name might give the impression that here, too, a system was in question—a system which other philosophical and ethical systems might change, and by which they might be changed. Yet the reality designated by the word Christianity is something quite different from phenomena of this kind, for they are concerned with things, with non-personal forms, whereas in its innermost heart Christianity is a living *Person* —the love of God appearing as a person, in human form, to be precise: the Son of God manifested in human history. Accordingly, to be a Christian is not merely, or even primarily, to accept certain truths and adhere to a certain law, although necessarily it is also these things. It consists primarily in a meeting with a person. Being a Christian involves a subjective relationship between man and God. It is a personal experience.

We want to examine this question further. The statement that Christianity is the love of God manifested in the world might at first sight seem like an empty phrase, for if Christianity is really the love of almighty God present in the world we are assailed by the problem of how history can be so gloomy and disastrous, destructive and murderous. Can we be right in calling Christianity the love of God in the world?

Thus, if we are to understand the definition of Christianity as love, it is important to make very clear the kind of love we mean. For love has for people so many different and conflicting meanings.

We can, nevertheless, reduce the various concepts of love to two: the one we encounter in Holy Scripture, the other in the Hellenistic world. In view of that, the latter has been the significant concept for natural humanity as a whole. *Eros* played a decisive role in the Hellenistic world: he was the universal ruler of God and men. He subjugated to himself everything that breathed and, indeed, by that means gave it happiness. *Eros* is an emotion in which the lover devotes himself to another, in order to stir the other and draw the other to himself. By this emotion the other is put at one's service, and helps the one to fulfil his being. Such love springs from the need of the individual. Its yearning for another is the expression of the loneliness and incompleteness of the individual. It is a symbol of its poverty. It reaches out towards the other in order to win wealth and security through the other.

But the kind of love testified to in the New Testament is a movement by which the one gives himself to the other, but in it the one gives himself, his own wealth, to the other, so that the *life of the other* is fulfilled. Such love springs not from want, but from plenty. It does not put the other at the service of the one, but the one at the service of the other. Its basis is the lover's joy in giving. It wants to give fulness of life and security to the other.

When we say of God that he is love, we are speaking of the second of these kinds of love. This self-giving love, love that puts itself at the service of the beloved, has become manifest in Christ. It has made itself present in the world in order to liberate men from wretchedness and indigence, from the insecurity and dangers of life. It has put itself at the service of needy man. Its service to man reached its ultimate and supreme potentiality in its self-sacrifice on the cross. It revealed its highest proof in the out-pouring of its blood. The highest form taken by its service was its offering of itself. 'God so loved the world, as to give his only begotten Son, that whosoever believeth in him may not perish, but may have life everlasting' (John 3, 16). This love is not God's response to the love-call of man. Rather, it is the spontaneous and primordial word of love spoken by God to men. It originates exclusively in the heart of God. It strives to lay hold of men and draw them into its own glory.

We have still to guard against a misconception of far-reaching importance. The love through which God lays hold on men has given no promise of a secure and full life within human history. The promise it gives points rather beyond human history to a life on the far side of death. When Christ took leave of his own, he called upon them not to be afraid: 'Let not your heart be troubled. You believe in God; believe also in me. In my Father's house there are many mansions. If not, I would have told you; because I go to prepare a place for you. And, if I shall go and prepare a place for you, I will come again and will take you to myself; that where I am, you also may be' (John 14, 1-3). In this appeal to them to conquer fear, Christ does not offer the prospect of a secure life on earth. On the contrary, without stressing it, he discloses to the disciples the vision of a life exposed to pain and death. He calls on them not to fear earthly failure. He promises a full and secure life beyond death. Behind this world of death he shows them the possibility of a full life. God will guarantee to man what man longs for—safety and plenty—not within the human time-scale, but beyond it.

The love therefore that has become present within human history through the incarnation does not take possession of men so as to bring them to a safe and abundant life on earth, but to carry them home through death to the safety and plenty of the divine life. It opens a view to a greater future, but it makes no immediate promise for the present time, within human history. Nevertheless, it also throws a clear light upon this present time, for light falls on this present moment from that future into which it has opened the way.

Love, which in Christ has become present in human history, has in Christ become audible and visible. In his words it has spoken to mankind and in his actions it has put its mark on the world. When Christ withdrew from the world, the word of love that God uttered in him did not fall silent again, and the symbol of love God displayed in him did not disappear. His word of love was to remain audible and his symbol of love to remain visible throughout the centuries until the end of human history, until the moment when his words of love shall no longer be given to man through the frailty of human utterance, but shall pass directly from him into man's ears, and when his loving gestures shall be visible to man no longer through the poverty of human symbols but in their unveiled splendour.

The principal means by which God's love is made audible and visible until that time are preaching and the administration of sacraments in the Church. The hand of love stretched out to mankind in Christ is stretched out towards them perpetually in the sacraments. The word of love calling men in Christ's words, forever calls them in the words of Christian preaching. Thus in the Church there dwells that love which appeared in Christ and so became present in history. At this point it becomes clear that we cannot separate the Church from Christianity—that it is, indeed, impossible, to differentiate between them. Any such differentiation would be based on an erroneous idea of the essence of Christianity.

We have seen that in its most hidden depths, Christianity is the living Christ.

We can now make a fuller definition: In its inmost essence, Christianity is the living Christ who is present in the Church continually until the last day. Christianity, therefore, is in actuality the Church. To speak of the essence of Christianity is to speak of the essence of the Church.

When we think of God's Church in this way, we see that it is the place, the instrument and also the visible entity through which God, having made himself present in the world through Christ, remains present in it. From this we can see that the Church is the normal community of those who seek the countenance of love, which is God, which has in Christ become present in the world and remains forever present in it. It is, too, the community of those who, in Christ, grasp the hand of love stretched out to them in the darkness. These things are done in faith and in the sacraments. Combining the view of the Church that says it proceeds from God with that which says it comes from men, we can say that the Church is the confederation of love in which God bestows his love upon men through Christ, and men, by faith, possess themselves of the love bestowed upon them.

Such an encounter between God and man leads to those who live in the Church also being bestowed upon one another. The Church is therefore a community of brothers and sisters. The baptized are united together after the manner of kinship. Love has gained power over them. Such is the fundamental law of their community: it is the essential basis of their unity. It is the heart of their relationship. But let us emphasize once more that the ultimate foundation of their community is no mere emotion, no mere idea or ideal of love, nor are they united only in a common task; together they do not merely make up a working-party in which all are interested in a common duty. The ultimate foundation of their unity is rather a living heart, the heart of Christ, in which beats the heart of God.

The unity of all the baptized in Christ surpasses in intimacy and strength all the communities of this world, for these take their intensity from the strength of this world, from physical or intellectual things. The community of Christian believers is however held together by the powers of heaven.

A deeper aspect of this fact becomes visible if we take into account the part played in the Church by the Holy Ghost: it is through the Holy Ghost that Christ remains present in the words that are preached and the setting of the symbol of his death in the world. The Holy Ghost is best understood by thinking of him as the bond of love who, in the divine life, surrounds the Father and the Son; or as the breath of love, breathed by the Father towards the Son and by the Son towards the Father; or as the pledge of love, given by the Father to the Son, and by the Son to the Father, in which is guaranteed the Father's love for the

Son and the Son's for the Father. As the *Hagion Pneuma*, the *Spiritus Sanctus*, he is the sacred, heavenly air, the celestial atmosphere, in which the Father and the Son live.

After his Ascension, Christ sent this Spirit to be his invisible representative in every community that holds the Father's word of love given by him to the world and the Father's token of love accorded by him to the world. In the stream of love which, through the sending by Christ of the Spirit, flows continually into such a community of men, Christ himself remains present. The Holy Ghost, the almighty love of God, like an all-powerful bond, surrounds Christ and those who are united with him. He is also present in the innermost being of every believer in Christ; in him, he calls continually through the Son to the Father. In the human words that the Christian addresses to the Father, the Father hears the loving words of the Holy Ghost. In man's very silence, the Father hears the Holy Ghost speak (cf. Romans 8, 26).

The love of God that has been made present in Christ, and by him has been given in the Holy Ghost to the Christian community, does not operate in mankind as does a natural mechanical force, but rather calls on the spirit of man and tries to gain power over him without violating his freedom, it tries to make its way into human hearts in such a way that man takes it into his heart quite freely. It seeks to become sovereign over mankind, without man losing his mastery, which originates in his freedom. Through the Holy Ghost the love that has been made present in the world in Christ seeks to become sovereign over the world, trying to set up its dominion as it has already set it up in the community of the faithful, which should be the place, instrument and manifestation of its universal dominion.

If love is the inmost kernel of Christianity, a paradox becomes apparent, for Christianity has the appearance of being an organization: duty and law play an important part in it. Indeed, it not infrequently appears as though duty and law played a decisive role in Christianity, as though nothing lay beyond and behind them —as though they were an end in themselves.

Duty and law do, indeed, have a place in the confederation of love represented by Christianity. They have an indispensable function within it. This becomes clear when we take into account the kind of love God's love is. When it calls upon mankind, it is a compelling appeal. On earth, love's appeal is accompanied by responsibilities and duties. Yet when God, who is love, bestows himself upon mankind, he bestows upon man a ruler to whom, because he is his creature, man is subject even in the deepest fibres of his being. In relation to this it behoves mankind to show obedience.

Thus as far as mankind is concerned, the love of God in Christ is a compelling love. It does not like to see men living in wretchedness and want, peril and danger. It longs to give him a life of security and plenty. It longs to give him a share in its own sovereignty. It is therefore an imperious love. All God's commandments are mandates of his love. Love, the love that longs to call mankind out of poverty of life, speaks in all God's laws, imploring man not to content himself with a life of want and moreover inviting him to expect and aspire to a demanding and full life.

All God's threats, too, become intelligible from this point of view: they too are but manifestations of love, although in them love to some degree masks its face. In them God warns man that if he does not grasp the proffered hand of love, he will remain imprisoned in the wretchedness of life. The judgement God threatens is therefore but the ultimate outcome of a life not formed according to the love of God, and therefore of a restricted autocracy in man, of autonomy so complete as to exclude God's kingdom. The ultimate fruit of this way of life is hell.

The Church's Mass is accordingly the permanent form in which the love of God, manifested in the world in Christ, remains perpetually audible and visible. It was created by Christ for love's service. Those who carry it on are empowered and obliged to perform the service of redeeming and pacifying love in an order indispensable for the continuance of the community. For the sake of love's array, there is in the Church authority, sovereignty, law. Ignatius of Antioch therefore saw in the bishop the manifestation of the love active in the Church. St. Peter in his first general epistle warns his brother bishops against lording it over their communities: they should rather render fraternal service to the members of the Church. In this way everything done by him who holds office in the Church becomes a service done for the faithful.

So for instance in absolution, the Church performs, through the administrator of the sacrament, a sovereign act—fundamentally, a fraternal service by which a sinful member of the Church is rescued. The dignity and eminence of those who hold office in the Church consists in this: that they are empowered to serve, and committed to a service which, in scope, surpasses any possible service in this world. The love manifested in Christ is lord and ruler of the Church. The imperativeness of its dominion may take effect in expression of direction and command. Every rule and command in the Church has the same tendency: to make compelling, appealing love audible to men. Thus it is clear that any lust for power in the Church is apostasy from her fundamental nature. Lust for power denies both sense and nature. On the other hand, the Church cannot dispense with law, because love requires order.

What we have said up to now has been concerned with the objective nature, the being, as it were, of the Church. From this essential nature spring the deeds of Christians. The God present in the Church is a God of action, who wants active, lively men. Because God is present as love in the Church, the activity of anyone belonging to the Church must be an activity in love. Not all love is the expression of the God who is active in the Church, but only that love which is in keeping with the divine. Paul exhorted his readers in Ephesus to 'walk in love, as Christ also has loved us and hath delivered himself for us, an oblation and a sacrifice to God' (5, 2). Augustine compressed this truth into the short formula: *Ama et fac quod vis:* Love and do what you like. This formula is not a charter for unrestrained behaviour, but a call to complete unity in love. Augustine said: Let yourself be wholly and completely formed by love. Vanquish all selfishness. If you are ruled absolutely by love, all your decisions will be free from selfishness and prompted by love. It is love that is crucified with Christ.

He who is characterized by love will want nothing selfish or tyrannical. As far as wishes and actions are concerned, he can give himself over to the love that forms and rules him. God himself is present in such love, and thus the man becomes a revelation of love: he reminds men of God, who is Love, and acts in the deeds of men.

St. Augustine's words do not abolish the commandments or empty them of their force, for the commandments show the ways in which love takes its effect. They answer the question as to how love should operate in the concrete situation of the life of man. Thus, for instance, the fourth Commandment explains the way and manner in which those who have become brothers and sisters through Christ in the Church, should treat one another when they stand in the natural relationship, one to another, of parents and children. So, too, the sixth commandment explains the way in which the members of the Church should conduct themselves towards one another when they are man and wife. Likewise, the seventh commandment interprets the manner in which the faithful, who are characterized by love, should deal with one another, if they have respect for their personal dignity, in the matter of control over earthly property. It explains too the eighth commandment, telling how those who are marked by love should treat one another if they pledge themselves to one another.

The love in which the faithful come together is that kind of love in which the lover gives to the beloved. Such love is impossible without sacrifice. It is therefore expressed by the sign of the cross. In it, the Lord's cross takes effect. It is not a reaction to proven friendship, but rather an emotion spontaneously awakened in the human soul in respect of another. This love is not passive, but active and self-giving. Sometimes it is a first step—it begins a new life. It is not primarily a response to a world filled with love, but a pledge to a world characterized by hate. It has within itself the power to transform the world. Because it is not a response to proffered love, but a new beginning, it is also not restricted by the hate offered it. It suffers all things, endures all things, refuses to be embittered. Kindled by God, it rises ever higher from the hearts of those who love. It knows no frontiers. It knows no other barrier than death. In this it resembles the love of Christ, which is present in it.

The ultimate foundation of its inexhaustible power is that the inexhaustible love of God acts in it. Through Christ and in the Holy Ghost, it pours out from God into the community of the faithful, and is proffered by each to the other, so that each becomes for the other a mirror of the love of God.

By this we do not mean that it necessarily succeeds, that it does not come to grief on the battlements of hate. The love of Christ itself was wrecked on man's hate. The love of the faithful, which extends the range of the love of Christ, must also expect to be wrecked on the walls of the selfishness of this world. Indeed, Christ himself suggested that the love of God made present in the world will not attain its objective within history.

Surprising as it is, men hold fast to destructive hate, and defend themselves against redeeming love. But love restrains itself and leaves men their fateful freedom. When it entered human history, love laid aside its might, its omnipotence, before its gates (Guardini). Its dominion will not be set up by force in this world, for that would be contrary to its nature. Because of human opposition, love succeeds only partially in this world. Even human history attains its goal only outside its own development. Within history itself, hate's magnificent uproar speaks louder than the voice of love, made audible by Christ and spread abroad by the Church. The sight of the slain, the tortured and the tormented, constantly masks in the course of history the tokens of love displayed by Christ and perpetuated by the Church.

Nevertheless, where love's rule has once been set up, it has an eternal future before it. It may be crucified, or tortured and put to death, but the cross and death are for it a path to everlasting life. Beyond earthly existence, love's dominion will be set up unconditionally. At that future time love's power will burst forth and no one will be able to withstand it. At that moment, even the most resolute hater will be dashed to the ground by love, not because love itself aims at destruction, but because he who thrusts at it suffers a recoil of terrible violence. Love will unwillingly judge him who hates.

At that time, God will ask men a question; by his answer to this question every man will judge himself. The question will ring out: 'Hast thou made love thine own? Hast thou lived for the love Christ hath revealed on earth?' Everyone who can reply affirmatively to this question will participate in the life of salvation—the life, that is, of plenty and security. Everyone on the other hand, who at that moment bears the impress not of love but of hate, will be expelled from the human community to the borders of existence and will have to live there forever in loneliness and inner strife. The shadow of this future is already cast upon the present. It has power, too, here and now. To the question as to how we can master our age, there is but one reply: Through love, which is God, which has become present in Christ, which has been spread abroad by the Church and which, in the end, will become ruler of all things. Hearts that glow with it can bring salvation. Nothing else can do so. Justice alone is not enough, although it is indispensable. Injustice has a fatal destructive power. Justice is essential, but it does not suffice. It cannot heal the deep wounds of humanity. It may, when it rules alone and rules ruthlessly, inflict yet deeper wounds. It can flourish only in the climate of love, because only where love prevails are men ready to grant one another justice. Only love can save the world and bring it out from disunion. The healing of divided and wounded mankind will succeed in so far as love is made sovereign. The lustre of the end is reflected in its dominion. Wherever love prevails and, in its dominion, heals, there is manifested a lustrous sign of the world to come.

Whoever is shaped by the love God has placed in the world, knows that he is responsible for seeing that the dominion of redeeming love is established in this world. He will not expect to be relieved of his responsibility, until one goes before him whom he can follow. He will, rather, seize every opportunity, to set up the rule of love wherever he is. By doing so, he kindles and tends the flame without which the world cannot live.

He knows of course that complete salvation cannot be won in this world because the rule of love cannot be made complete within time; full salvation lies beyond earthly things. It appears when time with its hates and its lies is swallowed up. Until that time those who believe in Christ are conscious of a duty and responsibility of making the love manifested in Christ known and apparent in the world. Even when hate heaves itself up in ever-higher billows, they remain confident that love will one day come to its full sovereignty. In all the afflictions and hardships of life, in the torment and agony of existence, in every failure and débâcle, they see accordingly the way in which the dominion of love progresses until it reaches its final form and emerges in undisguised sovereignty as the only mighty and precious thing.

In the exposition which follows, the foregoing outline of the essence of Christianity is amplified. In enlarging on it, we shall not try to pursue a pre-determined train of thought, logical from first to last, but to examine everything within a certain radius that seems to us to contain the core of Christianity. In this way, we shall see the same things many times over, but on each occasion from a new point of view. If we approach a point along a spiral path, we are able to discover something new continually about that point, and see what we have already discovered in an ever-changing context, with a more profound understanding.

CHAPTER TWO

CHRISTIANITY:
AN HISTORICAL REVELATION

Christianity is of great significance for everyone: it concerns us all personally and can also help us to understand our own times. Our concern with it is not merely that of interested spectators, but that of people whose very existence is at stake. What then is Christianity about? How does it appear to us when we apply ourselves not merely to obtaining a general view of it, but to working out its characteristics in detail?

If our efforts are to be successful we must exercise powers of discrimination, for many of the elements of Christianity are confusingly like other religious phenomena. Kierkegaard, the nineteenth century Danish theologian, was right to lay great emphasis on the power of discrimination for, if it is lacking, it is scarcely possible to avoid the danger of confusing Christianity with other religious systems. Discrimination is indispensable. If however we go far enough, our account of the characteristics of Christianity will also fix the limits of other religious phenomena.

First, we might make a fundamental differentiation by saying that Christianity is an historical revelation, whereas all other religious systems are built on myth, unless, like Mohammedanism, they are based on Christianity, or, like Buddhism, they exhibit genuine religious traits. Thus our attempt to uncover the essential characteristics of Christianity must begin with our comparing and contrasting it with myth.

What is myth? Our first approximate answer might be: The deification of nature. The gods of myth are personifications of natural forces and events. Their genesis and form may be accounted for by saying that in them the experiences, visions and yearnings arising from the depths of the human heart are predicated of nature. They give promise of fulfilment and so for those who follow nature religions they assume the functions of God.

Man may expect from nature what the Christian expects from God: he may, therefore, deify nature because as a result of having come from God it bears in its inmost being the stamp of the divine. There is more to nature than man can observe or register on instruments. It has another, mysterious side. This other side cannot of course be perceived by everyone. A truly positivistic thinker and observer would not be able to recognize and experience the numinous in nature—its mysterious, occult power—but that does not prove it does not exist. We might explain the situation as follows:

Imagine a completely unmusical scientist. If a tune was played for him on the piano and he was asked to interpret and define scientifically what had just taken place he could, if he was a first-rate physicist, express it in a precise scientific formula. Because he was only a physicist and was quite unmusical, he would feel that he had thoroughly explained what had happened. If it was objected that he had overlooked something, and that something the heart of the matter, he would smile incredulously. Because he was quite unmusical, he would lack the organ, the critical faculty, with which to observe the tune itself. The tune could not be expressed by the methods available to him, with the faculty with which he comprehended reality and believed himself able to comprehend it thoroughly. Yet it does exist. Similarly, there is a mystery in things that we cannot identify with our intellects and instruments, a mystery that is in the world because the world comes from God. It is with his religious faculty that a man perceives and feels the numinous power, the inner mystery of the universe that originates in God.

Nature is completely controlled by its relationship with God. This relationship is, however, especially strongly felt in certain situations, where nature summons up and reveals its power: in death, birth, fertility, love, light, darkness and so on. Man can now separate the mystery of the cosmos from the God from whom it originates, from whom it flows constantly in eternal streams. He can explain the world by direct reference to its divine character, rather than by calling it autonomous. If a man sympathetic to the world is endowed with creative ability, he can model the mystery at work in the cosmos in sharply defined shapes. Of course, these shapes are simply figures of the mystery of the cosmos. By making them, the man who does so is enabled to comprehend the depths of his own being and to envisage the original creator, whose likeness he sees in the characteristic of the world he has made.

It was in this way that the gods of the myths came into being in the minds of men. Nature, especially when it is strongly active, affords him the material from which he can create his gods. Thus the gods of love, light, darkness and so on came into being. Man may also relate his experience of the numinous directly to great natural phenomena, such as, for example, the sun. He then sees it as a god. Other men, not endowed with the power of creation, recognize such mythical beings as also valid for their own use. Thus the gods created in the mind of one man also become important for other men and even for a whole community. The mythical gods are, it is clear, not merely phantasies. They have a real potency, for in them reside both the might of the nature they represent and the vigour of human minds.

Mythical gods never have definitive forms. They are always fluid, like man's experience itself. The creators and worshippers of these man-made gods tell various stories about them. But it cannot be said about them that they really possess a history or give rise to one. We can talk about them in fairy-tale form: 'Once upon a time', but not in historical style: 'There was at that time'. It does not matter when they lived or even whether they ever lived. They have in fact never lived as historical and personal forces. They are after all personifications of the eternally-moving cycles of nature, which has no history. The power in the myth is the power of nature. In the imagination of those who believe in myths, the life of the gods of myth follows exactly the same constantly recurring pattern as the life of nature. Recapitulation is the foundation of myth.

Christianity is fundamentally differentiated from myth by the historical character of its revelation. In Christ—a figure historical in the time-sequence to which we ourselves belong—God has made himself present. In Christ, God himself entered history, so as to be present in it as a person who acts and speaks, so that he might

35

be met with bodily in human history, and one could hold out a hand to him and converse with him. We can date the revelation of God exactly: it occurred in the reign of Caesar Tiberius, of Pilate the governor, Herod, Annas and Caiphas.

God's advent in history filled history with divine splendour. It changed human history. The incarnation was the central point in the story of mankind: what went before it was the prelude to it, and what follows it is consequent upon it. Its pre-history extended over hundreds and thousands of years. Its consequences will flood hundreds and thousands of years with light. Great happenings are not quickly over. The incarnation of God was in preparation from the first moment of human history. Everything that happened before it was preparatory to it.

If we are to understand Christ and his importance for men and human history we must look briefly at the events leading up to his coming and its after effects. The pre-history of the incarnation is the story of man's guilt and God's grace. At the beginning of human history stands man's attempt to gain control of his own life. Man could not bear to live in obedience to God under the restrictions thereby entailed. He attempted to liberate himself from God and God's dominion and take charge of his own life. To a certain degree, this attempt was successful, but success was bought at a high price. Liberation from God did not bring men true freedom, but rather slavery. When he fled from God in order to stand on his own feet, so as to be wholly his own master, he came under the sway of a power antipathetic to God, under the sway, that is, of Satan. Man had no choice but this: either he must subject himself to God and in obedience to God participate in the fulness and security of the life of God, or set himself free from God, so forfeiting his share in the fulness and power of the life of God, and so fall under the tyranny of demonic powers antipathetic to God. There is no third path. No man can find a way out of this situation, because no such way is possible, either in heaven or on earth.

For mankind, the dominion of Satan means disaster, for it is Satan, the devil, who brings confusion to all things, who destroys life and brings the universe to ruin, who makes chaos. When man fled from God, he flew into the chaotic situation brought about by Satan, in which death and pain, fear and apprehension are supreme.

The man who is free from God and controls himself is plunged into the chasm of uncertainty and peril, homelessness and fear.

The dominion of death takes its most terrible form when man, having fallen under its sway, discovers in himself its craving to kill and destroy. This lust is the reason why the paths of human history resound with the groans of the dying. They are lined by the bodies of slaughtered millions. Thus the first sins had importance for the whole of history. Their destructive influence extended to every future century and millennium and the generations who lived in them. The history of humanity is the story of the sin at its beginning.

Flight from God's sovereignty was of disastrous significance for the whole of creation. It was of cosmic importance (Stauffer). So, by sin, the whole of creation was delivered up to destruction. The catastrophe which was unleashed on the world by sin means that the world and the things in it are no longer the image of everlasting life and can no longer assist towards everlasting life, but are rather bound to manifest and serve transitoriness. The whole cosmos is characterised by the tokens of perishableness. Death has left its mark everywhere, the signs of it are omnipresent. Even Beauty itself must die. The world cannot mediate for man, who, therefore, longs for everlasting life. It offers him only death. Even when it promises him life, it bestows on him a transitory life, ever-threatened by death. If it gives him his bread, water and air, all it spares by doing so is a life which is a slow death. A man in the world is a man in a place filled with the breath of death. When he strides over the earth, he walks on graves. He can therefore himself create nothing truly eternal. In accordance with the law governing all earthly things, everything his hands and mind produce is characterized by transitoriness. He builds death into everything. Therefore every work—although seeming to the superficial and naive eye to have been made for eternity—falls into decay. Nature itself exercises its power to serve this universally valid law of temporality. With fire and water, stone and iron, it hurls itself on man and his works to bring them to nothingness.

So then, all destruction reveals the inner nature of this world. Decay is not merely an accident that might be avoided by the exercise of greater caution and dexterity. Even if this or that thing

37

might be saved from destruction, there is no means by which the downfall of the works of this world might ultimately be avoided. Decay reveals the inner nature of things, the transitoriness that, since the separation of the world from God, has been the deepest-laid characteristic of their being. Thus, by his sins, man has brought about a helpless and hopeless state of affairs in time and in the universe. Within history and the universe there is no power that is a match for this doom. Death and transitoriness are the greatest of Great Powers, and subject all things to their dominion. Silently, they give their inexorable commands. Silently, all men and all creatures in the universe obey them and fall, as the law commands.

The absolute authority of these powers is mandated to them by him whom Scripture calls 'Lord of this world'. However much man would like to rebel against their enslaving dominion, he cannot shake them off. Having called them in, he must put up with them.

However, although the chaotic situation man has brought into being cannot be altered from within, it can be changed by the power of heaven. In point of fact, although God did not hinder man's attempt to shape his own life, because he respected man's freedom, he has not left him without help in the chaos he himself has made. Ever since the first moment of disaster he has constantly spoken and acted in human history to call back to himself—that is, to divine rule and, therefore, salvation—the men who have fled from him. In an unbroken sequence of historical acts, God has sought to lift the disaster from history. From the very first instant he has worked to re-establish his dominion, which men had cast off, and so establish anew the happiness of men.

We call these historical acts of God 'divine revelation'. If we are to use the word revelation, we must define it more precisely. Creation itself is a revelation of God, for in it God displays himself, his proper glory, his divine power, and the wealth of his life. The whole creation is a manifestation, or reflection, of God, veiled and disguised, but yet lifelike. He who possesses the faculty we mentioned earlier can therefore perceive the voice of God and signs of his presence everywhere throughout the universe. The confusion introduced into the world by human self-glorification has obscured and marred God's majesty in the world, so that it now requires great effort to see traces of the divine countenance in the chaos. But they are, of course, still there, even under these circumstances. Anyone who cannot see them is himself responsible for his failure (Natural revelation).

The kind of revelation we are principally concerned with here, however, is that self-revelation he has performed within the universe. In the revelation which is here meant, God reveals his inmost nature, which he had not hitherto allowed to appear in creation, or which had not hitherto been clearly revealed in it (Supernatural revelation). We shall see later that the inner self that God disclosed in the kind of revelation we are referring to here, was his existence in three persons.

This kind of revelation, then, was effected by God in historical acts. He did not disclose eternal and universally valid truths, enlightening each and every man, but he chose certain men and used them as instruments of his work in the world. The instruments God chose were frequently very imperfect. In his choice God takes no account of worldly majesty—a thing which in itself shows his otherness to men. Those who are chosen know that they have been touched and called by a personal power which is not of the world and which they cannot escape. And yet they remain free. God renounces force. He restrains himself. Thus, through his revelation, there comes into being a bond between God and men within history. Often the chosen rebel against the task asked or expected of them, but God does not change his plan. If man refuses and does not carry out God's instructions, God starts again so as to reach his objectives by another route. So man's rebellion becomes the occasion of a new revelation (Guardini).

Owing to the historical nature of revelation—for it takes place at a definite moment in human history—it fills the time at which it occurs with new meaning. The time so endowed leads to a special goal. Chronology, therefore, plays an important part in Scripture. It was not pleasure in symbolic and mystical numbers which led to the detailed listing of the genealogies and ages of the patriarchs, the emphasizing of the dates of the calls of the prophets, and the establishment of the dates of the life of Christ by giving particulars of the ruling Roman Emperor and governor, Jewish

39

princes and high priests, and by the reckoning up of the sequence of generations, with Christ at the end of them. Numerical symbolism of the ancient east, with its arbitrariness and exaggerations, may play some part in the fixing of dates but what mattered was the establishment of the historical place of the revelation. It was done by the means available to the sacred writers. They are the garments of revelation, borrowed by the sacred writers from the culture of their times. They are the forms under which the God who reveals himself has manifested himself. The details of time and place prevent us saying of revelation that it occurs everywhere and at all times. They make us say of it: it happened then and there.

The revelation of God in history took place by degrees from its first stage to its culmination in Jesus Christ. The call of Abraham played a crucial part in this series. Abraham lived in Ur in Chaldaea, in a civilization rich in religious practices and observances. At this time, the religion of the Veda, with its extra-temporal opinions and claims, was flourishing in India. Abraham was called to leave his home and seek another. He was not told where this lay. He had to set out believing that the Lord would lead him through the darkness to the land he had destined for him. Great promises were linked with God's command: Abraham would become the ancestor of a great nation; his name would be renowned; from him, a blessing would spread over the whole earth. The call and the promise were not left as empty words: they were followed immediately by the beginning of the events which it was God's will to consummate in him. Abraham submitted to the Lord's command, leaving the lands familiar to him, and starting out on the road to the future. The word of God established a covenant between God and Abraham, the consequences of which were immense both for the nation of which Abraham was to be the forefather and also for the whole course of human history. From the point of view of religious history, Abraham was the universal father.[1]

Half a millennium later, God spoke with new emphasis words of promise and obligation to Moses, a member of one of the tribes descended from Abraham, the majority of whom lived in slavery

[1] cf. Guardini, *Die Offenbarung*, 1940.

in Egypt. He, too, was given a command of historic significance. Whilst tending the flocks of his father-in-law, Jethro, on Mount Horeb, he received a command from God to lead the tribes of Israel out of Egypt. The testament with Abraham was given a new form. Afterwards, if anyone wanted to praise God for his revelation (as, for instance, in the Psalms) he had to tell the story of the deliverance from Egypt. The divine testament made with Moses formed the basis of God's covenant with the whole nation, which was established at Sinai.

Thus, at one and the same time, the form of the nation chosen by God was established and its way of life fixed. It was not a way of life natural to the national character, but one conferred on the nation by God. Characteristics of the new national life included its vocation, its resistance and the grace and judgement of Jahweh. It did not grow out of the life of the race as a national state—out of security, unity and power, the winning of a place in the history of the world—but out of attention to God (K. Barth). It was God's will to bring into being a holy nation, attentive to him, which should convey God's promises to all men throughout history and make them clear to all. The nation found it difficult to fulfil such a task continuously throughout its history. It was constantly tempted to live and shape its natural life after the fashion of the nations around it.[1]

God raised up men whose task it was continually to call back his people when, unfaithful to their duty, they fell into the ways of the nations surrounding them. These men were the prophets. Under God's mandate, it was their duty to explain to the nation that the disasters that overtook it on account of its worldly way of life were signs of the judgement of God. The people had to learn that rebellion against God meant self-destruction. At the same time, it was the prophets' duty to threaten new disasters for the future if the nation did not mend its ways. They had to foretell the judgement of God. They had, too, to prophesy that destruction would not have the last word. Disaster would serve salvation. A Messias, a Saviour would appear. He would take the form of a servant of God, but would establish God's rule. God's final accounting with the rebellious and mutinous nation—and, indeed,

[1] Leist: *Zeugnis des lebendigen Gottes*, 1943.

with all men who had deserted him—would be collapse and destruction.

The last in this series of forceful preachers was John the Baptist. John saw as already come what earlier prophets had threatened for centuries and what had been ignored and laughed at by their contemporaries, primarily because it would come to pass only in the distant future and therefore did not imperil the present. The time of the merciful judgement had come, the moment of corrective grace, in fire and the Holy Ghost. The history of this world had reached its end, and that end was Christ.

In the fulness of time, God sent his Son. No longer did he call into human history from without, as he had done earlier, with urgency and menace, with power and judgement, promise and blessing; he came into it himself in his Son. It sounds incredible, but it is true: God revealed himself in the child born of Mary, wrapped by her in swaddling clothes and laid in a manger, because she could find no room in the inn; the child whose youth, unlike that of the mythical and legendary saviours of the ancient world, passed almost completely without the accompaniment of outstanding wonders. God revealed himself in a man who hungered and thirsted, who grew tired and slept, was angered and surprised, wept and mourned, suffered and died—whose life ran its course according to the basic pattern of every man's life. Yet God himself was this man. This man's ego was God's ego. His life followed a precise pattern which was given him by God. Every phase of Christ's life was guided by the imperative of a divine command. It was a part of God's eternal plan for the universe that Jesus should enter Zacheus' house, however great the scandal he gave by doing so, for salvation had to come to that house on that day. He had to leave Capharnaum because he was sent to preach the good news in all the cities of Israel. Each day and hour held its task. In a dispute with the Pharisees who wanted to induce him to leave Herod's domain, Christ emphasized the historical character of his work. He said to them: 'Go and tell that fox: behold, I cast out devils and do cures, today and tomorrow, and the third day I am consummated. Nevertheless, I must walk today and tomorrow and the day following, because it cannot be that a prophet should perish out of Jerusalem' (Luke, 13, 32-33). When the hour determined by God struck, suffering came, neither earlier nor later. In Gethsemani, he prepared for the last events of his life. Before the coming of the hour of darkness, nothing could happen to him, despite the burning hate all around him and the ever-present intention to kill him.

Christ's death and resurrection are clear indications of the genuineness of his earthly life. In the myths, too, there is talk of the death and resurrection of saviours. But those deaths and risings are merely symbolic of the processes of nature, and can therefore be repeated continually. Christ's death and resurrection, however, were no allegory, but a unique, unrepeatable historical event. It is not the idea of death and resurrection that is in question, but the fact of death and resurrection. He who had risen appeared as a real man. When Paul wrote on this question to the Corinthians, most of those who had seen Christ were still alive. His death made it clear that he had really lived within human history. God took man's destiny on himself. When John says that the word was made flesh, he is testifying to the fact that the word took human nature with all its characteristics—the nature that had been man's from the beginning. The destiny that God took to himself in the incarnation included death. By this is proved the genuineness of the incarnation (Guardini).

At the same time his death showed that in his revelation of himself God acted in a truly temporal way. Revelation effected an historical link between God and man. God took on himself the risk of having dealings with rebellious, malicious, cunning, brutal man. Christ's death meant that the God-made-Man was really, although only in a certain sense, frustrated. Man did not accept the saving love offered him in Christ, or the light of God that shone on him in Christ. He was so enamoured of his darkness and hate, loneliness and homelessness, that he saw him who longed to give him security and fulness of life, love and light, as an alien and an intruder, and killed him.

God could have crushed rebellious man, but had he done so, his revelations would have had no historical features. It is, moreover, to the point here that God has left man his freedom. If man was to be free, God had to lay aside a measure of his power before the portals of history, so that man would not be crushed by his splendour.

A real historical relationship was only possible between man and a God who had accepted human weakness and divested himself of his divine power. In the course of our deliberations, we shall see that God was indeed frustrated by the opposition of men, but that his frustration brought salvation to men. Nevertheless, because Christ, in his own death, confirmed man's mortality, salvation is possible only through suffering and death.

As Christ is God manifested in human history, it is vitally important for us to meet and know him. In him, God extends his saving hand to man in the chaos of this world. In him, God turns his face towards man out of the maze of time. But this gives rise to a problem. It is not enough for man merely to apprehend the truth preached by Christ. Obedience to the law he propounded is necessary for salvation and redemption. But it is not sufficient. To be redeemed, we must lay hold on Christ himself.

This leads to the question: How can men of later centuries lay hold on Christ when he assumed an historical form and therefore the limitations of an historical figure, of whom it can be said that he lived at that time and in that place? It is of course that fundamentally characteristic feature, the historicity of Christ, that gives rise to this problem. Obviously we can only succeed in meeting with Christ if the limitations on life in time can be lifted. They have, in fact, been lifted: Christ himself has made it possible to lift them through the mediation of those signs we call sacraments. In the sacraments the historical life and death of Christ are mysteriously relieved of their historical limitations and in some way—whether actually or dynamically, symbolically or really will be discussed later—brought into the present.

The most far-reaching of these acts is the Eucharist. In the Eucharist are made present both the death of Christ and, in an indirect but real sense, the life of Christ which, both before and after his death, was inextricably bound up with it. It makes it present not in its historical, but in its supra-historical mode—a mode that is beyond our experience. Such bringing into the present of things from the past is possible only if different modes of existence are possible: Paul differentiated between the historical mode and the spiritual mode (that is, the mode brought into being by the Holy Ghost) of an historical event.

The fact that Christ was at one and the same time the goal of all that happened before him, and the starting point of all that was to happen after him is important for our understanding of the historical person and life of Christ. Christ was the fulfilment of the promises made by God at the beginning of human history and made ever more expressly during its course, for he was the promised Messias, the one who should bring the reign of God. But he was not yet the consummation of all things. He was, rather, a precursory fulfilment—he was himself another promise, a promissory fulfilment. Good Friday, the day on which he died, and Easter Day, the day on which he received new life, bore within themselves the germs of a great future.

Christ showed that his own life and his own task were a promise relating to the future, when he said to his disciples at the moment of parting that they would perform greater works than he himself had done. The works he proposed to them would be greater not because the disciples would accomplish more difficult things, or even more apparently striking things, but rather because the disciples would bring to perfection what Christ had begun. The disciples' task was to perpetuate Christ's mission over hundreds and thousands of years. They were to make the revelation that the Father had accomplished in Christ, his words and his deeds, audible and visible to all men living after his days. It was their task to fulfil this mission until the moment when Christ should come for the second time, until the moment when history should come to an end.

In this same parting conversation, Christ gave his apostles the task of picking up and carrying on his own mission, at the same time promising that he would come again and consummate his work. Christ's second coming would take place at the end of the history of mankind. But it also occurred during the course of history of the world. Christ saw death before him, and his promise that he would come again referred also to the second coming in the resurrection.

Actually, his return at the resurrection and his return at the end of time together form a single, protracted event, taking place over centuries. Indeed, the first coming of Christ should also be included in this single complex event, for there is an inner, indestructible, organic unity between the beginning, when God

45

first came into human history, and the consummation, which will be effected in the last coming of Christ.

This connexion should not, of course, obscure the great difference between the first and last comings of Christ. In the first coming, Christ manifested himself in the weakness of mortal human nature, which so veiled his divine glory that the splendour of God in his countenance, the fire of God in his words, and the divine light in his actions were barely perceptible. Most men failed to see God's majesty in him. At the last coming, Christ will appear in a different form: in a human nature shot through with the light and fire of God in such a way that no one could fail to see their radiance. Then Christ will come forth from concealment, so that he is seen completely openly in this world and no one can overlook him.

Between the first and last comings of Christ—which are, essentially, a single advent of God in the world, occurring in various forms—there is that coming which was the resurrection. This took a form midway between the others, for in it Christ had neither the weakness of mortal human nature nor as yet the glory of him who should come at the end of history.

Concealment is characteristic of the whole of the interval between the resurrection and the second, final coming of Christ. It lies like an opaque veil over his countenance.

But even in this intervening period Christ is not wholly concealed. Anyone who has that faculty we spoke of earlier—all the faithful, that is—can also distinguish a coming of Christ that takes various forms in this interim. Although he is still hidden, Christ comes into time as truly in the mystery of the sacraments as he did in the mystery of historical reality.

What was true of the first coming is also true of every sacrament, but especially of the Eucharist. For in every sacrament, and particularly in the Eucharist, the life and death of Christ are, as we have seen, somehow made present. An indication of this is afforded us by the liturgy of the eucharistic sacrifice. In the Introit we celebrate the coming of Christ effected in every Eucharistic celebration. In the Introit we announce the entry of Christ in words that are far from empty of effect but which rather act, in a mysterious way, when we pronounce them. Christ enters this world in the eucharistic celebration as saviour, redeemer and judge. Introit texts point out the various aspects of his coming. Christ's coming in the Eucharist is an echo of his first advent and a token of his coming at the end. Past and future act together in the eucharistic celebration. In it they are made one. From the past comes the death of the Lord, and the life linked so closely with it both before and after it. From the future comes the last coming of Christ.

In reality, all historical events are comings of Christ, for all historical events are ultimately acts of Christ, the ruler of all things, in whom we worship the Father of Heaven. Christ comes as much in catastrophes as in the happy events of history.

We shall understand this more fully if we remember that Christ is the active beginning of a new state of affairs in the universe. Therefore, his death, too, is the beginning of a new state of things in the universe. So, too, his resurrection is the preface to a new era. Collapses and failures show that the death of Christ marked the beginning of a new epoch in history. They are all after-effects of the death of Christ. They are images of that collapse that occurred at the centre of all history. They are at the same time precursory signs of the final collapse of human history.

In just the same way, happy events in history are after-effects of the resurrection of the Lord, images of that life which Christ received at the resurrection, of immortal life in plenty and security, and precursory signs of life in the transfigured world of the future.

Thus we can say equally well both of the disasters and the successes of history, that Christ comes in them, although in a veiled manner. Within and behind the life of the world there is enacted the mystery of salvation. What takes place in the mysteries, and what takes place in the face of the world, are both expressions of that event which will crown the whole of human history. For him who has eyes to see it, there shines forth both from the mysteries and in the outside world, something of that which is to come, when the whole of human history shall at last be swallowed up.

So then the coming of Christ which in its historical manifestation took place at a certain datable moment, extends over the centuries and millennia until it is consummated. Then Christ himself will be able to say about the whole of his life the words he said provisionally about his earthly life on the cross: 'It is consummated'. The preliminary consummation effected in his earthly life will then reach its ultimate fulfilment, for the second coming at the end of time will be the beginning of an everlasting world order no longer menaced by failure and death.

CHAPTER THREE

THE WORK OF CHRIST

Unlike all other religions, Christianity is based on an historical self-revelation of God, in which God entered into human history. Compared with it, all other religions are nature religions, and their saviours personifications of natural things, powers and events. This is true even of those religions which grow out of the civilization of a nation, for such religions are but nature religions on a higher plane. Christianity is differentiated from them by the fact that at its heart there stands an historical figure, the person of Christ. That is why the Christian speaks so often of meeting Christ in faith. To encounter Christ is simply to surrender one's ego to God who, in Jesus Christ, has entered human history. Christ is fundamentally unlike all other religious figures in that he offers only one interpretation of life—or, rather, in that he claims that he himself is the fulfilment of life. He who would attain to fulness of life can do so only by laying hold on the God manifested in Christ. Christ is the figure within history in whom man reaches full awareness of himself. He comes to himself, to fulness of life in Christ, because in him he is touched by God and receives divine fulness of life and vitality. In giving him these things, God reveals himself as love. In Christ love calls men compellingly and commandingly, to bring them out of their misery and danger. Love seeks by its compelling appeal to establish its rule in the world and so bring salvation to men. The rule of love—which is God—we call the *kingdom of God*.

The idea of the kingdom of God is essential to our understanding of Christ's life work. God made himself present in Christ in order to establish his kingdom. It is of great importance for our interpretation of Christianity for us to understand this concept clearly. What then should we understand by the phrase the kingdom of God?

This concept has two sides: on the one, the being, majesty, nature, authority, dominion—the kingliness of God, and on the other, the province, the sphere, in which his majesty and sovereignty are operative. The two sides are closely interrelated and cannot be separated, for those over whom God reigns are the sphere of his dominion. The two elements often merge into one another. The accent is, however, on the first. The phrase 'kingdom of God' describes a state of things in the world in which God, who is personalized Truth and Love, Holiness and Justice, rules, and the world is as a result transformed. It is, then, a concept concerned with kind, not place.

The Kingdom of God has not been set up in opposition to the kingdoms of this world. Its establishment does not lead to new imperialism or militarism. It does not come into conflict with the kingdoms of the earth. We cannot speak of geographical cr political boundaries between the kingdom of God and other states. It is not so orientated that it touches and pushes back or threatens the frontiers of terrestrial powers. It is coincident with no earthly state and lies athwart all earthly kingdoms. It is not advanced by the political success of lands or peoples, nor yet by mankind's economic, cultural, scientific or artistic advance. Secular history is not the same thing as sacred history. A step forward in the first does not mean advance in the second. The kingdom of God advances where the love and truth manifested in Christ advance. Earthly progress may mean either advance or retreat for the kingdom of God; the disasters in world history may be either disasters or advancements for the kingdom of God. Even glory for the Church cannot necessarily be taken as a sign that the kingdom of God is thriving. It may even mean a reverse for the kingdom. Conversely, oppression of the Church does not necessarily mean that the kingdom of God will be impeded. It may even signify an advance for the kingdom of God. Sacred history is not secular history. It takes place within and beyond human history. The relationship between them cannot be determined whilst earthly time endures. It will be possible to discern it only when God reveals it at the last judgement. All we can say is that every historical event favours the advance of the kingdom of God in so far as it favours the advance of love. At this point we can pick out the frontier of the kingdom of God—it has only one frontier, the barrier the self-aggrandisement of the creature—hate—set up against love, the rule of God.

When Christ began his public ministry, he started with the proclamation of the kingdom of God. It was the beginning of his preaching, and it was his theme throughout his life. When he cried to those who heard him: 'The time is accomplished and the kingdom of God is at hand. Repent and believe the Gospel' (Mark 1, 15), they did not find his message strange. Preparations for it had been under way for a long time. Over centuries, the promise of the coming kingdom of God had been strengthened and clarified (cf. Isaias 65, 17; 52, 7; Zach. 14, 9; Jer. 10, 10ff; Ps. 47, 3ff). The hopes of all believers were directed towards the promised kingdom. The Lord's words were exciting and disturbing because what had been promised and longed for had come at last. It is easy to see why the news excited and disturbed those who heard it.

Under the old testament the kingdom of God rested on a double foundation. It was based on the creation: God is the king of men and things because he is their creator. They are, through and through, wholly dependent on him. Thus they are by nature subject to God's rule. Nothing on this earth has unquestionable autonomy, because nothing on this earth exists of itself. The existence of everything is a continually imparted gift of God.

At a particular time and in a particular part of the world God did set up his dominion in creation with a deliberateness which over-stepped the usual pattern. He did so in order to choose a nation to convey his revelation of himself to mankind. This people was subject to him in a different and more marked degree than any other of the races of earth. The reason for this was that it was his will to effect his salvation through this people as through a pliant tool.

The kingdom of God took concrete form in the making of the testament. The testament was the form in which God displayed his dominion and sought to have it recognized. The sealing of the testament was itself an act of God's sovereignty, in which he took the initiative. He fixed the definitive terms of the testament. The social order established by the covenant was the order established by God. The law of the covenant was the law of God.

The nation submitted to his dominion. God took possession of it and showed it the paths it must follow. He protected it against its enemies whilst it was loyal to the testament. He executed ruthless judgement on it—famine, disease and war—when it fell away. But he never quite abandoned it, for his judgement was merciful.

The old testament is the history of the kingdom of God. It shows how God's kingdom advanced, and how step by step God established his dominion over self-willed mankind. Although the dominion of God does not abolish human freedom, yet there is a fateful contest between the kingdom and human self-will. The temptation to rebel against the kingdom of God was so much the stronger because the seductive gods all around the chosen people proved so powerful—indeed, sometimes seemed to be stronger than the God of Israel. They led the peoples who trusted in them to victory. The question constantly arose: What is our God? Is he really the Lord of lords? Many texts in the Psalms and Prophets read like answers to this question: our God, they say, is mightier than all gods, although it may not always look like it. In many old testament texts it is possible to find traces of the fact that they were meant to help in the conquest of doubts as to whether or not the heathen gods were mightier than the God of Israel.

Together with trial of the power of God went the temptation to fall away into the sensual cults of surrounding paganism. Recognition of the sovereignty of the one God was always overlapped by admiration for the pagan gods within the cultural circle of the chosen people. God strove ceaselessly to bring the wanderers home, back to himself in repentance and penitence.

Because God and man constantly come into contact within history, history itself has an ultimate and implicit importance: at every crisis within it there arises the question: God's glory or man's? God's honour or man's? The sovereignty of God, or the sovereignty of the gods? At every stage it was made apparent that if the people sought its own honour and chose the rule of the gods, it lost both honour and dignity. When it decided in favour of God's honour, it itself received honour and glory. If it chose God's kingdom, it decided for salvation for itself, for God is a gracious sovereign.

God exercised his dominion through earthly officers: first through the Judges, then through the Kings. Through the prophets he called the rebellious nation back time after time. It was the prophets' duty to keep the nation conscious of the fact that God was its king and that disasters overtaking it were the judgement of God. They were the active and ever-watchful conscience of the nation. They threatened punishment for backsliding, and warned that God would summon up hostile nations and natural forces to wreak vengeance on faithlessness and recalcitrance. If the nation broke the covenant, they said, it would be abandoned to destruction. Even their most terrible threats, however, were intended to bring the nation to its senses. God's will for it was not death, but life. He would not, however, be disregarded and he strongly condemned defiance. Yet even his judgement was a call to repentance. The prophets promised that a small fraction —a remnant—of the nation would be saved, because it heard and accepted his appeal. For it would be fulfilled the promises which the majority rejected in obstinate pride.

God's intention to give the chosen people a glorious future within history came to grief on their obstinacy. Although his promises will still be fulfilled, their fulfilment will not be outside history. The kingdom God promises is a transcendent kingdom. His promises of a kingdom do of course refer also to something on this earth, but their real and ultimate fulfilment is blended of colours and images which cannot be fully realized in the world we know. That is why it is so difficult for men to believe in a kingdom of God.

The transcendental nature of the coming glory of the kingdom was most clearly shown by Isaias. Isaias foretold a world in which God's kingdom would be established in its perfection. According to Isaias, God would set up a ruler in the world, so that his dominion might be realized in the world. But God's delegate in the world would have a difficult path to tread, a path that would lead him into places so dark that the regal dignity shining forth from him would be totally obscured. He would look like a servant of God, fulfilling his mission in affliction, suffering and death. But through his death he would bring the kingdom to its ultimate and indestructible form. God, who until then had been king only of his chosen people was proclaimed by Isaias king of all nations. Last in the series of prophets was John. He saw that the time of justice and grace was at hand. He foresaw the arrival of the ruler sent by God, the ruler who would be greater than all previous ambassadors and would establish God's kingdom, in the most perfect form it can know whilst the world as we know it endures. In his coming, the kingdom of God would be more powerful than it had ever been, although, of course, it would still not have reached its final form, but would be a foreshadowing of it as it will be in the world to come. John saw that the kingdom of God would burst in like a judgement on human pride. Only those who would turn back to the Lord in repentance and conversion would escape its terrors. Blood relationship with Abraham would not be enough for membership of the coming kingdom of God. It would be founded not on blood, but on spirit—on the Holy Ghost.

The last and greatest prophet of the promises of the old testament about the kingdom coming from God was Christ himself. When he entered history, Roman world domination had led to the old testament promises of the kingdom being widely understood in a purely national sense. Men hoped for the restoration of the old glory of the kingdom of David. Their hopes turned, too, towards temporal power and greatness, for such hopes are natural to this world. Christ's disciples shared these same expectations with regard to the kingdom. Slowly and laboriously they exchanged their former hopes for thoughts of a kingdom transcending the world. An important role was played in Christ's disputes with the leaders of the community, by their passionate devotion to hopes of an earthly kingdom. They defended themselves fiercely when Christ wanted to disabuse them of their notions of an earthly kingdom and preached a kingdom that should transcend the world. They believed that in so doing he was cheating the nation of its highest hopes. Christ revealed that the prophecies of the kingdom did not mean what men thought they meant, and that their real meaning ran counter to men's hopes. Christ it was who first revealed their true meaning. Christ's preaching clashed with earlier, inflated longings, and as a result his followers became ever fewer, until the leaders of the people became openly hostile, and decided that he should die. They came to believe that the interests of the nation would best be served by Christ's death, for death would prevent him from debasing and undermining nationalistic hopes for the kingdom.

Christ not only preached but also established the kingdom of God. He was the 'Son of man' who, according to Daniel's vision, had received 'power and glory and a kingdom'. He brought the divine kingdom into the world. It was revealed in him so that now any man who has the right kind of vision can see it. When, on the grounds that 'the Lord (*Kyrios*) hath need of him', he ordered the commandeering of the beast which, it was said, the Messias would ride, he was laying claim to royal dignity.

He did not want to be a king after the nationalistic and materialistic pattern of the demagogue longed for by the mass of the people, who promised themselves worldly well-being and earthly glory through him. He denied no earthly king's authority and offered no rivalry to any of the world's rulers. Yet he carried himself with regal pride when, with death looking him in the face, he was asked whether he was a king. He was indeed a king—but of a completely different kind from that meant by the pagan Pilate, who reckoned only with the powerful ones of the earth. Christ gave his disciples, too, the impression that he was a king, although it is clear they could not understand what kind of kingdom his was.

Christ established the kingdom of God by his words and acts— by words of power and signs full of the Spirit. The whole of his life was a revelation of the sovereignty of God. God had laid his hand on his life and predetermined its course. Christ bowed so unreservedly and unconditionally to his Father's commands that fulfilment of his Father's will became meat and drink to him. He lived on it. He preached words of truth and displayed tokens of love given him by the Father. The way God had marked out for Christ was, from its beginning, a way of sorrows, and God's control over Christ's life was shown most clearly in his death. At that time, the Father ruled so absolutely over Christ's life that his holiness and justice, love and loyalty showed him to be he who alone is mighty. At that time God's holy justice and righteous holiness so imbued Christ that he was ready to die at his command. Christ submitted himself as completely to the will of the Lord God

55

as was possible for a created being, and in so doing accepted God's dominion over his life. In dying he relinquished all control over his own fate. Thus he whose task it was to establish God's rule in the world became the servant of God, without either beauty or authority. Although he could help others, he was incapable of doing anything for himself. Yet it was at the moment of his greatest humiliation that he performed his duty most effectively. His death was full of the light of the new heaven.

Christ was transformed by a wonderful act of God. God gave him up to death, not in order to destroy him, but in order to reveal the face of his divine glory in Christ's human nature, and through Christ, to reveal it to the whole chaotic world. As a result of the fact that in Christ God realized his authority as far as it was possible to do so within creation, Christ became filled with the glory of God. He was ruled by the glory of God. The road to that glory ran through death, and in death, the mode of Christ's mortal life was completely transformed. He became immortal. At the resurrection he received radiant and potent life. He received a body no longer subject to the laws of mortality, but rather characterised by the immortal glory of God. Christ's body was thus the perfect expression of the glory of God that filled it. In it, the glory of God had become flesh. Thus, through death, Christ's human nature had attained perfection. The way of death was shown to be the way of life, and the resurrection—and the ascension so closely related to it—was Christ's coronation as king of everlasting glory.

The setting up of the rule of God involves the suppression of the powers opposed to God—the devil, death and sin. The devil is the adversary, whose existence God permits. He is the enemy and destroyer of everything divine in the universe. He tries to, and succeeds in, leading men to revolt against God and glorify themselves. But he does not in fact lead them to the freedom he promises, but into slavery under his own tyranny. Ever since the first temptation he has carried on the war against God's sovereignty by every means of temptation available to him—by cunning, tricks, lies and violence. Self-glorification is the motive for everything he does. Yet the power to bind and disarm Satan and the devils has been given to us in Christ.

Of this power thus given to us in Christ, the devil showed an immediate awareness. He prepared an extremely powerful counter-attack. The effort he made is obvious from the many cases of devil possession occurring during Christ's lifetime. They were not accidental, but were rather Satan's attempts to preserve his threatened authority. His determination to defend himself by attacking was shown even more clearly in the cases of demoniacal possession than in the onslaughts he made personally against Christ. He was the hidden instigator in the background in all the acts of hostility towards Christ, from Herod's persecution to the deadly hatred of the leaders of the nation, from the betrayal by the Apostle to the frenzied cries of the crowds that demanded his death. These same crowds at first followed him, but now they had been whipped up against him by clever nationalist propaganda, so that they forced a judge who was convinced of his innocence to find him guilty. Satan, the power of evil in bodily form, was behind all this hostility. On the Mount of Olives, he made use of man's natural fear in the face of pain and death (Stauffer).

Christ, however, did not succumb. The greatest triumph in his victory over Satan was that he did not fight with the same weapons as the devil himself had used. He drove the devil out with the use neither of earthly nor demoniac powers, but by the finger of God. He did not permit hatred to move him to hatred, nor lies to lies. He conquered the forces of the devil with divine powers alone—with the might of truth, holiness and love. By doing so, he gave glory to God. By doing so he took a path in earthly affairs never before used. It was a way so strange that his contemporaries found it incredible (Stauffer).

In dying, Christ carried this struggle to its ultimate limits. By dying, he glorified the Lord God to the uttermost. As a result his death—by which Satan had planned to bring down his dangerous opponent—led to Satan's own dethronement. Satan is, of course, not yet destroyed, but he has been mortally wounded. Like a beaten army, he can still do a great deal of harm. He can still make himself responsible for a great many rubbish-heaps and ruins. But final victory is now impossible to him. He no longer has any prospect of ultimately ruling the world. He faces, rather, utter and irremediable defeat.

Hand in hand with the overthrow of the rule of the devil goes the overthrow of the dominion of death. In his resurrection from the dead Christ had shown very clearly that he had dominion over death. Once for all by his own death he conquered death for all men, for in his resurrection it was revealed that to him death was a way to new life. Because he died as the head of creation, his death became for everyone the bridge between mortality and immortality. His resurrection was a manifestation of the world to come in which life, not death, has the last word. He himself called this era the time of the rule of God.

The despoiling of death involved the despoiling of suffering, death's precursor. Suffering found its way into human life in the same way as did death itself. Christ inaugurated a new age, in which death and suffering themselves serve the transition to a new life. He did not remove these destructive forces from the world, but he has made them serve eternal life. Later we shall look again at the place of suffering in the redeemed world.

Finally, through his life and death Christ has overcome that mark in man's life, his subjection to death and suffering, his remoteness from God. He has aroused in man a consciousness of sin, and it is he who keeps it alive. He has made the position extremely clear. He offers no comfort for sins. He accepts—and condemns—them for what they are: hostility towards God, demoniac expression of pride and hatred towards God. He accepts men for what they are—sinners. But he takes away sins fully disclosed to him. When he says: 'Thy sins are forgiven thee', he renews the whole man. Sin taken away by him is not merely forgotten: it no longer exists. The fact that the sin had historical existence cannot be denied, it may still have disastrous effects in the historical sphere and may even mar the spiritual life of man, but its guilt is taken away, because the sinner is no longer remote from God. Christ takes men into the fellowship which he has with the Father. In fact, the rule of God which Christ establishes means salvation for men, because it re-establishes their relationship with the Father. Just as separation from God was the cause of man's original distress (the symptoms of which are life's sufferings, pains, anxieties and fears), so the re-establishment of the rule of truth, love, justice and sanctity did away with that original distress. The purpose of the kingdom of God is the giving to man of divine life and fulness of those things for which his inmost nature longs. When God's rule is established over man, man himself attains perfection. The winning of salvation is possible only to him who shares in Christ's destiny. By doing so—and only by doing so—does man share in the life of Christ, and in the rule of God, made present in history by Christ, and so extended to the individual.

Sharing in Christ's destiny means sharing in his obedience to his heavenly Father, and because in the case of Christ himself the final proof of his submission to God was his death, the man who shares Christ's obedience, will demonstrate his complete devotion by sharing also in Christ's creative death.

He who shares in Christ's creative death does so, as we have already indicated, in a dual way: both mystically, and in historical reality. Mystically he does so through the sacraments, and especially through the celebration of the Eucharist, for the Eucharist is the re-presentation of the death of Christ. He who shares in it comes, by that very fact, under the influence of the death of Christ. He makes himself subject to that divine decree in which God sent his beloved Son to his death. The most perfect way in which we can partake of Christ's death is in communion, for the celebration of the death of Christ has the form of a meal. It is through the Eucharist that the rule of God is established in this world.

The second way in which we share in the death of Christ is through our sufferings in this world, for it is in these that the sufferings of Christ are extended to the faithful. Suffering may be creative because through suffering the rule of God may be extended, for suffering provides an opportunity of obeying God. Suffering tests our obedience to God.

Although Christ has established the dominion of God, he has not yet given it its final form, which is still to come. There will come a time when the reign of love, truth, holiness and justice will appear in its unveiled splendour. That moment will be the last of human history. Until then the reign of God, although really here, will be concealed, as, too, will be our share in that dominion established by Christ.

Within human history the kingdom of God seems powerless and defenceless because it is veiled. As Guardini said, on entering into human history God laid aside a measure of his might before the portals of the world. He did so, so that men would not be bewitched and overwhelmed by him, but might walk with him by choice in a way worthy of their freedom and dignity. One result of this is that men can rebel against God's sovereignty. Being called and fitted by Christ to do so, they can also submit to God's rule. They can submit to the God manifested in Christ, but they are not compelled to do so. Of course, if they do set themselves up against God, they must inflate their self-importance still further, for in Christ God presses men hard. If a man will not bow to God he has to fight ever more determinedly against him. As a result sin has become more powerful in the course of the centuries ushered in by Christ. As Guardini said, in comparison with the sins of pre-Christian times, which were those of a man not yet fully grown, of a child, sins have now become those of a grown man, an adult. He who, in these times inaugurated by Christ, rebels against God is trying to withdraw himself from a state of affairs brought about in the world by God himself. He denies the conditions of any life according to Christ. He is trying to live as if still in the pre-Christian era. From this point of view, a sinner is an anachronism.

In Holy Scripture, and especially in the Apocalypse of St. John, we are given a less clear picture of our human condition. According to it, men are so enamoured of their obstinacy and personal splendour that they refuse to be called back to God's glory by Christ. They prefer autonomy and the loss of salvation if salvation can only be theirs by submission to the rule of God.

Thus the destructive power of sin is still active even in the new era inaugurated by Christ. Indeed, it has become even more destructive. But this does not mean that Christianity is a failure. It was not Christ's purpose to rob man of his freedom by words or deeds, but rather to give him the opportunity to advance out of the rottenness of egoism and self-glorification into the realms of the life of God. If a man does not decide to obey Christ's appeal to him, he will be so judged. He falls still deeper and more disastrously into sin.

It is now obvious why, even in these Christian times, the result of man's rebellion is, that it is not love that rules but hate; not justice, but injustice; not philanthropy, but cruelty; not forgiveness, but vindictiveness; not devotion, but violence; not sacrifice, but lust for power and possessions; not truth, but lies. All these harmful forces are growing as an avalanche grows. The result is that the Christian era, too, is characterized—despite its real nature and inner dynamics—not so much by stillness and peace, progress and happiness, as by catastrophe, corruption, decadence and collapse. The snowball growth of revolt against God is matched by a snowball increase in God's judgements.

In the great discourse on the judgement recorded for us in the thirteenth chapter of the Gospel according to St. Mark, Christ spoke of God's justice. Judgement began with the fall of the Holy City and continues in the catastrophes of history, and will continue until the final breakdown at the end of the world. The view of history Christ gives is a glimpse of the slowly growing mountain of catastrophes together making up the story of man.

The belief in progress characteristic of modern times is based not on demonstration but on a vague emotion. It has no Scriptural basis and is contradicted by the facts of history.

What we have said so far is enough to show clearly that Christ made no promise of improvements in the condition of the world. It would be completely wrong to expect of Christianity that it should concern itself directly with the economic, political or social organization of the world. Christ's message is directly concerned not with the state of mankind within time, but rather with its condition beyond time. Its purpose is not the improvement of creation, but its transformation to make it conform to the antitype of the risen Christ. By doing so, of course, it releases a flood of light into history itself. The way in which it does so is our immediate concern.

Although, by being prevented from doing so by the opposition of men, the rule of God has not assumed its final form within human history, it will come to perfection beyond time. Anyone, therefore, who looks for the rule of God, fixes his hopes on the future—fixes them indeed on a future beyond time, a future absolute in its futurity. For such a man the emphasis is on the future form of God's rule. Modified slightly, Claudel's words are applicable here: 'The crucial question is not by whom but for whom we are born' (*Le père humilié*).

The fact that his hopes are for the future, however, does not mean that the Christian has no place in the present. In his book, *Gesundheit und Heiligkeit*, Goldbrunner tries to explain the relationship between expectations for the future and life in the present by the use of a simile: 'Hope, the Christian virtue, is not merely something felt. It is a gift of God, something actually present in the soul of the Christian. A piece of news—the announcement of some future happening—produces a change in the life of the mind. In Bergungrün's novel, *Am Himmel wie auf Erden*, we are shown every phase of life being infiltrated by news of an impending event, which imbeds itself in every thought, feeling and desire. The news is a reality—it really exists.

When a bride-to-be receives the news that her bridegroom is on the way home the whole world around her is transformed—or, rather, she sees and feels everything around her differently, because she herself has changed. Everything seems to tell her that he is coming soon. Her youth and strength renewed, she contends more easily with difficulties, taking many things more lightly because they can no longer touch her heart. Her whole being is directed towards that day. But, in spite of her thoughts being fixed on the future, she lives in the present: every task is painstakingly performed because it must be done well enough to pass the test of examination by him. She is all expectancy. Her sense and perception of time are changed: she lives in the future and yet is in the present. The future has entered the present. Her life consists in impatient waiting.'

The future juts out into the present. Its veiled outline is present in every age. The exorcism of devils, healing of the sick, forgiveness of sins, raising of the dead, and preaching of the Good News are all signs of its veiled presence, for such signs are evidence for the presence of the kingdom of God before the end of the world. Among them, too, are the sacraments—signs given by Christ himself by which he frees men from their sins, and fills them with his life here and now. They are tokens of God's sovereignty, put into the world by God himself. They are visible signs to the faithful of the fact that it is no longer evil, but God—his holiness and justice—that rules men. Chief among them is the Eucharistic sacrifice. Such divine signs, made apparent in the midst of the reign of demoniac powers, remind the faithful that God's hand is secretly on the tiller of history and that the reign of love and truth will one day break in and destroy all forces antagonistic to God. These signs are therefore the pillars on which the future rests.

Just as God revealed himself in Christ's humiliation and death on the cross, so too he further reveals himself in the medium of the cross until he comes again. The truth of this is seen not only in the re-presentation of the death of Christ in the Eucharist, but also in the sufferings of the faithful, for their sufferings show their unity with Christ. The might, power and glory of Christ the head operate in the sufferings of his members. He who, condemning the world, bears witness to Christ before the world in suffering and death, reveals by his testimony the reality of the rule of God. If at the moment of succumbing to the powers of the world, he proclaims that God is his lord, he will, like the protomartyr Stephen, fall beneath stones. His enemies will look only for their own triumph and the death of him who bears witness to Christ. God himself will sanction their victory; but in sanctioning it, he will both permit the destruction of the witness to the faith, thus bringing his mission to an end, and also will put his seal on their blindness. For there will then no longer be anyone to open the eyes of the blind. He who succumbs will see the heavens open and Christ sitting on the right hand of the Father. Those who see faith in Christ on his face will see the power of Christ in his death.

So then, he who believes in Christ does not expect paradise in this world. He is an initiate: Christ has opened his eyes to the diabolical potentialities of sinful men and to the questionable worth of worldly goods and worldly struggle. He is sceptical about all undertakings intended to bring about a paradisian future by revolutionary progress. In the face of such attempts and hopes, he looks like a realist among enthusiasts and utopians.

He knows that there is no permanent progress in this world, but that the history of man proceeds rather by an endless switch-back of disasters and new beginnings, destruction and reconstruction. He is, therefore, not driven to despair by history's rubble-heaps, but is prepared to exert all his strength to avert once more the threatened chaos. Such things convince him that the path of human history was never subject to a fixed control and never bound by the laws governing living organisms, but that rather as a result of its freedom and the creative powers of God, every age, nation, and civilization is capable of being renewed and healed.

But although he knows that even the greatest efforts are not crowned with any final success, he does not resignedly lay aside his arms, for he lives in the hope that what human strength cannot bring about will yet come to pass, for he trusts that God himself will bring it to pass. All man's successes are tokens of something that is to come. God will one day establish the reign of truth and love—will establish himself as absolute sovereign in the world and over human life. This prospect faces human history in the midst of all its sufferings and sorrows. All afflictions are birth-pangs: in them there is brought forth the new creation, the heaven and the new earth. In them, God sows a seed which will one day bear fruit. The world to come will be brought forth by God revealing his unveiled presence in the midst of mankind. The work of Christ will then have reached its final consummation. What he began in his earthly life will at that time reach its perfection. That day, the dawning of which we saw in Christ, will then have fully come, and no decline shall follow.

Because the principal signs of the last times ushered in by Christ will be the new heaven and the new earth, the post-historical phase of God's rule is usually called by Scripture, the coming age. In spite of the far-reaching modifications made by Christ, the age inaugurated by Christ's life and death and enduring until the consummation of the world, bears more outward resemblance to the pre-Christian era than to things as they will be after the world has come to an end. There is a closer connexion between history's pre-Christian phase and the world that began with Christ than between the historical phase of God's rule and its post-historical stage.

Yet God's sovereignty is being ever more perfectly realized throughout the duration of history in the Church. The Church is not identical with the kingdom of God, but is rather the instrument created by Christ for the construction of the kingdom. Everything Christ did by his life, sufferings, death, resurrection and ascension, together with the rule of God in this world, he has left to the Church to make temporally effective through its preaching and the administration of the sacraments. In its preaching and its acts it extends Christ's authority over sin and the devil. By its words and its signs it establishes the rule of God. Thus the Church is both the organ and the veiled manifestation of the reign of God in the world and in history.

CHAPTER FOUR

THE PERSON OF CHRIST

I : CHRIST THE WAY, TRUTH AND LIFE

Christ was given a mission greater than any task ever given to man. His message of redemption was not for this man or that, not for this group of men or that, but for all men, at all times—indeed, for the whole of creation. His mission was for all times and places. He was so made that he was capable of undertaking this task although it embraced the whole of reality. Although he has not yet brought redemption to its fulfilment, he has laid the foundations of it, doing so in such a way that it is certain to reach its consummation. The first stages he has already completed contain within themselves the seeds of their ultimate perfection. He is, therefore, the answer to all those questions which move men so profoundly —those Stauffer has called history's 'open questions', the problems of death, suffering and sin.

Christ's pan-historic and pan-cosmic importance compels us to ask: Who is this man? This question is of cardinal importance for mankind; there is, indeed, none more important. Its answer is of greater moment to man than anything else, for on it, all alignments and groupings of men depend.

In full awareness of the range and depth of his being, we are now going to try and grope our way to an understanding of his nature. We shall be helped in this task by the writers of the New Testament, who saw him face to face, heard his words and witnessed his miracles. What did they learn about him? What impression did he make on them?

The basic answer to questions such as these is that Christ was a profound mystery. Although ultimately every person living is an insoluble mystery, the mystery of Christ is of a different order from that of any other person in the universe. We can—within limits—come close to solving the mystery of the personality in which another reveals himself to us, but he can also obstruct our view, not completely, of course, but to such an extent that we cannot form a correct picture of him. In this respect a person is different from an impersonal thing. For we can understand a thing completely as long as we have enough intelligence. But we can perceive the inmost wishes, thoughts and will of a personal being only in as far as the personal being chooses to reveal himself to us. Even then, he cannot reveal himself completely. There is a small part of every person unapproachable by any other person, with the exception of God alone. We shall consider this point again later.

Even that part of the personality open and accessible to others is not accessible to everyone. To know a person, we need a special faculty, not merely intelligence, but also love enlightened by understanding, a gaze warmed by love. Something of the kind even holds true as regards knowing impersonal things. A man who is indifferent grasps nothing properly. He overlooks things that stare him in the face, even when an object captures his attention and arouses those physiological reactions by which seeing is effected. Real perception occurs only if a person applies himself attentively to seeing. For it is the inner self that performs the act of seeing, using the eyes as its tool. If the mind is distracted it does not see even if the eyes are turned towards an object. So then, for real seeing, we need interest, sympathy, love—a kind of relationship, as it were, with the thing seen.

This is especially true in the case of knowing a person, for the nature of a person is both higher and less easily perceived than those of impersonal things in nature. Penetration of the secret of personality therefore demands a greater effort. Only he who gives himself in love to the person he is trying to know can approach and perceive the mysterious heart of his being. He—and he alone—can penetrate the covers and veils and comprehend the true nature of the other. He who hates is denied such insight. Even he, however, does more than the man who is apathetic: he at least does the other the honour of noticing him. But he sees him only partially, as pitiful and mean. Goodness and nobility are hidden from him. His view is therefore wrong, for there is probably a remnant of goodness in every man so long as he is a pilgrim in this world.

There is, then, a close connexion between knowing and loving. Holy Scripture and, occasionally, secular authors, such as Plato, express it when they use the word 'know' as a synonym for the words 'unite in marriage'.

The mystery of the person of Christ can only be penetrated by those who love him. Cold intellectual consideration, historical research and philosophical reflexion cannot bring us to a full understanding of Christ. But they are neither indifferent nor unnecessary, for they bring Christ before men's minds. Historical examination and analysis of the Gospels and other information about Christ contained in the New Testament draw the attention of mankind to Christ. They make man face up to the question: 'What think you of Christ?' They force him to decide whether he will accept or reject Christ. If he accepts him, he comes to know by experience who Christ is, as far as it is given to man to do so. Unless he accepts Christ, any true understanding of the New Testament is impossible for him.

The way to a genuine meeting with Christ is not therefore that of rational and discursive logic, at the end of which stands assent to Christ, for only the eyes of love can pierce the mystery of the beloved.

In Scripture, loving acceptance of Christ is called living faith (in contrast to dead faith). In the last discourse, recorded by St. John, Christ explains that only he who unites himself with him in love can see him, that only to him can he, Christ, reveal himself (John 14, 18-24). It is a prerequisite of such loving contemplation of the Lord that the Lord should in some way reveal himself to man. Such contemplation makes possible understanding of the secret of Christ's person. It rests on a decision of the human heart, aided by light from the mind, just as on another plane does the turning of the lover to the beloved.

In this it resembles—in spite of the many differences between them—other life processes which do not fit into a strict pattern of cause and effect. Consider for example the art of swimming: it is not the necessary consequence of earlier lessons. Important as the lessons may be, the art of swimming cannot be learned properly until the swimmer entrusts himself, although he is not entirely certain of the outcome beforehand, to the water, believing that it will support him when he dares to take the plunge.

So too, only when, having seen Christ, a man surrenders to him in loving and reverential obedience can he come to a lively understanding of the mystery of his person. To him who loves alone does the door to the mystery of Christ stand open. He who loves is he who frees himself from selfishness, from the entangling threads of his own *ego*, from his isolation from others, and especially from his isolation from God. Such a man will not be prepared to interpret himself and the universe by a scale of values and judgements of his own making, but will allow himself to be interpreted by God, by a reality different from all human realities, and will allow himself to be corrected by the divine. He who shuts himself off against God cannot understand Christ, for he lacks every prerequisite for so doing—he has not the right standards of judgement. The 'world' cannot manifest Christ, for he cannot reveal himself to the world.

When Christ stressed this fact in his last discourse, Judas Thaddeus asked him for the grounds of this incompetence on the part of those who believed only in the world: Christ gave an indirect answer, which was, however, an explanation: 'If any man love me, he will keep my word. . . . He that loveth me not, keepeth not my words' (John 14, 22-4). It is characteristic of the 'world' and of those with faith in the world that they barricade themselves against Christ, so making it impossible for the Lord to enter them. He compels no one, but leaves everyone his freedom.

It is obvious from still another point of view that he who is locked up in himself cannot understand Christ. Christ is the face God turns towards the world. But God is love. Christ is therefore love—God—manifested in the world. But the mystery of love can be understood only by one who loves. It is hidden from the unconcerned, indifferent observer, let alone from the proud man and the man full of hate.

Even denial of Christ is based not on understanding, but on feeling. It is dictated not by the logical working of the mind, but by the workings of the heart. The arguments introduced by the intellect are, whether consciously or unconsciously, justifications of previous decisions, prior judgements, against Christ. We do not mean that arguments against Christ are merely Sophisms. They are—or may be—real difficulties. The basis of the fact that there can arise real objections to Christ is that God has revealed himself under heavy veils and masks. If one looks at the veil, at the weakness of humanity, and does not exert the powers of one's mind to pierce the veil, the disgrace of the cross, one is compelled to deny Christ. Just like the indolent man, the man who glories in himself lacks this strength of mind. He who allows love to direct him will pierce the veils, which, in the form of the weakness of humanity, lie over the divine glory of Christ, and see the mystery of God contained in Christ as in a vessel. He knows the arguments against Christ, but love enables him to counter them. He knows that they relate to the veils through which shines forth the splendour of the Christ they hide.

What then does a man see when Christ reveals himself to him and he turns to contemplate him in love? His first experience is a strange one. He discovers he cannot comprehend Christ completely with those ideas and images with which he comprehends and understands any other man. Christ cannot be fitted into the categories by which any other man can be defined. He breaks loose from all our ideas and images.

The reason for this is obvious if we look at him closely enough. In him many antitheses are bound together in a seamless unity. He is the relentless enemy of all falsehood, and yet is ready to sacrifice his life in the service of untruthful man. He hunts down sin in its most secret refuge, and yet he is the table companion and friend of sinners. He devotes himself in love and care to everyday affairs, and yet, untroubled and carefree, lets them fall from his hands. He is bound to men with an intimacy closer than any other bond, and yet he seems a stranger, alien to them. They find him both close and confiding, distant and cold.

There is more to Christ's nature than we can describe by the use of psychology, biology, biography or history.

Christ cannot, therefore, be a fiction invented by man. If he were a figment of man's imagination, he would fit into human categories. But so little is he of man's inventing that those who bore witness to him, who wrote about him for us in the New Testament, saw him as a strange and, to them, compelling personality. This is shown particularly clearly by the fact that the inmost mystery of Christ remained unsolved by them throughout his life, despite their closeness to him. When, after Christ's invitation to them to rest with him they believed they had come very close to him, they were to see him slip away from them again (Mark 6, 31-45). It was particularly noticeable when the disciples wanted to give him something to eat. To their invitation: 'Rabbi, eat'; he replied: 'I have meat to eat which you know not'. The disciples then said to one another: 'Hath any man brought him to eat?' and he said to them: 'My meat is to do the will of him that sent me, that I may perfect his work'. The same thing lay behind the failure of the disciples, even those nearest to him, to understand his message regarding the kingdom of God just before the Ascension (Acts 1, 6-8). It was the change effected in them by the Holy Ghost that first showed them the way into the mystery of Christ.

From the fact that Christ remained an impenetrable mystery to his disciples as long as he was with them, it is clear that his nature was essentially different from what it would have been had they invented him. It was not a product of their creative intuition, but it was given to them by continuous, ever more astonishing, practical experience.

This is shown very clearly by the cases of St. Paul and St. John. It was a life-long problem to Paul that God revealed his glory in the weakness of flesh and the folly of the cross. The mental image natural to him of God, a fundamentally different picture of the redeemer-God, was that of a strong man, a mighty man, who should crush his enemies. There are traces in the Pauline Epistles of the struggle Paul had with his mental image of God before he was able to accept the knowledge of God that came to him from without. When he declared in the Epistle to the Romans that he was not ashamed of the cross (Romans 1, 16), his very words treacherously gave expression to the inmost thoughts that strove continually to come to light. The same thing is true of his declaration that the message of the cross was a scandal to the Jews and a laughing-stock to the pagans (I Cor. 1, 22-5). Men laughed at this sort of divine revelation, and the Apostle obviously felt deep within him a temptation to join in their laughter. How could a man help taking offence at a weak God who was condemned to death and executed by men? He contradicted every picture man had ever made for himself of the divine and the numinous. Paul's words about God when he proclaimed that he had been crucified, were not invented in the depths of Paul's heart—or any man's heart for that matter. They originated rather in an experience which came to him from outside himself and cast him to the earth. It was an experience that shattered the image of God formed by the human mind. Christ laid his hand on Paul before the gates of Damascus and changed him beyond recognition, so that he worshipped what he had previously persecuted, and extolled and preached what he had formerly condemned.

Exactly the same is true of the witness the Apostle John bears to Christ. Guardini has shown that John naturally possessed a great capacity for love, but had no kindliness because his love was for things and facts rather than for men. The result was that John had a forceful, impatient, fanatical nature. His ungracious love was equivalent to a capacity for burning hate. It was expressed outwardly in the trenchancy with which John came out against Judas. In his inherent religious convictions, John came near to gnosticism, that creed which takes a dualist view of everything. According to gnosticism, everything contains elements of both the divine and the diabolic, of good and evil, light and darkness, matter and spirit, love and hate, male and female. The whole physical world is built up of things combining elements of both series. These elements themselves are metaphysical realities. In St. John's Gospel it is clear that John remodelled his natural temperament and original religious convictions in the light of his experience of Christ. But traces of his original thoughts are obvious in the Gospel.

If St. John had created Jesus in his own mind, he would have produced a gnostic picture of the world. Out of hatred for his enemies he would have made an image of a fiery, fanatical redeemer. But the characteristics of the picture of Christ given us in the Gospel are fundamentally different from that. John did not create his Christ: he received his image of him from outside himself. The Christ he reports is not a mythical figure, but an historical person. He does indeed often dress his testimony to Christ in the garments of myth, but this results from his choice of language, for his language is that of a gnostic. The matter of his witness to Christ is, however, essentially what he had seen and heard. Indeed,

73

John laid great emphasis on what he had seen and heard: in his first Epistle he wrote: 'That which was from the beginning, that which we have heard, that which we have seen with our eyes, which we have looked upon and our hands have handled; I mean the word of life of which we bear witness unto you; for the life was manifested and we have seen and do bear witness and declare unto you the life eternal, which was with the Father and hath appeared to us. That which we have seen and have heard, we declare unto you; that you also may have fellowship with us' (I John 1, 1-3).

If Christ's personality was mysterious and strange to the trusted disciples, it was completely incomprehensible to those furthest from him, to the mass of the people who felt hostile to him. His message about God, Man, the kingdom and the world was such that it contradicted everything the majority of the people expected of God and the promised kingdom. The result of this was that most of the nation was angered by Christ and his message. He destroyed images and hopes that had become dear to them, and they therefore took offence at him. The anger he engendered gradually sharpened into a hate that they longed to wreak on Christ in any possible way. There was nothing contingent about their hate: it could not have been avoided or overcome by greater exertion or display of skill on Christ's part. It was unavoidable, for it expressed the opposition man feels to God, when God approaches him after he has barricaded himself against the divine and become enamoured of himself.

Man—proud, self-willed, sure of himself—could not tolerate having to worship God in the puny and helpless form of a man, and especially not that of a man who had been condemned and executed. His resistance and opposition, his rage and hate did not originate in any harmful influence Christ had on the human mind. Even when it became apparent that Christ was also the guarantor of secular order, of social life worthy of mankind, men were scandalized by him on the sole ground that the God they encountered in Christ was different from the image of God—or, rather, the gods which they had made for themselves, no part of which they were willing to relinquish. Christ's execution was not the result of a misunderstanding or tactical blunder. It resulted from the kind of relationship bound to spring up between proud

74

man and a God who manifests himself in the weakness of man. Autocratic man could not tolerate such a God. The heart laden with sin comes to hate the living God (John 8, 43 f.).

Christ was conscious of the fact that he was a stranger in the world, and he had to endure this terrible feeling. He knew that he seemed strange not merely to some men, but to all. He was compelled to live in unconquerable loneliness. The fact that, as he said, he had nowhere to lay his head was but one expression of his essential 'foreign-ness' in this world. What Rilke said of every man's life was especially true of his: the world was a very strange place to him. All his life Christ had to bear the burden of seeming to belong to a different age both from those loyal to him and those who hated him, from both his friends and his enemies. He always seems out-of-date, because he and the pride of this world have nothing in common.

The world united in hatred against him. Its opposition to him was greater than its hostility to anything else, because it originated in the most telling of all of this world's antitheses, that between self-willed man and the God manifested in Christ. As a result, forces usually irreconcilably opposed found themselves united in friendship from their common antagonism to Christ. Faced with Christ, the pagan Pilate and Herod the Jew forgot the long and bitter enmity between them. All the world's domestic differences become as nothing in the face of common opposition to Christ. Towards the end of the second century, Irenaeus said that 'on the invocation of the name of Jesus Christ, who was crucified under Pontius Pilate, a division occurs among men.'

Christ expressed this in a saying full of the profound sense of loneliness which afflicted him in this world: 'If the world hate you, know ye that it hated me before you. If you had been of this world, the world would love its own; but because you are not of the world, but I have chosen you out of the world, therefore the world hateth you . . . that the word may be fulfilled that is written in their law: They hated me without a cause' (John 15, 18 f.; 25).

What picture of the life and work of Christ are we offered by the narratives of those who witnessed it? Each of them reflects the whole Christ, yet each reflects him differently. Each witness reports what he saw and found in Christ in a style peculiar to himself alone, dependent upon his own particular way of thinking, seeing and speaking. An essential element in the Catholic view of Holy Scripture is the belief that it originates in divine inspiration and that God is in some measure its hidden author. God the Holy Ghost used men—men who were still free—as his instruments. In doing so, he did not destroy human individuality, but held it in esteem. Part of human individuality, however, are human limitations and shortcomings. These too are therefore to be encountered in the Scriptures which God has composed through the agency of human beings. The revelation God made in the Incarnation is also made in a very real sense in the Scriptures. In them it takes a form essentially different from, yet comparable to that which it took in the incarnation. The Scriptures are the testimony God the Holy Ghost himself has given to Christ through Matthew, Mark, Luke, John, Paul, Peter, and James. Only this simultaneous presentation of all the different forms of the one testimony to Christ could present us with a complete picture of his person.

So then, let us pick out its characteristic features. The fundamental reason why Christ seemed out of place on earth was that he was from above, whilst everyone else is from below. Christ was born 'neither of the will of the flesh, nor of the will of man': he was sent into the world by the Father. He had a genealogy strictly in accordance with the human pattern, yet at the same time he transcended all humanity.

He is depicted as the fulfilment of all the promises of the Old Testament—the promises of the Messias (Saviour) and the reign of God. He himself was fully aware of this destiny. It was a heavy burden for him to bear to know that in him centuries and millennia had reached their goal, whilst in him too centuries and millennia took their origin.

This was made very clear by an event at the beginning of his public ministry (Luke 4, 14-21), after Christ had come out from the wilderness, emerging victorious from a struggle with Satan, whose design it had been to turn him from his duty and tempt him to surrender to the world. Christ went into the synagogue and asked for the book of the Prophet Isaias. Opening it, he found the place where it read: 'The Spirit of the Lord is upon me.

Wherefore he hath anointed me to preach the Gospel to the poor; he hath sent me to heal the contrite of heart, to preach deliverance to the captives and sight to the blind, to set at liberty them that are bruised, to preach the acceptable year of the Lord and the day of reward.' St. Luke continues: 'And when he had folded the book, he restored it to the minister and sat down. And the eyes of all in the synagogue were fixed on him. And he began to say to them: This day is fulfilled this scripture in your ears'. It was time for them to rejoice: for to those who saw this day of fulfilment, he said: 'Blessed are the eyes which see the things which you see. For I say to you that many prophets and kings have desired to see the things which you see and have not seen them; and to hear the things that you hear, and have not heard them' (Luke 10, 23 f.; Matt. 13, 16-17).

Christ was the Son of man promised in the Old Testament. In a wonderful vision, the Prophet Daniel saw a figure who looked like the Son of man standing before God, 'the Ancient of days', and receiving glory, power, honour and majesty. The Son of man was a ruler clothed in the glory of heaven. Yet he appeared in the form of a servant and did, in fact, fulfil the servant's office. He went in quest not of the great and powerful of this world, but of the world's little ones and the lost. He was the Lord of creation, and had less than the wild beasts. He did not know where he might lay his head, yet the Sabbath was his to do with as he would. He was tired and afraid—it even proved possible to execute him—and yet he was God's representative on earth and had the power of life and death. He who believed in him would be saved; he who did not believe in him would be lost. 'The Son of man goeth as it is written of him': It had been written of him that he would have to endure much suffering and humiliation: 'Behold, we go up to Jerusalem; and all things shall be accomplished which were written by the prophets concerning the Son of man. For he shall be delivered to the Gentiles and shall be mocked and scourged and spit upon. And after they have scourged him, they will put him to death. And the third day he shall rise again' (Luke 18, 31-3).

Nevertheless, he had authority over death. He could, indeed, be killed, but yet he was mightier than all men living, mightier than his judge and executioner. When Christ stood weak and helpless

77

before his judges in Jerusalem, he gave them a glimpse into a future which filled the court with fear and horror before this man they had accused and convicted. Certain of his power over death, he declared that he would come again on the clouds of heaven. The court did not laugh at his threat as they would have done at the fancies of a lunatic or megalomaniac. Christ made such an impression on them that they had no desire to laugh. They had to take Christ and his claims seriously, although his claims surpassed anything that might be said, promised, affirmed or threatened rationally by a man with a healthy mind. The judges began to hope that they could rid themselves of this man by executing him. But they slept peacefully for only a few days after his death. After a very short time they, terrified, saw come to pass what he had told them to expect. He returned. He was stronger than death. This first return forces us to take seriously his promise to come again to say the last word about human history, and to clear out all corruption and decay from his Father's creation, establishing the rule of God in its perfection. As Stauffer said, this second return will show that he is the Son of man, the universal, omnipotent Lord.

It is now clear that when Christ called himself Son of man, he was making very wide claims. The phrase is not an expression of humility and diffidence as the followers of the 'Life of Jesus' school once believed. Indeed, his complete self-assurance was super-human.

Christ's assertion that his mission was one of universal healing and blessing, points to the same conclusions. He ascribed to himself everything in the universe profitable and beneficial to man, and his disciples, too, attributed all to him. From this we can see his own opinion of his historic and cosmic significance. It is noteworthy that Christ's contemporaries, both his friends and his enemies, did not attribute these exalted claims to insanity. Christ must have made a great impression on them for them to take him seriously under conditions in which they would have laughed at anyone else.

Christ, then, is the fulfilment of the historical and natural development of creation. All movements converge on him. Just as the ultimate significance of history is to be found in him, and

78

cannot be finally understood apart from him, so also nature finds its ultimate significance in him and cannot be interpreted or classified apart from him.

Let us look more closely at a few of his claims: Christ called himself the Truth, the Way, the Light, the Bread and the Life.

Christ is the Truth: with the claim that he was the Truth, Christ maintained that his was the authentic interpretation of the universe, man and God. He who would know what man is, and what God is, what the universe and history are, must listen to the word of God. Christ preached not any intermediate, but the final truth. He revealed what man is in relation to God and what God means to man. He gives man a position of great importance. In his book *Krankheit zum Tode*, the Danish theologian Kierkegaard said in connexion with this: 'How infinitely real the human being is seen to be when he himself realizes he stands in the presence of God, when, as an individual, he is measured by the standard of God. A herdsman who (if such a thing is possible) is an individual to his cows is a very low kind of individual; as is a ruler who is an individual to his slaves. Strictly speaking, neither of these two is a person, for there is not a standard by which to measure them. The child whose only standard is at first his parents, becomes a person when, as a man, he can measure himself by the state. But how strongly the accent falls on the individual whose standard is God!'

Christ taught an existential truth—truth as it is determined by salvation and destruction. Acceptance of it leads to redemption; rejection, to damnation. The truth he preached demands unreserved acceptance from men. It is compulsive and it commits men to action. One who merely listens to it interestedly does not do it justice. He is like the seed which falls on stony ground, and not taking root, withers away. Interest in religion is not enough. The truth of Christ demands submission and obedience. In comparison with it the truths discoverable by man are precursory and secondary. They too however have their significance, and are necessary for life within the universe. Without them, man's social life would be impossible; without them, human existence would lack that guide which it needs in order to bestir itself in the world and to give a meaning to life. To this class belong the truths of science, philosophy and art. They serve civilization—the economic, political and social order. He whose only standard is the world may see them as the highest truths. He who takes God as his standard, sees that they are not final. Although these discoveries are worth all the labour they involve, they cannot answer the ultimate questions that worry every man. As far as they are concerned, the ultimate questions are still open questions. When science, philosophy and art try to deny that they are still open, and attempt to solve them themselves, their ultimate effect, despite all the enlightenment they afford men in this world, is to plunge men into darkness. Even in matters proper to them, they do not offer men absolute certitude, for they are subject to later change and improvement. Man therefore does not feel absolutely bound by his discoveries about truth. He sees that when they act alone, the order of things they bring into being is unstable. Christ on the other hand preaches a truth which answers the ultimate questions. He preaches it with absolute authority. He himself guaranteed the truth he preached, even to death. He demands the same pledges from those who hear and accept his preaching.

Christ, however, was not merely a preacher of truth—he was, rather, its revelation. The truth he claimed to be was not merely a formula throwing light on reality. It is rather the revelation of divine reality itself. It is the truth man must accept, by which he must live. It should be sovereign over him. It should be his strict, yet beneficent, ruler.

We shall find it easier to understand what is meant by the truth in which we should stand and worship God, if we accept the help the Greek word *Aletheia* offers us. *Aletheia* signifies that which is not concealed; overt reality and, more precisely, the reality about God. Christ has made once more accessible to men that which, on account of sin, had become and remained inaccessible to them. Through him, it has become again possible for men to reach God; for he is the revelation of the Father, the countenance the Father turns towards the world. In Christ, men can once again encounter God in history. In him, God stretches out his hand to men. Incredible and paradoxical as it sounds, he who grasps Christ's hand, takes the hand of God. In Christ God has ceased being a remote figure, and has drawn near to us, for in Christ God permits men to lay hold on him in faith and love.

In faith, man devotes himself to the divine Person given him in Christ. Because in Christ God has become accessible to men—for he has appeared to them in Christ—he who looks on Christ sees God. He who hath seen me hath seen the Father. Such 'seeing', is more than mere interested 'taking cognizance of': seeing here has the more intense and profound meaning 'to join *or* unite with'. Christ's saying is therefore very important for it means: He who binds himself to me in love, thereby binds himself to the Father. The Father comes to him and takes up his dwelling in him. He is moulded to God and becomes, as it were, God-shaped.

Christ, then, preached to mankind a truth different from the truths of this world. The life of the man who accepts Christ in faith is not restricted to this world. To him, therefore, earthly life is not ultimate and final. The result is that earthly losses too, are not final and absolute to him.

It is this which makes possible Christ's command to those who believe in him: 'Let not your heart be troubled' (John 14, 1). With these words in his farewell he charged his faithful followers not to be frightened by the death that was drawing near. Christ was bidding them not to fear the dangers of the world. On another occasion he spoke to them to the same effect: 'Fear ye not them that can kill the body and are not able to kill the soul' (Matt. 10, 28).

Christ's command not to be troubled and afraid, but to endure and overcome natural fears of dying and the perils of life, did not signify any belittling of worldly uncertainties and threatening dangers. On the contrary, Christ made plain the abysses in which the life of man may be swallowed up. He showed his followers that they must reckon upon death and dying. He stripped them of all their illusions. He offered them no prospect of a life of security and plenty in this world. He told them they must expect to come to grief through the opposition of the world, and that they would certainly founder on the reef of death. He showed them that there are critical situations from which men cannot escape. But at the same time, he warned them not to fall involuntarily into the dangers and perils of life, but to ascend from the abysses of fear and anxiety to a life of confidence and trust.

In giving his followers no promises regarding this world, he refused them what the world desires. It longs for life, fulness and security of life, within its own frontiers. Christ stated positively that he would not confer such earthly gifts. Yet he did offer those who believed in him fulfilment of their deepest longings and needs. Whilst refusing them fulfilment and plenty in this life, he did not demand of them that they should repress or suppress their longings and needs, for that would lead to a cramping and narrowing of their lives. He challenged them rather to long for the highest things; for although they cannot know fulfilment in this world, Christ nevertheless offered them the prospect of fulfilment, for he laid bare the way to that reality that surpasses all earthly things, in the presence of which all earthly things, though they be noble and great, seem pitiful and small. He revealed the way to the truth of God and the splendour of his love.

The prospect of dwelling in God and his love is a rich one for men (cf. John 14, 2). Christ himself is preparing for his followers a dwelling in his Father's house. He is empowered to, and capable of doing so because, as Son and heir, he has the right to dispose of his Father's house. In setting before his followers the prospect of a dwelling place, he promised fulness and security of life to go with it. A dwelling is more than a place to live, for a place to live merely affords protection against injury from the weather. A dwelling, however, affords fulfilment of life's longings. It expresses the inmost nature of him who dwells in it. The dwelling which Christ is preparing for his followers, is of a kind suited to them, so that they will feel at home in it. By speaking of many mansions, Christ promises that the full potentiality of 'dwelling' would be exploited; he promises the perfection of home. He who takes possession of the dwelling prepared for him will be in a very final manner at home there—so perfectly, indeed, that he will never feel out of place again. He will be at home in the place his heart tells him is home: in the love of the Father. As long as a man is not yet there, he is driven onward by the unrest of the wanderer and pilgrim. When he has once arrived, he will never again feel unrest, for he will have attained fulfilment of all those things in him which call for fulfilment. Such are the vistas opened by Christ's saying that he is the truth.

The scope of the truth revealed by Christ and the power with which he is endowed become still clearer if we remember that

God is love, and that the divine truth manifested in Christ is therefore truth about love and that he indeed is self-sacrificing love. In Christ, love is made present, accessible and tangible. However hidden or veiled it might be, it is active in history, in living and dying, in the sufferings and hopes of men, present as the power that stirs all things. Even when hate bursts forth violently, the love manifested in Christ has its hand firmly on the tiller. In the midst of the ravings, roaring, ragings and blasphemies of hate, man can reach out to the love that is never far off and grasp the hand that love, manifested bodily, holds out to him. In the abysses of hate, he can enter the realms of love Christ has opened to him. If hate overwhelms him as it overwhelmed Christ, he does not slip into the empty and bottomless pit, but into the arms of the omnipotent love made present in the world by Christ.

In laying hold on love, he also saves himself from defeat at the hands of hate, and answers hate and slander with their opposites. The love revealed in Christ preserves those men who cling to it from the perils of their own self-seeking and self-glorification. When he lays hold on Christ in faith, uniting himself to him, he makes himself one with love. When he is ruled by God, he is ruled by love. When he is moulded by God, he is shaped by love. In this way, his being and his life are fulfilled. As we shall see below, because of his descent from God, who is love, man bears in his inmost being the stamp of love. The life in keeping with our nature is, therefore, the life of love. Love gives meaning to life.

He who stretches out to the love manifested in Christ and, submitting to it, unites himself with it, thereby attains to the ultimate meaning of life. During the time of his earthly pilgrimage he sees only its dawn, but after death he reaches its perfection. Man cannot fail to see the meaning of his life fulfilled if he surrenders himself to the love manifested in Christ. Thus, experiencing the fulness of the final plenitude, whilst still in the midst of all the perils of this life, Paul could hymn the song of triumph: 'And we know that to them that love God all things work together unto good; to such as, according to his purpose, are called to be saints. . . . What shall we then say to these things? If God be for us, who is against us? He that spared not even his own Son, but delivered him up for us all, how hath he not also, with him, given us all things?

Who shall accuse the elect of God? God is he that justifieth. Who is he that shall condemn? Christ Jesus that died; yea, that is risen also again, who is at the right hand of God, who also maketh intercession for us. Who then shall separate us from the love of Christ? Shall tribulation? Or distress? Or famine? Or nakedness? Or danger? Or persecution? Or the sword? (As it is written: For thy sake, we are put to death all the day long; we are accounted as sheep for the slaughter.) But all these things we overcome, because of him that hath loved us; for I am sure that neither death, nor life, nor angels, nor principalities, nor powers, nor things present, nor things to come, nor might, nor height, nor depth, nor any other creature, shall be able to separate us from the love of God which is in Christ Jesus our Lord' (Romans 8, 28; 31-39).

When in the farewell discourse, Christ gave his followers the commandment not to fear, even when life foundered on the strand of death, he also set before them the way to the truth of God (that is, of love) he had revealed to them. He himself is this way (John 14, 4. f). There is no other. Everything else called a way is a parable of this way. Men wander through the world by many ways, seeking the fulfilment of their lives. They seek by many ways to reach fulfilment of what their hearts long for, but both individuals and societies find it takes trouble and effort to find a way that will put an end to their struggles. Ultimately, however, all this world's ways are blind alleys. They stop short inside this world. They do however lead to a human Thou in which the human I believes it finds relief from its loneliness. They lead to community in state and nation, to rank and property, to power and glory, to the peak of civilization, art and science. Yet he who follows them feels himself driven on further. He is led to the discovery that there is no road to lead where the longings of the mind and heart drive. All ways in this world turn back on themselves. They lead men in circles. If merely the ways of this world existed, men's wanderings and pilgrimage would be without final hope. There would in fact be for men only limited hope, and therefore, no real hope at all. When he notices that a road does not lead to his goal, he turns his wandering steps to another, but only to come soon to the realization that it, too, makes no eternal promises. Thus man's situation is finally irremediable. He can attempt to persevere with determined courage in this irremediable position. He can take it on himself to endure a life without final hope, but if he does so, a vista of nothingness lies open before him. Nihilism forms the horizon of the man who knows only the ways of this world. He is a man without hope.

Into this situation Christ tossed the word of consolation and promise: 'I am the way'. I am the true way, the only way. He is a way different from every other in the world of man. His way leads out of history and the universe. It leads to a reality beyond time and the cosmos. It is not a prolongation of any earthly way, but a completely different kind of way. The reality that lies at its end is present in every time and place, yet it is qualitatively different from every time and place, for it is the divine *ego*. The way Christ reveals to his followers really leads to its goal. Its goal is, moreover, the highest goal there is, a goal which, once reached, satisfies every desire.

Christ does not merely show the way: he is not merely a signpost; but he is himself the road. Man walks that road in faith: laying hold on Christ in faith, he puts himself on the road to the Father. Christ is man's only way to the Father and to fulfilment of his own being. But he who walks this road called Christ, which leads where no way on earth can lead, is not thereby spared the ways of the world. Over them, he wanders from one place to another, from one goal to another, for he is a steward in this world. Yet whilst he is wandering over those ways of the world allotted to him, he is also walking an invisible way leading him from time to eternity.

Christ is the light. But what is light? It illuminates the world, so that men can see the world and orientate themselves in it. It throws light on the paths of the world, so that man may walk on them. It is the brightness which enables man to find his way about. But all earthly light is menaced by darkness and is constantly being swallowed up by it.

Radiantly as the sun shines over the world, bathing all things in its brightness, it yet sets again, so that the world sinks into shadows and night. The terrestrial sun can only conquer the darkness for a given number of hours, and even during the hours in which it gives light to the world it does not completely subdue the darkness: even the most brilliant daylight is a mixture of light with darkness. Furthermore, no sun can conquer the darkness in human hearts and minds.

The light which man yearns for in his inmost being is never seen in its perfection in this world. Man longs for a light upon life, yearns to know the meaning of life, the solution to life's riddles, the answer to the questions Why? and Wherefore? He longs for a life whose meaning is clear. Light leads man to freedom—freedom from oppression and fear, and especially from the fear that the meaning of life is escaping him, or that it has no meaning. Only a life with such freedom can really be called life, for it alone will be a life of joy and happiness, peace and prosperity. Anyone who could give man light, would be giving him real life. Without the light that illumines life, life itself remains an insecure and fearful thing, cursed and maimed.

In his play *Le Père Humilié*, the French playwright Claudel shows us the longing that is in human hearts by making the hero, who, although taken for sighted, is in fact blind, say on being bidden to open his eyes: 'Can you guarantee that I shall see justice? If I shall not be able to see it, it will not be worth while opening my eyes.'

R. M. Rilke in his poem *Die Blinde* has movingly portrayed the confusion which loss of sight brings to the very heart of man, and the enlightenment which, in spite of—or rather, because of— the extinguishing of his physical sight, blinding may afford him. The cardinal importance of this poem for our understanding of human life makes it worth quoting, in spite of its length. Man's blindness forms the dark backcloth against which Christ, the light, displays his full brightness:

Stranger: Are you not afraid to talk of it?
Blind Woman: No. It is so far off.
               It was someone else who once saw it
               Lived so wildly
               And died.
Stranger: And had a hard death.
Blind Woman: Dying is cruelty to the unsuspecting.
               One needs to be hard

86

When even a stranger dies.
Stranger: She was a stranger to you?
Blind Woman: Rather—she had become so.
Death alienates even mother from child—
Aye, but it was hard in the first days.
My whole body was a wound.
The world, in which things bloom and ripen
Was torn from me by the roots,
With—it seemed—my heart,
And I lay open, like ploughed land
And drank the old rain of my tears,
Streaming gently, unceasingly
From my dead eyes.
As clouds would fall
From the empty heavens
If God had died.
My ears were acute, and ever open.
I heard things inaudible:
Time, flowing over my hair;
Silence, ringing like fine glass—
And I felt: close by my hands passed
The breath of a large, white rose.
Constantly I thought: Night
And: Night
And believed I saw a broad band of light
That would move like day's
And believed I moved to the day
That lay long since in my hands.
I woke my mother when
Black-faced sleep fell heavily on me.
I called my mother:
'Come here! Bring light!'
And I listened.
Silence. Long. So long.
And I felt my pillow turn to stone—
Then I saw something shine:
My mother's woeful tears.
I will not think about it any more.

'Bring light! Bring light!' Thus cry I
Oft in dreams: The room has fallen in.
Lift the room off my face and breast.
You must lift it—lift it high!
Give it back to the stars!
I cannot live like this—with the
Sky on me.
But—am I talking to you, mother?
If not—then to whom? Who is it back there?
Who is behind the curtain?
Winter? Mother—Storm? Mother—
Night? . . . Tell me?
Or is it day? . . . Day?
Without me? How can it be day
Without me?
Am I then missed nowhere?
Does no one ask for me?
Are we quite forgotten?
But you are there—
And you still have everything, have you not?
Your sight is still all right.
Though thine eyes rest—
Yea, though they be never so tired—
They will wake again. . . . .
But mine are still.
My flowers shall lose their colour.
My mirror freeze over.
In my books the lines will run together.
My bird will flutter in the alleys
And injure itself on strange windows.
I am joined with nothing any more.
I am abandoned by everything.
I am an island.

Stranger: And I am come over the sea.
Blind Woman: How? . . . To the island? . . . Here?
Stranger: I am still on board my boat.
I brought it gently to the shore—
To you. My pennant moves—

It flutters towards the land.
Blind Woman: I am an island: I am alone!
I am fertile.
At first, when the old paths were still
In my nerves, worn there by much use
I suffered much.
Everything fled my heart.
At first I knew not where—
But then I found it all—
All my feelings, all I am,
Is brought together, and presses,
And screams to my dead and walled-up eyes.
All my suborned feelings . . . .
I do not know whether they were so for years
But I know about the weeks: they came back broken
And knew no one.
Then the way to mine eyes was closed
I could no longer find it.
Now everything goes round inside me
Safe and carefree: my emotions,
Like convalescents, go happy
Through my body's dark house.
Some are readers of memories.
But the younger of them
Look out, for where they reach
My outer wall, my wall is glass.
My brow sees.
My hand reads poems in other hands.
My foot talks with the stones it walks on.
My voice profits from every bird.
Now I am deprived of nothing:
Every colour is translated
Into noise and smell.
Endlessly, beautifully they sound.
What is my book?
The wind turns the pages of the trees,
And I know what words are written there,
And often repeat what it reads.

And death, which breaks eyes like flowers
Cannot meet my eyes . . . .

Stranger: (In a low voice). I know. . . .

Into the darkness of humanity, Christ cries: I am the light of the
world! He is the authentic, the true light, of which all earthly
light is an allegory. What earthly light signifies, but can only
partially effect, Christ brings to perfection. He is the light in
whose luminosity the glory of God and the meaning of the world
are illumined for men. His light has streamed forth since the
first moment of creation.

By his light, men have ever been able to see themselves for
what they really are: the creatures of God. They have always been
illumined by the light of God and it has, therefore, always been
possible for them to understand themselves aright. The world
has always been a revelation of God to them. But they have closed
their minds to that revelation and therefore lost true understanding
of themselves and the world. They have slipped into the folly
of believing themselves capable of governing themselves; fallen
into the darkness where they no longer understand themselves,
because they are no longer willing to regard themselves as God's
creatures; fallen into the darkness where they must lose their way
and stray into error. In their delusions, they rob themselves of
the true life, the life of happiness and freedom. Darkness and
death are near neighbours. Once mankind has fallen into darkness,
its representative and ruler is Satan. In depriving men of true
knowledge of themselves, he deprives them of real life. He is a
murderer and a liar.

Since the incarnation, the true light has shone in the darkness in
bodily form. Christ is a torch shining in the darkness of human
history. The healing of the man born blind was a parable of this
truth. It is possible for us to regard that miracle merely as a gesture
of help, given to a man by a Christ whose heart brimmed over
with merciful love. But if that were its only meaning, it would in
fact be a meaningless event in a world full of thousands and millions
of blind men who find none to heal them. It must, therefore,
have a wider significance. It reveals Christ's function, for human
history and for the individual man. Christ fills man's life with

light, so that we can see who we are. In Christ, man comes to have a true and sober view of himself. He realizes he is a creature of God, lost and now saved. He sees himself as God must see him, and so comes to possess a right standard by which to judge his life. As long as Christ is not the source of his understanding of himself, he lives a life of illusion. Those who see properly are those enlightened by Christ. Everyone else suffers from dreams and delusions, dreaming of supermen, of men who are as gods, of the earthly paradise.

Christ gives men true knowledge of themselves and of the world. The man who sees the world by the light of Christ does not imagine pictures of men and things that cannot be fulfilled in time. He does not count on perpetual progress, with a continually rising curve of well-being and harmony. He sees both the world and men clear-headedly, without illusions. He is a sceptic. But the sinfulness of man and the rubble-heaps of the world drive him neither to resignation and hopelessness, nor to the despair from which he can be saved only by amusements and diversions. For in his words of love Christ gives man something in which he can have final and unreserved hope. That something is the love of God, visible to men in the light of Christ in the midst of the darkness of the world, in the midst of earthly perils and dangers, of all human malice and meanness and the ruins and desolation of history. By that light, he can see which way he must turn if he is to escape despair. In its glow he too can turn in love to mankind and the things of this world.

The light that comes through Christ is not a natural phenomenon like the light that comes to earth from the sun. It is a spiritual thing. Christ is the light and the bearer of light, because it is he who is the source of revelation. It is man's responsibility to perceive and accept the light, but he may stand aloof from it in his self-glory and pride. Self-glory prefers darkness to light, and the man who glorifies himself refuses to see himself as a creature, and insists on controlling his own destiny, even if that involves leaving the riddle of life unsolved and the questions Why? and Wherefore? unanswered; even at the price of a life which falls short of perfection, being without liberty and happiness. Self-glory prefers the life of night and despair to light and the happiness it brings, because enlightenment can be attained only by submitting to him who reveals the light. He who despairs—whether openly or not—is therefore responsible for his despair. Despair is sin. The man who allows himself to be enlightened by Christ, the revealer of the light, thereby gains the true life. For Christ is the life. In him life is made manifest. The life manifested to the world in him is not like anything else we call life. All life we know is mortal: it is a prolonged death-agony, for death is in the midst of it. It is therefore not true life: compared with the life of God it is an allegory of life. The man who partakes only of this life can therefore with truth be called a dead man, for it is a life which needs continual protection against the onslaughts of death. Even then, death will one day drag it into the abyss, for it is subject to the laws of mortality. It must founder on the reef of death. There is no escape for it from that.

The life manifested in the world by Christ is, unlike any earthly life (or biological existence), the real, immortal life, for it is the life of God. Only God is truly alive—indeed, he is himself Life. He is the uncreated and inexhaustible fulness of Life. His life cannot be divided into a series of separate acts, subsequent to and dependent upon one another: it is rather the highest concentration of the fullest form of life. There is nothing more alive than the life of God. When in Christ the life of God was manifested in the world, there was made present in the world a life which no onslaught of death could endanger. Mortal man may now become a partaker of that life: mortal man can reach out for a life bearing in itself the plenitude of immortality. To the man who gives himself to Christ in faith, Christ gives the prospect of eternal life beyond mortality. For in spite of the life ruling in his inmost being, Christ took upon himself the law of death, which is the law of mankind. By his death the life in him was set free: in the resurrection it broke out into his human form, so that his human nature became imbued with the life of God and began to partake of its fulness and power. Anyone who lays hold on Christ in faith is made a partaker of this life of abundance and power, so that he survives the collapse of life in its earthly form. Indeed, the breakdown of earthly life becomes for him the way to the immortal, eternal life of God.

Baptism marks the beginning of our sharing in this new kind

and fulness of life, for it gives the death-blow to mortality and brings into being the new, immortal kind of life, which he who shares in the life of Christ possesses within himself. What is begun in baptism is furthered by the other sacraments; they too separate man from the way of life of the earth and establish the divine life within him. It continues throughout the afflictions of life, until life's complete collapse. Death brings the ripening of the seed sown in baptism: it liberates the life of God implanted in man. In death, there is the same fulfilment as a grain of wheat finds when it falls to the earth and dies. The grain of wheat must accept death if it is to yield much fruit. If it were to refuse to die, it would remain alone. Man must accept death if the life of Christ he has received is to attain its perfection. For through death, he reaches out to immortal life. The resurrection of the dead is the proper hope of the Christian.

Christ is the bread of life: he is the true and essential bread. What earthly bread is intended and attempts to give men—but can give them only partially—Christ gives in its fulness. Bread is meant to feed life. It can, however, feed only mortal life, and mortal life it can sustain only temporarily. Earthly life fed even on the best bread will one day pass away. Earthly bread is an allegory of Christ: he who understands it properly sees it as an allusion to Christ. The Flemish poet Gazelle described the symbolic character of bread and its fulfilment in Christ in these words:

> Who can see wheat
> And not remember
> How noble a food it is
> —And not remember?
> And wine—
> Who can see wine
> And not remember
> How noble a drink it is
> And not remember?
>
> Who can a Christian be
> And not remember
> That Christ himself he eats and drinks
> And not remember?

93

Christ is the bread which provides life that is truly immortal, the life for which man hungers and thirsts. They who hunger for the true life are being called by Christ, who promises them satisfaction of their hunger and appeasement of their thirst. The man who does not experience this hunger and thirst has grown hard, and does not really know what his heart wants. He has no experience of hunger which differs from the hunger of the belly— hunger which others know to be of the heart and soul. Such hunger cannot be appeased with the foods the world provides. In this world man cannot satisfy his soul, but has to live in longing. Any possible earthly fulfilment of that hunger would only be temporary and partial, and could only keep the yearnings of his heart alive. To those tormented by such a hunger, Christ cried: I am the bread of life! He calls the troubled and the burdened and those who know the ways of the world, those who know what life's real needs are, those who, as Stauffer says, know the toilsomeness of man's work, the lamentations of women, the tears of children and, above all, the burden of guilt; those wise in the ways of the world who are too sensible to expect the healing of their greatest woes by the world. They must come to Christ and find their satisfaction in him.

What Christ was proclaiming when he said I am the bread of life, he explained in an allegory when he summoned the multitude to a great supper. The meal in which he satisfied their earthly hunger, was a sign of the meal he would give them to appease their mental and spiritual hunger. There was no one to bring help that evening. The disciples showed themselves perplexed by the situation. They could find no way out of it. Without remedy or advice, powerless and helpless, we face the hunger of our own and every other man's soul. Yet satisfaction is possible: there is one—Christ—who can satisfy it. The baskets that were left after that meal were an allegory of the abundant satisfaction that Christ, and through him, God, would give them who in their hunger and thirst would come to him. They will be able to eat and drink without restriction until they are filled.

What Christ did that evening in an allegory, he brought to preliminary fulfilment at another supper—at the last supper on the day before he died. At that supper he gave his followers bread

94

to eat and wine to drink, different from those with which any other host has ever entertained his guests. Under the appearance of bread and wine, he gave them himself to eat and drink. By so doing he gave real fulfilment to his saying that he was the bread of life.

But, despite its reality, this food too, had and has an allegorical character. It points to a future time when Christ will give himself to his followers, no longer under signs, but in unveiled reality. Until that time his followers, in obedience to his command, use the sign in which he offers himself as provision for their journey, their bitter and difficult wanderings along the paths of history, their long and perilous pilgrimage from time to eternity. When their pilgrimage is ended, Christ will give himself to them in his unveiled splendour, so appeasing the hunger of heart that cannot be appeased by anything given it on earth.

Eating his flesh and blood is a pledge of the final satisfaction that will be ours in the future. It is a guarantee that men, who cannot be freed from hunger in this world, will one day be completely satisfied. This will come to pass when man, who yearns continually for union with another, and ultimately for union with that highest Other, God, finds in God his eternal fulfilment. Then Christ will show himself to be that bread which is the immortal food of everlasting life. Those who have reached perfection will eat an eternal meal in the Father's house, and in it will find a satisfaction endlessly renewed.

CHAPTER FIVE

THE PERSON OF CHRIST

II : CHRIST AND THE CHANGED WORLD

The historicity of Christ sets him apart from all other saviours. The strange and incomprehensible thing about him is that he led a truly human life, with all its bitterness and disappointments, and yet he was far above everything human, far above human miseries and afflictions. His followers never thought it necessary to console him. He was different from everyone else. They were restrained by awe of him: they sensed his pre-occupation. He went forward to his death with regal assurance: when death threatened, he needed no consolation, but at the last supper the disciples from whom he was soon to part needed consolation from him. At the moment when the last clouds were gathering over his head, he said to them: 'Let not your hearts be troubled' (John 14, 1). In these darkening hours, he opened his heart to them and explained to them that it had long been his wish to feast with them (Luke 22, 15). He celebrated this last farewell as though it had been a festival. He blessed the woman who anointed him against his burial, and by doing so incurred the anger of those about him (Mark 14, 3-9). Christ rose above despair. He met with absolute confidence difficulties which would have beaten other men to their knees.

Hölderlin pointed out the difference between Christ and other mythical saviours, by saying: 'But modesty prevents me from comparing thee to the men of this world'. Despite his love for the gods of the Greeks, Hölderlin knew that Christ was fundamentally different from them, from Grecian Apollo, for instance, or Dionysus. They belonged to the world: they were personifications and, as it were, crystallizations, of the things of the world. Christ comes from the realms beyond the world, from the sacred domain of the personal God. He is the Son of man, who is clothed with the radiance of God, and endowed with God's glory. He does indeed walk the paths of death, but not as others walk them. He shows himself to be mightier than all the living, for he shows himself to be the Lord.

The word Lord, *Kyrios*, shows us a new aspect of Christ and helps us to come to a deeper understanding of his person.

The ancient world was full of *kyrioi*, both earthly and heavenly. Even the earthly lords were thought to have about them the lustre of heaven. The *kyrioi* originated in the oriental civilization of Mesopotamia, Syria and Egypt. From there, they emerged into that region where Christ lived. Even by that time they had undergone many changes. The ancient traditions of the east spread ever further during the Hellenistic period. In the time of the Roman emperors they were beginning to gain ground in the Roman dominions. Thus the Roman emperors were thought of as gods. It must be realized, however, that the deification of the Caesars was carried over from the servility of the eastern provinces, and encouraged by the flattery of the influential rhetoricians. Some of the emperors—Tiberius, Vespasian, Nerva and Marcus Aurelius, for instance—rejected divine honours emphatically, as an invention of the philosophers and historians of the Empire. Others allowed and even claimed them as did Caligula or Nero, for reasons of political expediency, or from vanity. The deification of the early Roman emperors was a mark of respect granted in the east to a ruler whether living or dead. Even when the deification of the emperor reached its climax under Caligula, Nero and Domitian, its primary purpose was political: it was intended to increase the reverence and obedience of the subject to the civil authorities appointed by God. This is shown very clearly by the fact that the greater the political difficulties facing the eastern provinces were, the greater was the emphasis put on the divinity of the emperor. After the pacification of the east, both Claudius and (with even greater resolution) Vespasian, rejected the temptation of deification.

This also shows clearly that no one, at least in enlightened and educated circles, believed in the divinity of the emperor. In educated society, the worship of the emperor was nothing but a political and courtly ceremony. They did not regard the temples of the official religion as churches, nor did they pray to the deified emperors.

To the foregoing explanation we should add that the background to the worship of emperors was formed by the myths. It could only thrive in the atmosphere of myth. When human reason pierced the mysteries of human life and history, myth was doomed. The masses, however, discerned in the ruler a numinous power: they saw in him the presence of the divine. Their belief was a distorted form of what Holy Scripture says about rulers—namely, that they are God's representatives on earth and their authority is held in trust for God, so that they are, as it were, his officials. The ruler's link with God was forgotten by the myths, and his divinity alone was remembered, so that he himself appeared to be a god. The concept of the ruler in myth is such as to lead men to see in him—in his well-being, his health and his victories—the embodiment of the well-being of the nation. As such he was worthy of divine honours.

When Holy Scripture calls Christ Lord, it does not intend to deify a great man. Many of the once popular schools of modern religious history have tried to explain the title *kyrios* used of Christ in this way, saying that he originated in a myth similar to those that led to the deification of the pagan emperors.

Just how far Christianity was from deifying any man in this fashion, and indeed, how opposed it was to the apotheosis of any ruler or hero, is clear from the fact that such actions would have been condemned as sinful idolatry by the Old Testament. The Old Testament offered the Christian community no encouragement to deify Jesus of Nazareth.

But neither did belief in the Godhead of Christ originate in Hellenistic paganism. On the contrary, when new-born Christianity came into contact with the deification of rulers and heroes, it opposed it, steadfastly rejecting it out of hand. This is clearly illustrated by two incidents at Caesarea and another at Lystra. Chapter twelve of the Acts of the Apostles (vv. 20-23) tells of the tension between King Herod Agrippa I on the one hand and the citizens of Tyre and Sidon on the other. The men of Tyre and Sidon were trying to appease the king for economic reasons. They sent ambassadors to Caesarea who were received with great ceremony: 'And upon a day appointed, Herod, being arrayed in kingly apparel, sat in the judgement seat and made an oration to them. And the people made acclamation saying: It is the voice of a God and not of a man. And forthwith an angel of the Lord struck him in retaliation because he had dared to rob the true God of the honour due to him: and, being eaten up by worms, he gave up the ghost.' This incident makes it clear that Christianity marked the end of such myths. It was clearly not itself a new myth. Both those who lived through the events of spring 44 A.D. (related by Luke in the year 60 or 62 A.D.) and also Luke the narrator himself, regarded the deification of a man as an act of sacrilege. Hence it is clear that neither Luke nor the Christian community in Caesarea transferred the titles God, Son of God, or Lord, to Jesus of Nazareth from the mythical cults of kings as they were known at that time.

Even earlier, Peter himself had forbidden his own deification at Caesarea (cf. Acts 10). When—in about the years 37-41 A.D.—he visited the Roman captain Cornelius, the Roman came out to meet him and threw himself at his feet. Proskynesis of this type was obviously meant to convey more than a normal greeting. Among both the Persians and the Greeks it was an act of reverence which was paid only to the godhead. By giving the apostle that outward sign of reverence, Cornelius greeted him as one endowed with supra-normal powers. But Peter rejected his greeting: 'Arise; I myself also am a man.' To the apostle, deification was a thing impossible because it was an unchristian thing. The incident shows the unbridgeable gap between Christianity and myth.

In a third incident we see that the early Christians were absolutely opposed to the apotheosis of heroes. When Paul and Barnabas healed a lame man in Lystra in the years 45-7 A.D., the multitude believed that saviour-gods had come to them: 'And they called Barnabas Jupiter; but Paul Mercury, because he was chief speaker. The priest also of Jupiter that was before the city, bringing oxen and garlands before the gate, would have offered sacrifice with the people. Which when the apostles Barnabas and Paul had heard, rending their clothes, they leaped out among the people crying, and saying: Ye men, why do ye these things? We also are mortals, men like unto you, preaching to you to be converted from these vain things to the living God' (Acts, 14, 11-15). This incident is a proof of the strength of the pagan belief in the appearance of gods on earth, but it is also at the same time an example of the way in which the religious convictions of the first witnesses to Christ led them to reject with horror, both the mythical faith in the epiphanies of the gods, and the deification of a mere man.

In the midst of a world which revered and adored both earthly and heavenly lords in great numbers, Paul and the Christians confessed the true *kyrios*. There were, to be sure, other gods and lords in heaven and on earth but 'to us there is but one God, the Father, of whom are all things, and we unto him; and one Lord Jesus Christ, by whom are all things, and we by him' (I Cor. 8, 6). 'To whom (the Lord) be glory for ever and ever' (II Tim. 4, 18).

When Christ is called Lord in the New Testament, that title is not an expression of any mythical creaturely power. Christ was not a mythical figure in whom a human community—whether it was a nation or a civilization—displayed its religious feelings and experiences. He is a fact of history. In confessing him and extolling him as its Lord, the Church gave expression to the experiences the disciples had of him. It recognized him as the Lord of all lords. All other lords were his precursors, and prepared the way for his coming. He realised what they signified. His personal authority was more far-reaching than the authority of any other ruler. He had authority over the powers of destiny, which controls all other lords. He had authority over death and suffering, over care and anxiety, over the powers of nature and the guilt of men; he was not himself subject to death, although all others were subject to it. 'Even kings must sleep, and the mighty on the earth must lie down like little children' (G. de la Fort). Even they, the lords of the world, were doomed to wither and die. When Christ took death upon himself, he did so of his own free sovereign choice. In the last discourse, assured of his ascendancy over the doom pronounced by destiny, he could say: 'I go away, and I come unto you' (John 14, 28). The lord of this world had no part in him (John 14, 30). He cannot lay on him the hand with which he throws all others to the dust. Christ went freely to his death: he took death upon himself, so as to be obedient to the will of the Father, that the world might know that he loved his Father and did the tasks his Father gave him to do (John 14, 31). It was no effort for him to fulfil what he had resolved. Strictly speaking, he died neither as a hero, nor as a martyr, for he knew where he was going and what awaited him beyond death.

Because death was for him the pathway to a new life far above all earthly ephemerality, his dying signified the shattering of the rhythm of nature. In his dying he put an end once for all to the eternally repeated pattern of life and death. He opened a way which led out of this rhythm. That alone made him the exact opposite of myth, for as the mythical gods are personifications of natural things and events, faith in them does not lead out of nature, but even further into it. Devotion to the myths leads those who believe in them to an ever closer union with nature and its deeds, so that they are swallowed up in the universal life of nature. He, on the other hand, who has Christ for his lord, trusts that he will be led out of the decay of nature into the immortal life of God. No one but the Lord, that is, Christ, has the power to do this. Christ demonstrated his superiority to the powers of nature in acts of power performed during his lifetime. In the miracles of the multiplication of the loaves, in the healing of the sick, the stilling of storms and waves, he reveals his ascendancy over those powers of nature which restrict and crush man. Christ seized nature and so changed it that it was compelled to serve mankind. But even whilst he was putting nature at man's service, he was opening a way to a life truly worthy of mankind. Although afflictions—which he alone can heal—invade, fetter and restrict the life of man, there is still possible a life truly worthy of mankind—a life which is in his gift alone.

Man has, of course, the ability to build a society for himself. He can even produce great and splendid civilizations without Christ, fascinating to his race, full of scintillating successes in science and art. But even then they fall short of perfection. In the ages before Christ men were *in adventu Domini:* awaiting the true saviour. In the centuries since the birth of Christ the works performed by men hostile to him have been tokens of human self-glorification and have, therefore, like all things antipathetic to God, carried within themselves the seeds of their own destruction. Just how little success men have in using the facilities of this world to build a way of life truly worthy of their race, we can come to realise through the failures and breakdowns of which the record of human history is so full.

In Christ's miracles—and especially in his resurrection—his sovereignty is clearly displayed. But it will attain its perfection only in the world to come, when death and suffering will be altogether eliminated from the life of man by Christ, and he will appear as conqueror and judge. He will rise far above the stormy seas of destruction, hate, slander and disbelief, as he who was, is, and is to come. Until then it may seem as though the rule of Christ is weak and contemptible, and as though other lords determine the course of history. In spite of appearances however, Christ is the true Lord of human history. He has its helm under his hand. All its threads come together in him. Every creature is his instrument. Every event and happening serves his will. The things that are hidden during the passage of history will one day be revealed in dazzling clarity; the majesty of the lord of heaven. In the midst of all afflictions and persecutions, the early Church was so convinced of His lordship that it placed his portrait as Lord of the universe in the apsides of its places of worship. This portrait showed him crucified and crowned as a king. By so doing, it acknowledged the authority of him who, although in a veiled manner, is forever king and, at a time in the future beyond human history, will exercise his sovereignty publicly in the world.

Not everyone is capable of faith in the lordship of Christ. He who glories in himself and believes in the world cannot acknowledge the sovereignty of Christ, for he can believe only in a sovereignty within the world, in a lord he can see and feel. Only a man who can look higher than the world and the powers of the world, who can understand that things beyond the universe are greater than the forces of earth, and that the Father of heaven is mightier than the mightiest man known to history is capable of acknowledging the sovereignty of Christ. Such a man will glory in his Lord. But he will see no occasion to boast in the same way of any other Lord as he does of the crucified (Gal. 6, 14). He will stand firm in all the vicissitudes of life, for he will know that his Lord is mightier than all things and will one day come to save him from them. He who believes in the world will mock at the Christian's Lord, because he seems despicable and helpless. The believer in Christ feels however that he is committed to his Lord. Everything he does, he does for his sake: in his Lord he greets men and thanks men, prays and works, lives and dies (Romans 14, 7 f).

He who has chosen Christ as his Lord knows that he has entered the service of a power who does not oppress and enslave those who serve him. There is nothing about him to make men fear that he will put an end to their freedom. He does not fall into the temptation to which all other lords are subject—the temptation of making slaves of those he rules, of using them as though they were his property and robbing them of their human dignity. Christ exercises his sovereignty in such a way as to reveal his own glory in his followers. His dominion is therefore of service to those whom he rules. He does them a service surpassing in scope and depth all the services performed on the earth, for he suffers them to partake of the fulness and potency of his life. His sovereignty is a service of that love which gives itself.

Christ was himself very clearly aware of his ascendancy over the world and over the ephemerality and temporality of men. He kept clearly in view that life which was his before time began, and which it was beyond the powers of the earth to arrest. He looked back to a point before all earthly beginnings, and forward to a point beyond all earthly ends. He knew he was united to the Father with an intimacy which was essentially and qualitatively superior to the ephemeral knowledge of God possessed by other men. His awareness of his life before time and after history was not obscured by the course of his earthly life. It was rather with him from the very first moment of his consciousness. It was expressed for example in the prayer: 'And now glorify thou me, O Father, with thyself, with the glory which I had before the world was, with thee . . . Father, I will that where I am, they also whom thou hast given me may be with me; that they may see my glory which thou hast given me, because thou hast loved me before the creation of the world. Just Father, the world hath not known thee: but I have known thee; and these have known that thou hast sent me' (John 17, 5; 24 f).

Before the world began, the Word was in the closest intimacy with God. Christ does not belong, as does everyone else, to this world. He is set apart from it as God himself is set apart from it. He belongs entirely to the sphere of the divine. The words he spoke were the words the Father was saying to the world; the things he did were acts of the Father. In his words and actions, the Father spoke and acted. 'Do you not believe that I am in the Father and the Father in me? The words that I speak to you I speak not of myself. But the Father who abideth in me, he doth the works. Believe you not then, that I am in the Father and the Father in me?' (John 14, 10 f).

Christ's awareness of his relationship with the Father made it possible for him to give his disciples promises about death: 'Everyone that liveth and believeth in me shall not die forever' (John 11, 26). Christ admits those who devote themselves to him in faith into that unity that he has with the Father. He prayed: 'that they all may be one, as thou Father in me and I in thee; that they may be one as we also are one' (John 17, 21-3). Christ lives the unchangeable life of God. Not only did his life stretch back to before all time, it was also characterized by the changelessness of the divine life. Conscious of this fact, he said to both his friends and his enemies: 'Abraham our Father rejoiced that he might see my day. . . . Before Abraham was, I am' (John 8, 56-8). When Christ made such pronouncements as these about himself, those who heard him did not mock him as though he were mad, for he made such an overwhelming impression on them that, although his claims were unusual and indeed surpassed anything possible to a man, they had to take them seriously. Just how seriously they took him is clear from the fact that they took up stones to put him to death.

Christ's consciousness of his relationship with God is obvious from the fact that he called himself Son of the Father. He is Son in a way in which no other can be called Son of God. God was to him what father and mother are to other men; everything he had and did he owed to the Father in heaven. The Father, on his side, has vouchsafed him everything that belongs to himself. Christ partakes in its fulness of the being of the Father. He is God by nature. The man Jesus Christ is as essentially divine as the Father himself. Hence no one can understand the Father as Christ understands him; and no one can understand Christ as the Father does. Indeed only the Father can understand him. 'I confess to thee, O Father, Lord of heaven and earth, because thou hast hidden these things from the wise and prudent and hast revealed them to little ones. Yes, Father, for so it hath seemed good in thy sight. All things are delivered to me by my Father. And no one knoweth who the Son is, but the Father: and who the Father is, but the Son, and to whom the Son will reveal him' (Luke 10, 21-2).

The word Son as it was used by Christ himself in calling himself Son, and by the disciples in revering and acknowledging him as Son, should be understood in an analogous sense. It does not mean that there is any kind of sexual differentiation in God. As we shall see, the picture of God given by Christ shows quite clearly that, unlike all the gods of the myths, God stands over and above all sexuality. The word Son is not meant to convey the notion that in his eternal existence Christ was masculine as opposed to feminine. It is rather a declaration by Christ, in the form of an analogy, that he possessed his Godhead, the divine life, consciousness, will and love from God. As far as this giving and receiving was concerned, he would have conveyed exactly the same analogical idea if he had used the word daughter. He must have been called Son, therefore, because this title was necessary for the expression of the public nature of his rôle in history; we connect man with public life and woman generally with veils of privacy. The fact that Christ is the Son of God makes him fundamentally different from all others sent by God, just as it makes him essentially different from all other men.

The fact that he is Son of God gives him the authority and right to use the things of God as he will. Whatever he does in the Father's house is right. He is competent in everything pertaining to salvation. He is the person in whose presence the meaning of all ways and times, all thoughts and destinies are made plain, so that all those who love God may be gathered in one. Satan struggles against him until all God's purposes shall be achieved. He lived and died so that good might be pursued and performed. It is his converse with God that determines the destinies of individuals, of mankind and the world. Because he is the Son, he is the Lord of the law of the old testament. He has complete authority to put it aside, and in place of the holiness enjoined by the law, to establish complete justice and a new order of belief and devotion. The constantly recurring words: 'You have heard that it was said to them of old. . . . But I say to you' (cf. Matt. 5, 21-48), show that he was conscious not merely of having received the fulness of power from God, but of being the Lord himself, and having the right to dispose of the things and institutions put in his power. He was greater than Jonas, greater than Solomon, greater than the Temple—he was indeed Lord of his own ancestor David. He had authority over the Sabbath established by God. He claimed the power to interpret conclusively the law of the Sabbath and to say what was permitted and what was not.

He could use Nature, the Father's creation, as though it belonged to him. For the sacraments, he took things of this world—bread and wine—and used them as vessels of his saving will, not merely temporarily but for ever. He had authority to forgive sins and do away with man's remoteness from God. When he lays hold on men and leads them home to the Father, he has no need to fear that the Father will repudiate him. He may prepare dwellings for his followers in his Father's house and he knows that the Father will sanction his doings.

In an impressive passage, St. Mark bears witness to Christ's authority in pronouncing the salvation of men and leading those who have strayed back to his Father's house: 'And it was heard that he was in the house. And many came together, so that there was no room; no, not even at the door. And he spoke to them the word. And they came to him, bringing one sick of the palsy, who was carried by four. And, when they could not offer him unto him on account of the multitude, they uncovered the roof where he was; and opening it, they let down the bed wherein the man sick of the palsy lay. And, when Jesus had seen their faith, he saith to the sick of the palsy: Son, thy sins are forgiven thee. And there were some of the scribes sitting there and thinking in their hearts: Why doth this man speak thus? He blasphemeth. Who can forgive sins but God only? Which Jesus presently knowing in his spirit that they so thought within themselves, saith to them: Why think ye these things in your hearts? Which is easier, to say to the sick of the palsy: Thy sins are forgiven thee, or to say: Arise, take up thy bed, and walk? But that you may know that the Son of man hath power on earth to forgive sins (he saith to the sick of the palsy): I say to thee: Arise. Take up thy bed, and go into thy house. And immediately he arose and, taking up his bed, went his way in the sight of all; so that all wondered and glorified God, saying: We have never seen the like' (Mark 2, 2-12).

The event St. Mark narrates here was so sensational as to be unnerving. The friends of the sick man and the sick man himself went to a great deal of trouble to reach Christ, being driven to do so by their faith and trust. They accepted both the struggle and the indignation of other men, particularly the owner of the house. How great their disappointment must have been when the Lord promised them what they neither asked for nor wanted, but did not grant them the bodily health for the sick man for which they had striven so laboriously! The public way in which Christ spoke of the sick man's sinfulness must also have been very painful to him. Nevertheless the disappointment was salutary. Christ showed how far this man had strayed and revealed the fact that all his other miseries were symptoms of that remoteness from God of which he himself was not conscious and from which therefore he had no desire to be saved. By this disclosure, Christ revealed the position of all those present. He declared that he would heal the sick man's deepest-seated affliction and would give him freedom from shackles from which no mere man could free him.

Those who witnessed this happening realised immediately from Christ's words that he was claiming to be able to give something that no man is empowered to give. Two possibilities were open to them with regard to the Lord's pretensions: if they could not accept Christ as the Son and heir of God, empowered to perform such acts, they would either have to mock at them or feel pity at them as the words of a madman, or they would have to condemn them as overweening pride. The first possibility did not cross their minds. Obviously Christ made so strong an impression of superiority and earnestness, so great an impression of dignity and greatness that there was no question in their minds of their having to deal with a madman. So then, for those who heard him but did not believe in him, there remained only the second course: they were compelled to condemn Christ for making himself equal with God. And this, in fact, they did.

This was an error of judgement on the part of Christ's

contemporaries. He proved that he was empowered and authorized to arrange man's relationships with God, that his hand was sure in matters touching on the inmost things of human life, and that God recognized what he did without his having first to obtain the divine approval of them. Such a claim on Christ's part was no empty form of words. He proved that it was his right to arrange the relationships between man and God by healing the sickness of the man, and by giving him what he had longed for from the beginning, but was only now enabled fully to comprehend in all its breadth and profundity.

In healing the man's bodily sickness Christ healed the symptom of that disorder which is made apparent in all our bodily and mental failings. He posed to his hearers the problem as to which was more difficult: to subdue such a symptom or to heal the deep-seated failing that produced it. He received no reply. There was no answer he could receive. Neither is easier, neither is more difficult. Neither of the two afflictions could be healed by man. Christ alone had power over them. By healing them he freed the man from the restrictions and entanglements of both body and soul and restored to him a life truly worthy of mankind. Men continually attempt to build such a life without Christ. They sometimes even have a great deal of success: here and there they rise to heights of greatness and nobility. But in Christ human dignity is afforded security surpassing any security it could find on earth, security of a quality which leaves far behind anything originating on earth. Ultimately there can be well-founded hopes of a life truly human, only where man gives himself in faith and trust to Christ.

Those who heard Christ did not of course, all allow themselves to be convinced by his proofs. The majority remained silent. There is nothing surprising in that. Christ's acts of power, by which he gave proof of what his Father had given him, could not be observed and understood like other occurrences in history. Anyone who regarded them as such would overlook the most important thing about them: the fact that God's glory and power is shown forth in them. Only he who has eyes can see in them the revelation of the mystery of God. Only he has such eyes who has opened his heart to God. Others see the happenings or hear about them, but do not perceive that they are mirrors of God's glory.

They either deny that they happened, or misinterpret them. They behave as did Christ's unbelieving contemporaries.

They chose not to understand. In general they did not fall into the temptation of denying the reality of Christ's miracles, and preparing a suitable propaganda with which to refute them. But they explained the miracles in which the power of God shone forth as delusions produced by Satan. They were able to do so because they were blind to the glory of God. They were as little aware of it as a colour-blind man is of the symphony of colours in a painting. They had been blinded by their hate. Their blindness towards God and the things of God reached its climax after the raising of Lazarus. When they received the news that Lazarus had been called back to life by Christ, they did not try to escape from their dilemma by the use of lying propaganda. They chose the way of power, resolving to kill Lazarus and execute Christ so as to remove from their own path and from that of the nation, both of these men, who were causing such difficulty. Where, in the deeds of Christ the Son, the glory of God and the love of the Father shone forth with great brilliancy, hatred and bigotry could see only corruption.

We might illustrate their reaction by means of a parable we have already used once before. The metaphor of the completely un-musical physicist will show us the different strata which are trace-able in things and happenings alike. If a tune is played through for him on the piano, he can describe what is happening and measure it, expressing it in a physical formula. Because he is completely unmusical he will think that he has grasped the whole of the matter with his formula. If he is told that he has overlooked the most important element in it, he will shake his head unbelievingly and declare that whoever told him such a thing was mad. Yet in fact he himself has fallen victim to an illusion. He has overlooked the most important thing—the melody itself. He cannot do anything but overlook it, because he is unable to perceive it. Where he errs is in thinking he can set out the whole reality of the matter with the means at his disposal, and by accepting as real only what he can grasp and comprehend. He who can observe the melody itself because he has the faculty of doing so, will not let the blind man take away from him the reality that he has understood. He will rather feel sorry for the other because, owing to his restricted capacity to see, his world is narrow and small. Indeed the very thing, which the blind man feels must be refuted because he cannot see it, appears to him who sees it, the greatest and best thing of all.

Because Christ is the Son, he is empowered to pass judgement on men. Universal jurisdiction was given him by his Father. In his judgements the judgement of the Father himself is made known. Because of his Sonship, the same honour is due to him as is due to the Father himself. He has no need to provide for his own honour: the Father will provide for it. Anyone who honours the Son, honours the Father; because he is the Son, the Father's honour is his chief care, and everything else is secondary to him. Because he is the Son he can take men to his Father's house and bring them before him as adopted sons and daughters, without fearing the Father's displeasure. Accepting them as his brothers, he assumes them into the Sonship he himself possesses. Because the fulness of the divine life is proper to him as the Son, he can bestow life that will survive death on those who unite themselves with him in love.

Just as Christ's contemporaries took seriously his claim to a transcendent sovereignty, so too they took seriously his claim to be the Son of the Father; it became the final justification of the condemnation to death passed on him by the Jewish court in Jerusalem. But he remained sure of his God even in death. Even when he was completely in the power of the hostile forces in the world, he knew him to be his God. For him, to die was to go home, to go back to his Father, who, after he had performed his pan-historic and pan-cosmic tasks, was calling him back to the glory with which he was garbed before either cosmos or history existed.

The expression *logos* will help us to come to a fuller understanding of the manner of Christ's Sonship. According to the Apostle John's testimony, Christ was the divine *logos*. In the beginning was the *logos*. We cannot enquire here into the history of the development of this title and its diverse meanings: we can only examine the elements in it which are most important for our study. When John decided to call Christ the *logos* the word had long been familiar to his contemporaries. At the time when John adopted it as a name for Christ, it was used with a variety of meanings, and by using it he told them something immediately intelligible to them: he told them that he had seen everything they meant by the word *logos* transcended in the incarnate Christ. The *logos* and *logoi* known to them owed their existence to the meditations of men, and were creatures of the human mind. But the *logos* to which he, John, bore witness was an historical reality. They were to rest assured that he had seen him, had heard him speak, and had taken his hand in his own. He had come to earth in bodily form.

What then was the meaning of the title *logos?* The sense of this word is very difficult to grasp, but we shall be able to begin to do so if we take into account its earlier history. It is more probable that John took the expression primarily and exclusively from the Old Testament and Greek philosophy, than that he adopted it from the Gnostic creed—although even this is disputed.

The concept of the 'word' in the Old Testament approaches that of John's *logos.* God made the world by his 'word'. The world owes its existence to the utterances of God, by which it was both called into being, and is maintained in existence. The Word of God is the act of God in human history, by which he calls men and leads them to the goals he has allotted to them. The expression 'Word' means the divine power and the divine activity in the sense of spiritual power and activity. The title *logos* therefore signifies that Christ is full of the spiritual power and activity through which nature and history were brought into, and continue in, existence. Thus it is clear that the translation 'In the beginning was the deed' would not be so far removed from the sense of the first sentence of St. John's Gospel as Faust believed. In the beginning, in fact, was the Word which is the deed.

In paganism a second belief was current about the word *logos,* used by St. John. It originated with Heraclitus and through Plato and Aristotle was handed down to the Stoic philosophers, to Philo's Jewish philosophy of religion, and finally to Neo-Platonism. This in itself is enough to show that there were many concepts conjoined in the word *logos.* The Stoics' use of the word is perhaps the most important for our understanding of the johannine *logos.*

To the Stoics it meant the cosmic mind, which is universal and occurs in individual men, so that the individual soul is a fragment or splinter of the universal soul. Thus the Stoic teachers were not far from the Platonist view that a single mind is embodied in everything, and in the universe as a whole. Plato thought that the fact that everything is the manifestation of an ideal, gives every single factor and the universe as a whole its meaning. Everything points above itself to a spiritual thing mirrored in it, to an archetype of which it is a copy. All things are shadows of such archetypal realities. It is the archetypes which are the true realities. The things we see are imperfect copies of them. All ideals are in reality one ideal. Plato called it the idea of the good. Such ideas are consonant with the concept of the *logos*. The *logos* is the embodiment of all ideals and prototypes which we see reflected in the things of the world. In it is realized the reality pointed to by individual things, and the cosmos as a whole. Thus, for instance, what bread or wine or water signify is realized in its ultimate perfection in the *logos*. They are distorted and atrophied copies of their antetypes in the *logos*. There is also in the *logos* a type of every man. The *logos* is therefore the universal ideal of God. From this point of view, the Greek *logos* is strikingly like the Word. In the *logos* God utters his thoughts about the world, as though in a profound and comprehensive language. So then, there is in him both cosmic potency and the cosmic ideal. Everything that exists was brought forth by the creative power of God and the formative thoughts of God. Fact and idea, power and spirit, are united and displayed in and through the *logos*. He is the eternal, universal consciousness, manifested in all things and in every happening. Thus the existence and meaning, profundity and form of the world, and the individual things in the world, are guaranteed by the *logos*. In the midst of the world's impotence and incomprehensibility, he represents the final guarantee of the existence and meaningfulness of the universe and humanity. During the course of man's earthly history, the real life and meaning of things and men are concealed. They will however one day be victorious over the darkness of earthly obscurity. Faith in the meaningfulness of the *logos* involves, together with the prospect of the ulimate revelation of the meaning of all things and all happenings, power to overcome all perplexity.

The potency and meaning of the world took bodily form in Christ. In the Gospel of St. John it is clearly shown that the personalized cosmic potency and mind were in existence before the actual existence of the world itself. The world began to exist, and from that moment was a distorted copy of that prototype which exists in the *logos* in personal form. The whole creation and each individual thing in it has a symbolical character, which is particularly obvious where the universe is differentiated, for instance, in the sun, the sea, and the earth.

The *logos* has a twofold significance for the world. In the first place, he is the ultimate norm of human entelechy. In the second place, union with him does not mean the restriction of human activity, but the gaining of the life that should be properly man's.

With regard to the second of these points it should be noticed that man will attain to his true life in so far as he approaches the archetype realised in the *logos*. In fact, the more he becomes like him, the more closely he approaches his own true being. The further he is from him, the further he falls short of his own archetype and his own true form. Apostasy from the *logos* is alienation from his own personality. Denial of the *logos* is denial of one's true self. When therefore, Christ calls a man to follow him, to enter his company, he is calling him to shape himself according to his own archetype and come to himself. When Christ binds a man to himself, he binds him to his own true life. When engagement to Christ seems a restriction on a man's life, he is in error. This error is rooted in human self-glory. Christ knows better what is of profit to a man than does that man himself. This state of affairs is in many ways analogous to human experience, for it is not unusual for a man to know the nature of a friend better than the friend himself, and therefore to be able to help him overcome all the difficulties in which he finds himself and to aid him in the perfection of his nature.

Because Christ is also the realisation of the ideals of the Good and the Beautiful, all embodiments of good and beautiful things in time are reproductions of the archetype found in Christ. Man therefore is good in so far as he is moulded to Christ. Denial of Christ brings confusion in morals, and art, and even in civilization itself. Apostasy from him is defection into formlessness and deformity.

It is now obvious in what way Christ is the final standard of human entelechy. Man will be judged, not by an impersonal standard of goodness, but by personalized good, embodied in Christ. In so far as he unites himself with Christ, he unites himself with the good. The further he retreats from him the more completely he comes under the sway of evil. If Christ rules in a man, good rules in him. If Christ does not rule in him, then evil does.

Because the *logos* bears within himself the prototype of every man, every man is a mirror of the divine *logos*. We can therefore meet the divine *logos* in every man. The way in which we treat other men shows the disposition we have towards the divine *logos* and thus towards God himself.

The relationship between the *logos* and the individual human being was illustrated in a way unique in the realms of history when he assumed a human nature and became like us. As a result of this, everyone can now enter into communion with the *logos* in his human form in faith and the sacraments, and by doing so can mould himself to the likeness of the Incarnate Word. Our dealings with the human beings who are united with Christ are in fact dealings with Christ himself, inasmuch as the life of anyone united to Christ is life with Christ himself, and Christ's likeness is mirrored in his personality.

Our relationships with those who are united with Christ show our attitude to the Incarnate Son of God. Hatred for men is hatred towards Christ; love towards men, love towards him. In giving or refusing food, shelter, clothing or freedom to those who are in need, we are giving or refusing them to Christ himself. Thus, Christ himself, the personalized divine *logos* in human form, is the ultimate standard of good and evil, and thus of the ultimate judgement of man.

St. John also maintains that he himself has seen the *logos*. The *logos* to whom he testifies is not an impersonal cosmic law, but the Son of God who has taken human nature within time. The Son of God has taken upon himself human life, human form and nature, so that whatever the vital essence is which forms a man into a man, it belongs to the ego of the Divine *Logos*, and this *logos* can thus act as a human ego, and work through it. Thus the man Jesus Christ has no human, but only a divine ego.

When John says of the *logos* that he has become man he is bearing witness to the fact that the Son of God has taken upon himself human nature with all the limitations under which man has lived since the fall of Adam. Christ is what we are, yet he is different from us, because his ego is the ego of God.

By the assumption of a human nature by the divine ego, God has established an emergency association with man: by the taking up of a real human nature into the life of the Son of God, a human nature has been brought to God. But, as the whole of mankind is bound together in one family, the bringing of one man to God orientates the movement of the whole of humanity towards God.

In connexion with this aspect of the incarnation of the *logos* we should investigate further what this event means. It would be best to start from the distinction which can be made between nature and person. Before we begin our investigations, however, we must be absolutely clear on one point: the nature of the hypostatic union, the union of two natures in Christ, is an impenetrable mystery. The term *Nature*—that is essential being, or substance—is used of the inmost reality of a thing, what makes it what it is; what gives man the form of a man, or an animal the form of an animal; that which is the basis and source of its life. Our nature is the basis of our physical and mental faculties—those things with which we perform our actions, with which we hear, see, speak, think and will. Each of our faculties is ordained to some particular task. We hear with our ears, see with our eyes, speak with our mouth. We cannot however identify a man with his faculties. As has been pointed out countless times, the cardinal thing is that it is not the eye that sees, or the hand that writes but I who see with my eyes, who write with my hand. It is therefore my ego which is the decisive factor. It is the ego which acts through the natural faculties and which controls and directs them. The ego is answerable for what is done. Nature and ego, nature and person are therefore to be distinguished from one another.

The problem of the definition of the relationship between the ego and the person will not be discussed here. We merely wish to emphasise that we are using the word ego in this context to designate an entity which is not only psychological but also metaphysical.

The antithesis between the ego and the nature may even lead to the ego misusing the powers of the nature by giving them a command against nature, forcing them to do things against nature. The nature is under the authority and sway of the ego. It is the property, the possession of the ego. The ego is the proprietor of the nature, which is therefore subject to the ego; yet it is very important to the ego, because it decides the wealth or poverty of the ego. But it is the ego which decides how this wealth or poverty shall be used. The person may be defined as the essence permeating, forming and controlling the nature; the being as an individual; the being as possessing individuality and free will. 'What the possession of such an ego implies we may see by comparing it with the life of a nation. If in the days of Christ, the emperor in Rome said: "It is my will that . . ." the whole earth shook. A few years ago, it only needed Ghandi to say: "I do not want . . ." for the whole of India to hold its breath. And if there were a power that ruled the whole world, the authority and power of the *ego* of him whose will it was that controlled it, would extend to the boundaries of the world. . . . We can now see the meaning of St. Thomas' words: The Person is the most important, most aristocratic, highest, most noble, most potent thing that exists in the sphere not only of creation, but also of reality as a whole' (Christmann).

If we take person to mean a being as endowed with individuality, power to control its actions, and free will, we must not overlook the fact that it is not complete in itself. The divine Persons, the most perfect beings with personal existence, exist only in relationship to one another. In the same way, the human personality can exist only in relationship with others. It continues to be itself only by going outside itself, reaching out to another. To do so is a necessity of its life. When we become conscious of its need, we express it in love and friendship. If this necessity of life is not expressed consciously, in friendship and love, the individual as such is not destroyed, so that he no longer exists, but, as a result of his unnatural relationships, he remains unfulfilled.

The incarnation of the *logos* meant that one particular human nature was so united with the *logos*, being conjoined with him in community of life, that it no longer had human individuality, was no longer the property and possession of a human ego; its only individuality was the individuality of the divine Person. It was no longer the possession and instrument of a human ego, but of the ego of the divine *logos*. It was no longer a human ego which spoke, acted, thought, and willed with the faculties of the human nature, but the ego of the Son of God.

Two further thoughts might be of value here in helping us to see a little more clearly the nature of the union in Christ's person. We have already said very clearly that the human ego lives only in its relationship to other persons. If, as has been said, an individual usually expresses himself in friendship and love, this means that he has to emerge from himself, leave and abandon himself, and enter into another and assume the other into himself. His actions, thoughts, values, desires and judgements receive their orientation and their form from that other; they will be steeped in the light and colours of the other. The one will live in the other. And what is true of friendship and love is even more profoundly true of union between man and Christ. Christ then becomes a personalized power ruling the human ego: 'I live, now not I; but Christ liveth in me' (Gal. 2, 20). The human ego is so strongly moulded to Christ that Paul could speak of the death of the old ego formed by the world and the springing up of a new one.

With this state of affairs we can compare what took place at the incarnation. In the incarnation, the yearning of the one ego for union with another became so powerful that its nature left its proper medium completely. But it did not of course live without a medium, without an ego. The medium however in which it lived, the ego that belonged to it, was no longer its own medium or ego, but the ego of the Son of God. The centre that was the source of its acts was God. It was so powerfully and mightily moulded by the ego of the Son of God that his ego thought, willed, loved, spoke, acted, died and obeyed in the human nature, so that it was not merely the ego, but the acting subject in the human nature. Another way to approach the mystery of the incarnation is as follows: the words men speak are a great force which can move, shape and form the hearts and minds of others. Not every word has the power to pierce the inmost heart of another. Many a one glances off, either because it is too weak to do anything else, or because it is prevented from doing anything else by a wall that it cannot pierce, by hardening of the heart or closing of the mind. When however it is able to reach the inmost heart of another, it can then enrich, impress, transform and remodel it.

No word is more potent than the word of God. It is alive, active and sharper than any two-edged sword. It pierces until it divides soul from mind, and limb from limb. It acts as a judge of the thoughts and sentiments of the heart. God has spoken many words. He spoke mightily to those who preached his revelation. He entered their minds with such authority that they were certain that no human or earthly power spoke to them, but one distinct from them all.

In Christ's human nature, the Father spoke his personal Word, the Word he speaks through all eternity, in which he shapes and displays all his knowledge. In Christ's human nature he sent forth his Son. This powerful and comprehensive Word touched and stirred his human nature to its inmost depths. The transformation and remodelling effected by God's personal Word is more far-reaching than that effected by any other. Christ's human nature, being imbued by the Word, was so completely shaped to the Word that it no longer possessed its own power and potency, but lived only in the potency of the *logos*. It became the echo of the human nature as a whole and in its parts.

In the incarnation, the ego of God assumed the burden of human nature and human life, in order to lift them out of the world. Christ fulfilled this task, so giving to the Father of heaven that glory which men had denied him at the beginning of their history. He served the *gloria dei* in a world which sought its own glorification, and by so doing he brought salvation to the world. He brought back to their Father those who in their own self-glorying had fled from God. He was the mediator between the holy God and sinful man.

CHAPTER SIX

CHRISTIANITY'S MISSION TO MANKIND

I : MAN AS A PERSON

The *logos* entered human history to save the lost race of man and bring man back to God. In view of the misfortune which has bedevilled human history even since Christ performed his redeeming work, we may ask whether that work was performed for individual men or strictly for society as a whole. Does God value the individual only as a part of the greater whole, or for his own worth and significance? To such questions as these, arising from the afflictions suffered by the individual, the true reply is that God's saving acts were directed towards individuals, but that the individual is redeemed only as a member of the human community.

In the light of the Christian revelation the individual is shown to have eternal personal significance and to be moving towards an eternal personal goal. He cannot be sacrificed to the needs of a greater whole—whether that whole be the state, the nation, or mankind itself. The fact that people have this individual worth is not apparent outside the sphere of revelation: it is a characteristic mark of Christianity.

Among the many answers suggested for the question: What is man?—Christianity's stands out because it ascribes to the individual a unique worth. Christianity maintains that a man's soul—and therefore his whole being—is of greater value than any treasure, and indeed, than all the riches in the world. Let us examine this point more closely.

The best starting point for our attempt to investigate and understand mankind is a sentence from the Gospel of St. John. In the preface to his Gospel, St. John declares that the Word was made flesh. In becoming man, the *logos* took human nature, together with all the limitations imposed on human life. As Guardini said,

God took man's destiny upon himself. He thought it worth while to make such an expenditure of time and effort for man's sake. He thought human nature to be valuable enough to be taken into a union of being and work with his divine ego. In this way God set the seal of his approval on man despite all his transitoriness and frailty.

The approval which God had already given man in assuming his nature was expressed most clearly in the death of Christ, in which God's efforts on man's behalf reached their climax. When God strove for man on the cross, it was love itself that was striving. God laid aside his divine glory and immersed himself in man's frailty, in order to be able to sacrifice himself for men within time and the world. In doing so he manifested the value at which God assessed man. In God's eyes man is obviously more valuable than anything else. In God's eyes the salvation of mankind is worth any expense of time and effort, even to the surrender of life itself. The salvation of mankind—and indeed, of the individual man—is more important than anything else in this world, more important than anything civilization holds dear. It could not therefore be sacrificed for any consideration.

God's endeavours on man's behalf, and his assumption of human destiny, established and secured man's worth for ever, for God assumed human life into his own eternal existence for ever. In view of this it is of the greatest importance that God's redeeming work does not compel man, but leaves him absolutely free. God entered human history in such a way that man was neither blinded by the divine glory nor bewildered by the divine might. God renounced his glory so that human freedom should not be infringed. He valued human freedom so highly that he would not limit man's responsibility at any cost. High as God's opinion was of the value of salvation, he would not force it upon mankind. Great as was the cost to God of bringing man into the breadth and height of his own life, he would not compel anyone by the manifestation of the intensity of his own divine life. If man prefers the pitiful and paltry life of the world, God does not forbid it to him by force. God is far from that love of power which so easily tempts anyone whose concern is for the welfare of others. A tyrannical attitude of this kind is the almost inescapable accompaniment of one man's concern for another. Yet it was altogether absent from the work of salvation God undertook for lost mankind.

God's way of thinking could lead to a disastrous conclusion, for it involves the possibility of man's repudiating all the efforts and endeavours God makes for him, and indeed, of man's evil reducing them to its own low level. The nearer the love of God, which offers itself for men, draws to a man, the more the man who has closed his mind to God resists it, even though he may not consciously want to do so. Thus, the love which has come to save men may be forced against its will to judge them because they who do not want to be saved become obdurate in their evil at love's approach.

God would rather founder on man's obstinacy than succeed by enslaving men. He wants free men, not automatons. Those who long to charge God with not taking the trouble from the world through his acts of salvation and establishing justice in the world, have the outlook of man rather than of God. They think less of man than God does and would wish men to be mere machines. They dream of a God who would beat man to the dust, of a man who is a cog in the mechanism of history, thus wrongly seeing the redemption as an act of celestial imperialism enforced by God on the world.

Such a view of man, and the indictment against God which springs from it, show a contempt for human freedom, and the human dignity that is grounded on it. God's opinion of man is fundamentally higher than that of such a prosecutor. He will not infringe man's freedom, even though he may be in danger of being frustrated by the evil proud freedom of mankind. God refuses to restrict man's freedom in any way.

We might ask what is the foundation of the high opinion God has of man. We can answer this question precisely. It is rooted in the fact that man is the image of God. In man, God is manifested. Man is God's representative on the earth within the limits imposed by creation.

According to the account in Genesis, what man reveals of God is his sovereignty, his ascendancy over the cosmos, his kingliness in all he does—in a word, his personality. Man, however, although he is God's likeness, is himself personal. He is essentially different from everything else by virtue of the fact that he is a personal being.

Although the fact that man is a personal being is of such fundamental importance and has so many implications for the true understanding of mankind, it would never have been clearly realised apart from revelation. In general, outside revelation, man is seen as a part of the world, a part of nature, the highest stage nature has reached. Only Christianity alone has grasped clearly the significance of his personality, and of the consequences flowing from it. Christianity sees personal individuality as the highest and most precious form of life, to which all other forms are subject.

The categories of nature and of life so highly praised in modern times fall far short of that of personality. As we have already seen to some extent, it is of very great help in attempting to understand the personality of man, to compare the manner of his life with one that offers a contrast to, and is subordinate to his own—the life of nature. As Guardini said, personal life and natural life are the two basic forms in which created life occurs. They are qualitatively different from one another. Personal life is not a variant form of natural life, or its highest peak. It is rather essentially different from it, even though it may be very closely bound up with it. All impersonal life is life according to nature.

By the word nature we mean everything near to or around us that presents itself as an object or an instrument to our minds and hands. Nature includes such things as the earth, water, the stars, animals, plants—everything that can be of use to us, or might turn on us in hostility and extinguish our lives and destroy our work. Powerful as nature so defined is in its exhibitions of construction and destruction, it knows nothing of what it is doing. It is blind. Even its greatest works are not performed as a result of its own free resolve. It is not master of itself. It is bound to its acts by the inescapable chains of cause and effect. It is under a constraining law. Nature, not conscious of itself, and not potent in itself, constructs a unified kingdom. The individual things it constructs are both like and unlike one another. They contrast with, and yet are bound up with, one another. The difference between them is a merely quantitative, numerical one: the difference, for instance, between two machines, or two cogs in a machine.

In the realms of differentiation of this kind, one thing can replace another or be changed into another, and thereafter everything is once again orderly. The difference between things is a qualitative difference only when one thing has a particular form which differentiates it from others of the same kind. Nature is built up of things superimposed upon and overlapping one another. But the things are not conscious of the law of their own being. They must submit to being used as tools by man. Indeed, as Steinbüchel has said, in being used and expended by man they fulfil their being.

Personal being offers a complete contrast with natural being. One of the characteristics of life as a person is, that persons are proper to themselves, and cannot be the property of other beings. This in itself makes persons essentially different from any other creatures. From the fact of belonging to one's self and of being differentiated from others it follows that personality involves isolation, life in oneself, and essential loneliness. Life as a person is incommunicable. It is independent of other lives.

One of the consequences of independence in life is that a person does things of his own will. A person is not like an animal or a plant, or a stone, forced to act as he does. A person resolves on his actions himself. His mode of existence is that of freedom. As a result, he has a true knowledge of himself. What he does, he does primarily for himself. With his actions he fulfils his own nature. His goal is within himself. He cannot be used and expended as natural things can be, as though he were a tool. It is possible for another to use and expend the work-potential or worldly property of a person, but it is impossible for him to use the essential self.

Because life as a person is fundamentally different from every other way of life, every person is unique and irreplaceable, and has an absolutely unique personal worth and significance.

All these are primarily objective factors. Their fundamental basis is that man is a being endowed with reason. Man's individuality, his self-possession and self-direction, are expressed in the individuality of the human mind and the way in which man exercises his will. In those actions, whether conscious or unconscious, in which man demonstrates his individuality, he shows himself to be a person.

The fact that man is a person is revealed by his self-consciousness.

The fact that man can say 'I' sets him apart from all other beings. This ability gives the meanest man the lustre of dignity which the noblest animal lacks. It endows man with a grandeur which makes him inviolable. As a result, every injustice and atrocity against man is an act of treason. The conscious and voluntary individuality of a person need not always be exercised consciously. It is part of the very nature of personality that a person is in control of his own thinking and willing. Man is a person because and in so far as he is a being characterized by his ability to say 'I'.

Objective, essential personality is the basis of personal action. If a man is truly aware of his personal life, he will express in action the potentialities within him and by doing so will become ever more fully a person. He will do justice to this characteristic feature of his being if he recognizes its essential character and, whilst depending on himself, remains master of himself. In this way the independent individuality which is his, because he is a man, will gain in significance, security, dynamism and animation. He does not remain dead and passive, but expresses himself in action. Life as a person does not consist in action or self-expression, yet it cannot really exist without action, without putting itself forward. In his acts, a man affirms, asserts and defines himself. The more resolutely he turns to himself for support, the more fully he enters into his own inmost being and the more interiorly he lives, the more powerfully and fruitfully he realizes his personal being, the nature which is latent within him.

The self-dependence characteristic of personal life has a kind of dynamism within itself. As Steinbüchel said, it finds its moral perfection in being true to itself.

Where we encounter such awareness of self, we speak of ego. The ego—and the ego alone—has the power to take possession of itself, to enter into its own inmost being, and dwell within the sphere of itself, to preserve its own inner life against all perils and dangers, and to safeguard its unique and irreplaceable nature. Its greatness and value lie in the fact that it is through it that a man gains faith in himself, is enabled to be true to himself, and by it he can review and evaluate everything else. It is the basis of his final indestructibility: iron may grind him to powder, fire may burn him, but he remains the victor, because even in collapse he preserves himself by his fidelity to himself.

If we are to understand fully the nature of personal being, we must look at one other point. Hitherto we have only taken into account the ego's relationship to itself. The fact that it is self-dependent, however, does not mean that it is locked up within itself and cut off from other things. Actually it is necessary to life as a person to look outwards to values and persons outside oneself, even to the point of uniting oneself with them.

This is obvious if we remember that as a likeness of God, man is in his very person the likeness of love, for God is love. Man is therefore in his heart love itself (i.e. man is an *animal orans*). Man's love is realised in his relationships with others. Man also realises his personality in his surrender to others. The individuality and self-sufficiency of the person are embodied in the way in which it behaves towards others. It is characteristic of the ego that it lives in the company of another or others. Human life is essentially life with others. Man is only truly himself when he is in communication with others. He is truly himself only in so far as he turns outward from himself to another or to some thing of merit. Only when he transcends himself is he fully himself. When he refuses to give himself to others and to things of worth, to truth and goodness—when, therefore, he remains by himself and locks himself within himself—he comes into conflict with himself, with his inner character, because such is not his real nature. Then he offers himself violence and perishes. Thus both immanence and transcendence are characteristic of mankind.

Paradoxical as it may be, it expresses the reality of human life to say that a man only does himself justice when he sacrifices himself, offers himself up. He who would preserve his life shall lose it. He who gives it up will preserve it. Man is and will be himself only in self-surrender.

If then a man is anxious that his self-possession and self-determination should not grow weaker and shrivel away, he must enter on the things about him, on things of worth, on things that are good and true and beautiful and take them into himself. Only thus can he live a full and rich life; only thus can he realize his potentialities as a personal being. He can fulfil himself, come to his true fulness of being, only in so far as he does not remain locked up with himself, but, in his thoughts and will, with the powers of his mind and his heart, comes out continually from his own heart and enters into the world in which he lives (i.e. he is an *animal rationale et animal orans*).

The most important—and at the same time most unavoidable—of man's encounters in the outside world are those he has with other human beings. The ego exists in and for its relationships with others and with the community. This is shown, for instance, in man's ability to speak. It is speech alone—whether audible or not—that makes the passage of human life meaningful. This truth was not discovered by the poets and philosophers: it is obvious from life itself.

We must go one step further: a man attains true and truly personal existence not in his communication with other humans, in inter-relationships within the human community, but in his relationship with God. Only thus can his personality be fully expressed. Every man who is truly alive shares a characteristic experience: as it was with Faust, so it is with him. Faust was driven on from one of the world's glories to another, never finding peace, and unable to say: 'Stay a moment, for thou art beautiful'. How should we account for this experience?

St. Augustine is able to help us here because he experienced it in its most intense and painful form. He knew the human spirit to be capable of receiving God within itself. He spoke of a capacity for God. On account of this capacity, the human spirit cannot be satisfied with anything on this earth; it can be satisfied only by him who is all things. Man, the *animal orans*, is orientated towards an infinite, divine Other, God, whose worth is limitless. An essential element in him remains unsatisfied as long as it is not satisfied by God.

Man feels this incompleteness as a yearning transcending any-thing else he has ever experienced. He feels constrained to look towards and press towards something beyond himself, and not to be content with himself and his experience of temporal things. He must, by his very nature, continually turn outwards from himself. If he tries to restrict himself to the purely human world or the bounded universe, he injures himself. Refusal to transcend himself and enter into a relationship with the eternal being of God, springing as it does from the idea of the self-sufficiency of nature, leads, because it is a contradiction of the inmost being of man, to his destruction. The man who will not venture into the wide realms of the infinite person of God, but choses unassumingly and modestly to build an individual or communal life within the bounds of everyday experience, digs the grave of both his own life and the life of the community. Man's insatiable need for God springs ultimately from the fact that he came into being through God. No matter how men try to explain man's origin, it remains true that he is descended from God. Physically, his descent is indirect, but spiritually, it is direct. The fact that he comes from God stamps his inmost being with certain characteristics. On account of his descent from God man is related to God and bears within himself God's characteristics, just as children bear within themselves the characteristics of their parents. He must therefore, if he wants to develop and fulfil his inherited nature, give expression to these characteristics which originate in his relationship to God. He can only do so by turning to God in his thinking and loving.

Man can, then, come to the fulness of his development, can become truly himself, only in so far as he devotes himself to God. He is in his inmost being ordained to God. Whilst he is not with God, he is incomplete. His inward orientation towards God becomes conscious and expresses itself in his consciousness as a yearning for God. Whilst then a man is not with God, his deepest longing remains unsatisfied. He arrives at the fulness of his development, he attains the fulness of his own being, not by remaining alone, nor yet by ranging over the whole cosmos, the material and spiritual universe, but only by travelling to the end, the endless road to God. No shorter road to his perfection is open to man than the unending road to the infinity of God.

The result of man's sinfulness, self-glorification and wilfulness is, that it has become possible for man to deny his orientation towards and longing for, God. The man who glories in himself experiences not only a force drawing him towards God, but also a compulsion, driving him away from him. God seems alien to him because he sees in God one who will accuse him and attack him for his self-glorying. He therefore attempts to quiet his continual yearning by making his own gods to whom he gives his heart. But untrue gods cannot fulfil him, and he turns restlessly from one thing to another until, in complete despair, he realizes that nothing will satisfy him. He who finally renounces all possibility of coming into any relationship with God is lost in that condition we call hell.

It is the spirit which makes him a person. It is his spirit which forms and moulds him, giving him the ability to apprehend himself and establish his position, and to penetrate into and shape nature. The ways in which the spirit devotes itself to others and to things of value are manifold. It is able to grasp the significance of things: it can enter the chaotic world of things and events, and discover the relationships between them. It can see and accept another's worth. Deep within itself it hears the voice of conscience and knows, as Guardini said, that it is the voice of God.

The leading of a personal life is a difficult and life-long task for man, because the fidelity to himself that he feels simply because he is a person, and the yearning for another which is in him— whether that other be human or divine—do not act automatically, but demand the constant exercise of the human will. As a result, in determining his own course a man is continually threatened by the danger of becoming wrapped up in himself and becoming proud of himself in the very act of entering his own heart. He may, on the other hand, be in peril of losing himself to another, to the community or to the world, even whilst in process of giving himself to others and to the precious things of the world.

The temptation to allow oneself to fall into the power of nature or the community, and lose oneself in them, is a constantly recurring one. The more strongly man feels loneliness, the loneliness that is the result of being a person, the more powerful will be the desire in him to free himself from it by dissolving and losing himself in the cosmos and natural human relationships. If he yields to this temptation, he loses his personality and becomes a mere 'man'. By doing so he loses the characteristics of personal identity and will, becomes content to accept public opinion mechanically—what 'they' are thinking and saying—and, without testing it against his own inner sense of rightness and justice, repeats thoughtlessly whatever has been said to him, and becomes content to do what everyone else does. He does it because 'they' do it. He needs someone to dictate to him what he should do. He does not dare to act unless someone gives him an order. The temptation to extinguish our personality in this way becomes greater as we find that making decisions is an effort, that it involves thinking, risks, and the acceptance of responsibility, that it is in itself hazardous and uncertain, and cuts a man off from his neighbours. Man can only fulfil his duty to live as a person, rather than as a plant or an animal, by continual struggle against such temptations. Self-preservation and self-surrender; self-surrender and self-preservation: so we might sum up the duty which falls to every man because he is a personal being. The nature of this task is such that during his life a man can never accomplish and fulfil it completely. It is for man an essentially interminable task. It is his duty to walk a metaphorical tightrope, remaining master of himself without becoming wrapped up in himself, and giving himself without losing himself. Although this task cannot be fulfilled perfectly during life, man may not and cannot shun it. He cannot resignedly give up trying but must constantly take up the task anew, knowing that during the course of his life he may never renounce it. Sustained by the hope that it will one day be discharged—on that day when God bestows on man life beyond time—he is thus enabled to strive for that self-possession and self-surrender, which can only find its true completion in union with God.

The difficulty of this task makes it easy to understand why man rejected it at the beginning of his history and has constantly rejected it since.

Man tried to absolve himself from the task that had been given him by undertaking only one side of it: at the beginning of his history he undertook to remain in possession of himself, without giving himself to God; he undertook to enter into himself, without at the same time turning outward from himself. By doing so, he broke off his relationship with God. This meant that he chose to live only in and for himself. The alienation of the first man from God had many consequences for the whole of mankind, for in Adam and Eve the whole of humanity was cut off from God. As a result, every man coming into the world—with the sole exception of Mary—lives remote from God in original sin (Romans 12, 5 f.).

Only Mary, the Mother of the Lord, the Mother of God, was, by a special act of intervention by God, freed from every stain of original sin, so that from the first moment of her life she lived in that communion with God in which all men will share only after the annulment of original sin. This is what we mean when we speak of the *immaculata conceptio*. Mary owed her earthly life to the same processes and laws as every other human being. But her relationship with God was established from her birth—or, rather, from her conception—so that she lived in the most intimate relation with the Father of heaven.

Because man is essentially orientated towards God, if he becomes wrapped up in himself to the exclusion of God, he offers violence to his own being. To do so can lead to the derangement and breakdown of self, and may even lead to the splitting of man's personality.

If relationship with God is the basis and guarantee of human dignity and greatness, then seclusion from God must involve both the forfeiture of human greatness and dignity, and the surrender of the pledge of man's irreplaceable worth. If man seeks his own honour, and denies honour to God, then he loses his own honour. When God is no longer honoured as the pledge and guardian of human dignity, human dignity is trodden under foot. Godlessness is the enemy of true humanity, for life can only be truly human in an atmosphere of faith in God. If faith in God dies, the forces of hate and the lie rise up and enslave man. Then Satan, the bearer of hate and lies, the eternal murderer, the father of lies, invades and abuses mankind, the image of God on the earth, through his servants, the instruments of his hate and his lies, using men as though they were things of the world, like plants or animals. The proud man who will not tolerate the rule of God is delivered over to punishment by earthly lords. Those who proclaim that God is dead, become the executioners in a purely human society. A world of godless demi-gods inevitably calls into being a world of underprivilege, and itself, quickly degenerates into a world morally sub-human.

For a short period it may of course succeed in restraining the diabolic powers of destruction slumbering in human hearts. But, as history shows, they continually break out and spread, flood-like, over everything that we call dignity and security. Thus in the realm of godlessness, the only kind of human life that exists is that burdened with trouble and distress. It can seldom withstand the trial by fire offered it by sorrow and temptation. It has not enough strength to withstand the inroads of vileness and violence.

Even if it is able to suffer the blows of fate and the temptations of hell, it is still poorer in one way than human life as guaranteed by God. The man who is united with God has a depth that the godless man lacks, for the latter is the poorer by the whole kingdom of heaven. The question arises as to whether it can survive such a loss, for it involves the forfeiture of life's ultimate meaning and security. A man cannot suffer such things as these without falling into melancholy, despair, fear and resignation.

He who tries to avoid these moods, finds himself struggling with all his might and consequently limiting his life. Trust, confidence and love are basic foundations and needs of the human heart, but they grow cold within such a man. Fear and despair are the companions of godlessness. If the godless man no longer feels them, that is because their voices are drowned by the voices of day-to-day distractions, such as the cinema, radio and press. They withdraw from the realm of the conscious, to the inner realms of the sub-conscious, and there lead an active life. As Goldbrunner said, they continually penetrate, disturbingly and cripplingly, into the consciousness. Melancholy and despair are sketched on the face of the man who lives without God. The godless life is an inhuman life. Godlessness leads to inhumanity.

Just as the vainglorious man digs the grave of his own greatness and dignity if he is untrue to the difficult task of living as a person, so he digs the grave of human community life. He then becomes subject to powers hostile to life in community—self-seeking, tyranny and the lie. Thus chaos enters the world of man. This may, in its turn, lead to a still deeper degradation. It calls forth the dictator to restrain the unbridled, and war, by all against all, swallows up everything. Dictatorship speeds the process of dehumanization in mankind, for it must undermine freedom if it itself is not to be bridled by someone yet more mighty. The result is that individualism disappears. Those who live under a dictatorship, are no longer a human community, but become a mob.

Standing aloof from God is accompanied by surrender to some

thing or person in the world. Any man who does not make the resolve to turn outwards from himself towards God, falls victim to the fascination of things: of possessions, honour and lust. His life is passed in caring for the things of this world. He exhausts himself with the tasks of the hour. With the passage of time, he himself passes, and nothing remains.

Modern existential philosophy—the roots of which are to be found in Nietzsche's philosophy of life—advises man not to look over and beyond the walls of the world, but to revere the mystery of the world as the greatest and most profound of mysteries. But these views are to be found earlier, and even in classical literature. Faust said: 'I know the orb of the world well enough; I am prejudiced against things outside. Fool! He who turns his dazzled eyes out there, and meditates on clouds like himself! He should stand fast, and look about him here. To the gifted man, this world is not dumb.'

In the poems of Rilke, too, we are called on to look to the world for nothing, but to give ourselves to it in devotion and faith. God is the mystery of the world, at once obscure and plain.

Very recently, this same idea was employed by Ernest Wiechart in his novel *Die Jerominkinder*, where we are told: 'Life was without glamour. Men went through their days with aching backs; care was a guest at their doors; yet life was fenced in, a dog watched and children grew up in the coarsest way, but blood of their own blood, who would care for a coffin and a wooden cross on the little hillock under the old lilacs and elders, in which the thrushes sang in autumn.' So life passes: in summer and winter, in the coming and going of the cranes, in the celebration now and then of a wedding or a funeral. We must beware: we should care for the fields and serve our own limited circle, the group of men into which fate has put us, and we should want nothing beyond that.

Such advice does violence to the human heart and spirit on which it longs to rise, and should be able to rise, to a reality beyond this world. As Spranger says, if we worship the world in this way, we shall sink into one of the many bogs put in our path by human life. But the Word has become flesh, taking on himself the destiny that has been man's since the coming of sin into the world, and demonstrating how abysmally far man has fallen, and at the same time sanctioning that fall for ever, for the world in which God was executed can never again become a paradise.

One of the chief despair-laden afflictions in life and the world is the homelessness that afflicts the human heart in the world. Man feels the world is his enemy, that it treats him with hostility. Nature does of course encourage his actions, but it may also be indifferent or even hostile to him, destroying the work it costs him all his energies to produce, swallowing up his life and seemingly thinking nothing of it. The sea, having swallowed up a ship and those it carried, smiles as though nothing had happened.

Nature is indifferent to man's tears. Man is an immigrant in the world—a refugee, a tramp, a homeless wanderer. Always wandering, he lives in it, never finding peace, never able to lay himself down in a sure resting place. This is why melancholy attacks him, arising from the depths of his heart and oozing out of the things around him. Virgil said that things themselves seem to have their tears, and Dante asserted that there is a great sorrow in nature. It overflows into man's heart, and he cannot find on earth the consolation and peace he seeks. Nature offers him one disillusionment after another. Hence, if he believes only in the world, he may fall victim to the temptation of thinking life is not worth while. He may go so far as to say: 'Nothing pleases me'. Pleasure deserts him, not because some particular thing has gone wrong, but because the whole of human life is a disappointment.

The believer in the world sees stretched out before him ultimate, unending emptiness and nothingness: he can find no final meaning in his life, and so becomes afraid. As history shows with disconcerting thoroughness, fear is the constant companion of anyone who knows no faith but that in the world. If he tries to escape fear by increasing his rate of work, by diversions and expenditure of effort, it still holds him fast. Even if by valiant fixity of purpose he succeeds in mastering fear, he does not succeed in really freeing himself from it. He may suppress it, but he cannot abolish it. As we shall see below, it escapes into the realms of the subconscious and, whenever man's will sleeps, wreaks great destruction in him. It expresses itself in neuroses, and man can escape the restrictions it places on life neither by exerting his will nor by resorting to medicine. He can do so only by conversion from faith in the world to faith in God—by turning to Christ.

The instability of the world is further shown in the fact of death. In death, human life is cut off, whether or not it has reached its full development. Death shows that man is not entitled to any real fulfilment of his longings within time. If there is no fulfilment beyond death, there can be no ultimate fulfilment at all, and human life is ultimately meaningless. Thus futility has the last word.

We cannot lighten the burden of such a belief as this, by saying that a man survives in what he does, in his accomplishments, his children, or his reputation, for there is no guarantee of such survival. Besides, man's longing is not for this kind of survival, but for personal survival. Every kind of impersonal survival after death is temporary, and soon passes away. The most important point, however, is that life often breaks off in a moment, before any of its fruits have ripened, before its richest possibilities are realised, or could be realised. All that remains is an unfinished work, flotsam, ruins. And thus futility is life's keynote, and the end poisons everything.

When the spirit and heart of man resist meaninglessness, their resistance is not the rebellion of human self-seeking—refusing to submit to the disappearance of the human ego, rebelling against bitter reality—but the protest of the spirit seeking for meaningfulness against absurdity. The search for meaning drives the spirit onwards, no matter whether its endeavours are successful or not.

In connexion with such considerations as these, the philosophy of existentialism argues that death is the inexorable end, the untraversable frontier, the wall on which life is dashed to pieces. It is as it reaches this wall of death that life should sparkle with its greatest brilliance. To the existentialist, death is therefore a superb opportunity—the finest opportunity ever afforded us—of experiencing real and full life.

To be called in this way to drive on towards the wall of death as though it were the highest of peaks, leads man to nothingness, and promises him the climax of his life in nothingness. It promises man his proper and full life in ultimate insecurity and uncertainty, and pride in that ultimate insecurity and uncertainty. But in fact full life dies in the icy blast of nihilism, for to be real, life demands not only firm resolution, but confidence in its ultimate meaning. This cannot be guaranteed by nothingness. It can be guaranteed only by God, as we shall see more clearly later on.

Christianity sees nihilism as a way of life in which man carries his tyrannical self-glory to its highest pitch of development—as the way of life of hell. Anyone who seeks a life of absolute autonomy has before him totally different prospects in respect of hell, from those which he who believes in the world faces regarding death. His life is shattered, not on the reef of death, but on the absolute power which is God. A life of opposition to God may reach a pitch of intensity measurable only by comparison with the absolute life force of God himself. If man's only thought is intensity of life, then Hell is the highest possibility open to him who repudiates God. Measured by him, the potentialities of the man who believes in the world are unimportant. Yet, of course, life in hell unmasks all men's attempts at gaining fulness of life through autonomy and self-glorification, showing them to be failures and illusions. The man who glories in himself, who sees nothing before him but a panorama of nothingness, loses life properly so called. His life is pitiful, and as he never knows it is so, he does not know life's fulness, because he thinks the little island on which he lives is everything, while in reality, the wretched life he does enjoy is bringing him only death. He has no hope. Thus, death is one of the objections to worship of the world.

Furthermore the gap between virtue and happiness, righteousness and success, morality and beauty, seems to show that man's life is not a thing of this world alone. The co-ordination of justice with success, virtue with happiness, immorality with unhappiness will be made—if it is ever made completely—on the other side of death. If, in spite of their experiences, men do manage to endure a life of worship of the world, they do so only by accepting an erroneous concept, whether consciously or not—the error of hoping, whether openly or not, that what is not yet, will one day be. At the foundation of their hope is the unspoken presupposition that the world is continually improving, so that happiness and virtue are being bound together.

There is nothing to prove this hypothesis. The hope that is based upon it is like the vague and unspoken hope of the boatman who encounters a cataract in midstream and assumes that he will be able to traverse the rapids in safety. It is the hope of the dreamer and the fanatic. History continually confirms the sentence of death which Holy Scripture and, through Scripture, God himself has pronounced on such hopes as these.

Finally, our conscience makes it clear to us that faith in the world is unacceptable. Conscience teaches a man that he is absolutely responsible even for the Fall, that no one else can assume responsibility for his actions, and that the Fall was injurious both to him and to other men. It teaches him that he may not be guided by expediency or advantages offered him by the things of the world, but that a call comes to him from realms other than those of the world of experience. The honest man cannot ignore this call. He feels himself bound to obey at any price and under all circumstances.

Such facts as these can only be explained by something outside the cosmos, which is but a mirror of a reality different from itself —the reality of God. If this is so, then man is a wanderer between two worlds, a pilgrim from the world of space and time to the reality of the living God. It is in God that he will find his true existence. He who believes in Christ does not surrender to the illusion that his deepest hopes will be satisfied within time and space. He is clearheaded and far-seeing, so he expects no earthly paradise. The promises of the revolutionaries of every age do not convert him to fanaticism. He realises that in every epoch they have been accompanied by the groans of the victims of murder and enslavement. He knows that a radical improvement of the world can only be brought about by effecting a radical improvement in man. But whilst men struggle against the hate, violence, lies and lust for power of others, they themselves fall victim to the same troubles and nurse within their bosoms their own judges and executioners.

The man who is far-seeing knows that sin—remoteness from God—is man's fundamental affliction, and that all his other afflictions are but symptoms of this primary disease. He therefore expects nothing from the world that the world cannot give. Because man is as he is—because he is a sinner, and remains a sinner—he fights constantly against love and justice. Hence life within time will always pass in uncertainty and want. Hölderlin saw this fact clearly, and made Hyperion say of human destiny: 'But we are given nowhere to rest: suffering mankind stumbles and falls blindly from one moment to another, like water thrown from rock to rock, undecisively for ever.'

But in spite of his clear-sightedness, the believer in Christ does not become a sceptic and nihilist. He does not reduce his demands to a level that the world can fulfil, but rather, in the midst of all the hopelessness of history, he holds on to his highest claims and does not doubt that they will be met. But he does not expect them to be met until after death, for he knows that it is from and in God, the absolute life-force, that man receives his true and proper life, in all its fulness, richness, security and intensity. It will be given to individuals, and to the race as a whole, only when God's sovereignty, the reign of truth and love, is fully established. When God's kingdom is made absolute, morality will be equated with beauty, and love with justice, endeavour with success, and merit with happiness. But this state of affairs is still in the future—and the way to it is called death and destruction (cf. John 14, 1-4). It was Christ who opened this way to us: the Son of God was made flesh and came to save the lost.

CHAPTER SEVEN

CHRISTIANITY'S MISSION TO MANKIND

II : REDEEMED MAN

As our guide to the understanding of mankind we have chosen a saying from St. John's Gospel: The Word was made flesh. There it is, all in one sentence: the infinite worth of man; his error; and his redemption. Man's worth was shown by God's taking human destiny upon himself, and making extreme efforts on his behalf. His perdition was shown by the fact that only by God's endeavours was it possible for man to rise from his abyss. The Cross offers the clearest proof of man's perdition. His condition is such that only the cross can bring him back to the glory of God.

The cross shows us the full horror of the human condition from two separate points of view. In the first place, man condemned himself utterly by the death of Christ. We can trace man's secret will to put God aside and to kill him in the very first sin and in every sin thereafter. Sin strengthens our feeling that we can no longer tolerate God. We do not remember that we are not God, but only mere creatures. Man's desire to kill God—a desire secretly at work in every sin—reached its highest pitch in the condemnation and execution of Christ. At that point, man succeeded in murdering God, sitting in judgement on him, condemning and executing him as one who disturbs the peace of the world. When God became man, he made it possible for man to fulfil the evil longing that until then he had kept a close secret, and which until then it had been impossible for him to fulfil. By executing Christ, man realised his most abysmal potentialities. Man is such that he is capable even of this crime of crimes. His self-glorification, pride and reserve towards God, and his hardness of heart were glaringly revealed in the condemnation of Christ. When God met him, he no longer fled from him, but struck at him as violently as he could for no other reason than that he was God. So corrupt is the world, so entangled in hate is man, that the love and holiness which Christ revealed cannot live in the world they themselves have created, but must die there. Love can find no home in the world of hate. There is nowhere for it to lay its head. It cannot live in the atmosphere of hate—it must die.

The fact that only the cross could draw man out of the abysmal depths into which he had sunk is a second proof of the completeness of man's perdition. The death of the Son of God who was made flesh shows what manner of thing sin is, and what efforts are necessary to abolish it from the world. Sin is such that he who would redeem man from it can do so only by mounting the cross. When the *logos* decided to take human destiny upon himself, he was resolving to die in his human nature, for only thus could he really experience the fate of mankind from within. He had to descend to those diabolical depths into which man had fallen through his godless self-glorification, if he were to take human depravity onto his shoulders and bear it out of the world. Only thus might the lost be saved.

The redemption was not effected automatically. It demanded that the ego of the divine *logos* take on himself the heavy burden of human destiny that oppresses every man born on the earth, and live it out in his human nature.

It might be asked how individual man can participate concretely in the redemption wrought by Christ. The answer is that he can do so by enduring his fate in communion with Christ. Christ entered upon a relationship with men and took upon himself the destiny of mankind so that mankind might endure its fate with him. The redemption Christ wrought did not mean that men would be freed as though by magic from death and sorrow, but that they could walk their way of death with Christ, so that it became a way of life, of the true and eternal life. The redemption is operative for individuals in so far as they enter into communion with Christ, so that their lives partake of Christ's life, so that their sorrows and death are one with the sorrows and death of Christ.

There is also the difficult question as to how we today can enter into communion with those who, in previous centuries throughout the world, have entered into communion with Christ. As we have already seen, Christ's historicity sets him sharply apart from the gods of the myths. Historicity implies limitation in time and space. It is not difficult to attain union with the gods of the myths, Apollo and Balder, Ishtar and Juno, for, as it is impossible to differentiate their living and dying from the rhythm of birth and death in nature they are born everywhere and die at all times. To unite with them it is necessary only to enter into the rhythm of nature. How can those men who live after Christ, who are limited to their own particular 'here and now', enter into real, lively communion with Christ, who is bound to his own 'then and there'? The communion with Christ in which the salvation of man is effected, is no mere communion of thought or will. It is, indeed, completely different from such communion, although communion of thought and will are consequent upon communion of being and life, of communion of destiny with him. Communion of life with Christ is more than relationship with a teacher, tutor, or instructor. We can unite ourselves with our own greatest men as with a teacher. We can look up to Plato and Socrates, Augustine and Thomas, Leibnitz and Rousseau, Kant and Nietzsche.

We cannot solve the problem by regarding redemption as the reception of higher gifts ministered by Christ and distributed through the Church. This of course is true and of great importance, but it is not all, nor is it the most important thing. According to Holy Scripture—especially St. John's Gospel and the Pauline Epistles—and to the theology of the Fathers of the Church, especially the Greeks, the redemption of individuals is effected in their relationship with Christ. How is this relationship possible? We, of course, can only have a very imperfect conception of it. Union with Christ transcends all other relationships of love and friendship possible to man. Its power and intimacy are greater than those of any other union occurring within the bounds of our experience.

How can there be such union with a man who lived long centuries ago and far away? We might attempt to picture union with Christ as dependent on his own life in the glory of the Father. In fact death was for Christ a passing over into the fulness and abundance of the divine life. From the time of his death, it became possible for Christ to remain forever with his followers, as he had promised.

Thus we might think of union with him as communion with the glorified Christ.

But even this explanation does not do full justice to our union with Christ, for salvation was earned for us so that we might become partakers in the life of the Christ who walked upon the earth, and who through death received glory, so that the events of Good Friday and Easter Day might take effect in us. As we know, our salvation is not yet made perfect. It will be perfected in suffering and death, and in the heavenly life of the faithful of Christ. Essentially, it consists in sharing in the rhythm of his life. Only if we do so shall we attain the salvation he offers us, and come to that place in space and time where we may pass over from the temporal, sinful life, to the eternal, holy life of God; from the life of self-seeking, to the life of love; from the life of loneliness, to the life of fulness and communion. Only he who finds the bridge which leads from earth to heaven can be saved. This bridge is the cross of Christ. There is no other way across the chasm. There remains the difficult question as to how we are to find the crossing. Heaven and earth are not in contact everywhere, so that it is not everywhere possible to step over from time into eternity. We can do so only in a few places. How can we reach these points of contact? They are exactly fixed and bounded in time and space.

Christ has made it possible. He has provided the means whereby the space-time restrictions of his death and resurrection can be overcome. We call them the sacraments. In the sacraments the life and death are in some mysterious way made present once more. They can overcome the restrictions of time and space.

The way in which the sacraments make present the temporal death—and, indirectly, his life both before and after that death—is disputed in theology. We can imagine either a dynamic or an ontological explanation. In the first case we must assume that the death of Christ is expressed in the sacramental signs, and through them is transmitted to those who receive the sacraments. Every event is of significance for the time following it. The death of Christ operates more powerfully on succeeding ages than any other event in history. What we can say of every happening—namely, that it never completely dies, but always shapes and forms the future, and remains potent for ever—is true in a surpassing way of the death of Christ. The whole of time after him is under the influence of his deeds and actions. This was already apparent in the fact that those who stood before the cross of Christ were divided into two main groups: the believers and the unbelievers; those who loved him, and those who hated him.

The potency of the cross of Christ is, as it were, brought to a focus at certain points in the world and in time. Its foci are the sacraments. In the sacraments, the power of Christ's living and dying are present in a concentrated form, as it were.

According to another interpretation the temporal event, the death of Christ, is present in the sacraments not only dynamically, but also essentially, in its true nature (Casel *et al*). The presence of the death of Christ is effected in a non-historical way, in a spiritual way, after the fashion of a mystery. This form of being is outside our knowledge and cannot therefore, be proved by experiment. But it can be demonstrated from our experience. When we imagine something that has happened, such as, for instance, a bloody accident, it has for us no terrible results. Its only effects are mental. The temporal event, the death of Christ, has in the sacraments not a bloody, but a mental and spiritual outcome. Of course, we must not, in making this simile, overlook the vast differences between the two happenings. When we call a temporal event into our minds, we make only the image of it present there but when we make the death of Christ present in the sacraments, we make it present in its full reality.

If we would compare these explanations and test their validity, we must first realise clearly that the sacraments do not all have the same form. We might claim that it is quite obvious that the historical death of Christ is made present in the Eucharist in its true form, not historically, but in a supra-historical, spiritual way. For the other sacraments, we might be able to prove only a dynamic re-presentation of the death of Christ.

To be valid, these theological explanations of the mystery of our redemption must show that in the sacraments, the death of Christ is made present, together with the life that preceded it and the life grounded in it—that they make the life of Christ accessible to us. In the normal way we are made partakers of him in the sacraments. We cannot now concern ourselves with the question as to whether

God knows and uses no other ways to bring men to Christ. He has, as a matter of fact, made available other extraordinary ways. However, in our context we can consider only the normal way given by God—the way normally open for every man to come to him. This way is the sacraments, in which Christ has made his life and death available to us. In other ways—perhaps, for instance in nature, in the rustlings of the forests, in the storms and calms of the sea, in the tempests, in the mountain heights, or the glittering of the sun upon them, he is not so attainable that we can find salvation in them. He who refuses to lay hold on Christ in the sacraments, the sign he has given us, in so far as he refuses to do so against his better judgement, finds it almost impossible to reach him. By doing so he also refuses the life Christ has given, and remains dead.

We lay hold by faith on the life Christ has made available to us in the sacraments. According to Holy Scriptures, Faith, in the fullest sense, is a movement of the human heart, by which we lay hold on Christ to surrender ourselves to him. Faith also involves assent to the truth preached by Christ, and the facts about God and love revealed by him. But in actuality, it is more than intellectual assent to truth or fact, or a series of facts. It is rather a way of life. Christ portrayed faith as an act, by which man lays hold on him, in order to be satisfied by him: 'I am the bread of life. He that cometh to me shall not hunger; and he that believeth in me shall never thirst' (John 6, 35). Thus, to believe is to come to Christ. Faith is, as it were, a turning of the human ego to Christ, based on a resolution of the human heart.

It would be very dangerous and wrong to believe that faith is necessary to the human heart, and to try to draw from that the conclusion that some men have faith because they have a need for, or talent for religion, and others do not have it because they lack this need. In this interpretation, faith is mistaken for something in the human being himself. A religious need, so-called, or a talent for religion, so-called, may be restricting, as well as helpful, to true faith. A need for religion may lead a man to accept a faith as the faith he needs, and it is precisely this which has given rise to most of the gods created by human self-love. It produces a picture of Christ, constructed and corrected according to the wishes of the individual, such as we find in many of the distortions of the Christian faith. True faith is not an expression of a need in the heart of man; it is rather a resolve of the will, born of a heart enlightened by knowledge and is, of course, able to satisfy the real needs of the mind and heart. It is this decision which makes men give assent to Christ. Its pre-requisite is recognition of the Lord, just as the pre-requisite of believing in a man, or loving him, is knowing him.

Faith is neither the logical outcome of philosophical or historical study (although it cannot exist without reasoning, without at least the minimum of thinking) nor the product of a talent for religion. It is a personal meeting with Christ, to whom one has been called. Because it is the call of omnipotent love, this call is binding on everyone, whether or not he feels the need to follow.

Assent to Christ—that is, assent to the things shown us by Christ, things different from the things of the world—can only be given by those who have the power to see things outside this world. The natural eyes of the mind are not enough. We can see with them the world and the interrelationships of things within the world. But as long as we have only these eyes, we are like a colour-blind man before a symphony of colours. When we stand before the things of God which are different from the things of the world, and yet have been revealed by the things of the world, we see nothing. If someone else claims to see this colour or that, the colour-blind man is compelled to shake his head incredulously and dismiss these claims as fantasies. Those who have the power to see cannot be moved by his protests, but accuse him of blindness. The power of sight needed to see the reality revealed to us by Christ is an enlightenment given to man by God. God enlightens man by sending him the Holy Ghost. The Holy Ghost produces in man an ability to see with the heart and spirit the truth about Christ. Thus it depends on God whether a man believes or not. But it also depends on the man himself, for God enlightens only those who will allow themselves to be enlightened. Thus those who do not believe, because of their evil will, are responsible for their disbelief. On the other hand, no one can come to Christ unless he is drawn to him by the Father (John 6, 44). How the divine initiative and human willingness and resolve are interrelated is a closely kept secret which we cannot discuss more fully here.

Obviously, however, because living faith is a resolve of the enlightened will, because it is a personal relationship with Christ, it is related to love, and, indeed, is at one with it. To believe in a living person, not in an objective truth, is almost the same thing as to love him. Love therefore is also part of a living faith. In love man seizes the invisible hand of the Lord—the hand of love—stretched out to him from the darkness. In loving Christ, he gazes with the eyes of love, the eyes of the heart, illuminated by the Holy Ghost, into the countenance of the love revealed to him by the incarnate Christ. Thus faith establishes and preserves communion with Christ.

More precisely, we might define this communion as man's entry into the life and destiny of Christ. This involves two things. If a man enters into communion with Christ, he is changed in accordance with the likeness of Christ. He lives therefore in the mind of Christ, established in him by Christ. The Christian is the representative of Christ in the world. Christ becomes the law of him who is united with him, just as the beloved is the rule of the lover's life, just as the mind is the ruler of the body.

This last comparison, of course, shows us also the limits of this union. The spirit cannot express itself perfectly in the body. The laws of matter limit its action. A man's face, for instance, is indeed a visible expression of his spirit, but it is not completely shaped in all its features and movements by the spirit. Man's countenance is, to an extent, formed by the spirit. In so far as what appears on the face falls short of what would be fully human, the spirit lacks the power to enforce its law on rebellious matter. Whilst we are pilgrims, the spirit cannot succeed in completely shaping matter so that it is its perfect mirror. But what is unattainable during the time of our earthly pilgrimage will be reached in the post-historical life, in that condition we call heaven. When we are in that state, the human body will be ruled completely by the spirit, so that it will be a perfect reflexion of the spirit. Then the body itself will be even more perfectly human, for perfect man is glorified man.

From this comparison we can also see what is meant when we say that Christ is the law of the man united to him. Christ works in such a man. In him, Christ reveals himself, so that he may in a true sense be called a manifestation of the dead and glorified Christ.

Just as the human body obstructs the spirit, so the human ego is an obstacle to the all-sovereign Christ, making it impossible for him to work or manifest himself perfectly in man. The obstacle the ego presents consists in its self-seeking and self-glorying, its sloth and self-will.

The man who is united with Christ is Christ, in so far as he is a mirror of Christ, representing him in every facet of his life. It is his duty to accept what he is, and express it in his disposition. And what he is, is the representative of Christ and so of the heavenly Father. In so far as he obstructs the working of Christ in his life, he falls short of the Christ-life. No one will succeed in allowing Christ to manifest himself perfectly in him during his earthly life, and so completely fulfil his task of representing him. Yet it will be performed successfully one day—namely, in the life beyond time, when Christ will so transform men that they will perfectly mirror him. Thus the perfect Christian is he who is perfect in heaven.

The man who shares Christ's destiny, also has something else, namely, community of life and being with him. St. Paul expressed this in the formula: We in Christ and Christ in us. This expression —which it is not easy for our minds to grasp—does not mean that Christ is ontologically present in the believer. For the Apostle Paul the word 'in' had a causal force, and his phrase 'Christ in us' therefore means that Christ works in us, and not that he lives bodily in the baptized. We are touched by Christ's actions and thus we live within the area of Christ's effectiveness. Christ's activity is, as it were, the atmosphere in which the believer lives and breathes. He is in it, as a fish is in water. Thus, we can speak of a dynamic 'presence' of Christ. There also exists an ontological presence of Christ: this is given us in the Eucharist, the sacrament of Christ's body and blood. But even so, the ontological presence of Christ is directed towards the dynamic presence: it attains its full significance in so far as a man is governed wholly by Christ.

When someone is wholly imbued with Christ and lives within the sphere of his influence, it is true to say of him: I live, now not I; but Christ liveth in me (Gal. 2, 20). Such a person lives through

149

Christ and has his being in him. He has received a new existence. Taken literally, the word existence means a coming-out (*ex-sistere*), a continual creation. A man has being because he proceeds constantly from the power which produces him, and for as long as being flows into him from that power in an unbroken stream. From the Father, through the Son and in the Holy Ghost, the divine being and life preserve those who are united with Christ, in so far as it pleases God, and in so far as man is able to receive them. Christ gives him a new point of origin. He fulfils his *ex-sistere*, because he is from Christ and lives by Christ.

Union with Christ is of an intimacy surpassing all other such intimacies. Yet it does not lead to the identification of the human ego with the ego of Christ. The mystery of the life of man consists in this: that he who is united with Christ is made so fully one with the Lord that he can really be called an *alter Christus*, yet he remains fully himself. He is not swallowed up in Christ's personality so that his individuality is extinguished. Yet, on the other hand, there is no strangeness between him and Christ.

It is possible to define the manner of this union even more closely. It depends on the fact that Christ has passed through death, and has been granted the life of glory. He who is united with him is therefore united with one who has been crucified, executed, exalted, glorified and made Lord of all lords. Union with the dying Christ is effected by bringing the believer in Christ into contact with the death of Christ. He receives a blow from the death of Christ: he receives, therefore, a death-blow. The death-blow given by Christ falls upon the sinful, mortal life: the life of the flesh, as St. Paul expresses it—the life subject to the law brought into being by sin. Thus the person united with Christ also has a share in the death of Christ. His mortal, sinful life is not, however, wholly extinguished; but it has received a death-blow. It is therefore only a question of time before it is completely destroyed.

The death-blow falls on it in baptism, and is furthered in all the sacraments. It falls particularly heavily on man in the celebration of the Eucharist. The death of Christ is also continually at work in life's afflictions. The life that has already received the death-blow is finally broken off in the death of the body. In death, there is finally completed what was begun in baptism and was furthered throughout the whole of life. So then, the man who is united with Christ is always dying. He ought not to be surprised when this is made obvious to him in life's troubles and afflictions, and in the leave-takings he must continually make in the world—the leave-taking of the adolescent from childhood, of the adult from youth, the ageing from the fulness of manhood, the greybeard from the autumn of life, the leave-taking of friend from friend, of lover from beloved, of each man continually, daily and hourly, from the glory of the world, for so he practises for the final leave-taking that everyone must make at his death from the world, and life in the world. For death is the lowest acceptable price of true life in its fullest form. The highest price is in this case the same as the lowest.

Just as the man united with Christ receives a blow from the death of Christ, so he receives a ray of glory from the glorification of Christ. He is directly touched by the splendour of heaven, the home of the risen Christ. In this sense we may say as a man is drawn into the death of Christ, so also he is assumed into the glorified life of Christ.

Both the process of dying and the glory of Christ are effective in him, and both are revealed in him. Whilst his partaking of the death of Christ is detectable in the afflictions and sorrows of life, so too his sharing in the glory of Christ is traceable in the joys and consolations of life. During his pilgrimage, the fact that he has a part in the death of Christ will be expressed more clearly in him than the fact of his partaking in the glory of Christ. During the period of his earthly wanderings, his partaking in Christ's life of glory will be only embryonic and rudimentary. It will reach its perfection in the life beyond time. The consciousness he has on earth of his part in the glorified Christ is, as it were, an earnest, a first instalment, an advance on the future. St. Paul testified to our part in the heavenly life of Christ when he said that we have been raised into the heavenly places with Christ (Eph. 2, 7). Heaven is not merely in the future, but is already present, just as the life of the butterfly already exists in the life of the caterpillar, neither more, nor less.

Union with Christ is not an end in itself. For man, Christ is not the goal but the way. The way Christ indicates leads to where all roads end, to the place from where no other road sets out, the face of the Father, that home for which the heart of the earthly pilgrim yearns.

The intimacy with which the believer is united with Christ, and through him with the Father, is effected in a continuous process by the Holy Ghost. The Holy Ghost is that personal love in which the Father bestows himself on the Son and the Son on the Father, the love which flows to the Father from the heart of the Son, and to the Son from the heart of the Father, the breath they exchange, the token of love in which the love of the Son is shown to the Father, and the love of the Father to the Son. Thus he establishes the relationship of love between the Father and the Son, doing so in the almighty power that is peculiar to God.

The Holy Ghost is now sent by Christ to his faithful. He is sent as love is sent from the lover to the beloved. Christ breathes the Holy Ghost, who is personal love, into every man who gives himself to him in faith. Thus the faithful are imbued with that love on which is based the relationship between the Father and the Son.

The love which fills the faithful is not merely that emotion of love which is familiar to man from his own experience. It is love itself, love in person. Such love lies beyond our experience. The following argument may help us to gain some idea of what this means: When one person turns to another in love, an emotion passes from him to his beloved. Let us pretend that whilst it is on the way from the one to the other it is called by him from whom it has come—and something surprising happens: it proves possible to recall it. It stops and turns, turns and opens its eyes, and asks him who called what he wants of it. Love has suddenly assumed a face, so that it is possible to converse with it. It has become a person. This fairy-tale concept pictures something which cannot happen within the reality known to our experience, but it does happen with God. The Holy Ghost is an emotion of love that is not faceless, and that therefore is personal. And he is the love which Christ breathes over those who are united with him. They are imbued with it and ruled by it. It lies as a bond between Christ and those united with him. It is in its power that man is made one with Christ. Through Christ, it establishes a relationship between those united with Christ and the Father, and so establishes communion with him. Because the Holy Ghost is omnipetent love, he establishes a bond with Christ and the Father which is deeper and stronger than any earthly bond.

The Holy Ghost, who has dominion over all those who are united with Christ, also lays the foundations of the interrelationships of those men who live in communion with Christ. He lies as a bond of union, around the plurality of believers, and draws them together into unity. Thus he establishes the community which we call the Church. The Holy Ghost is therefore the foundation of the life of the Church. The communion of the Church is thus formed by a continuous outpouring from heaven, by the unending flow of the Holy Ghost into her. Therefore, it surpasses every communion which has its basis in the earth, in blood and soil, in the human mind. Because the Holy Ghost is the basis of the community of the Church, those who are at one with her are united to one another by no mere dull accident of blood or physical proximity, but in the illumination and clarity of the Spirit. They express the community founded in the spirit, by giving themselves to one another in faith and love, in love illumined by faith.

Thus in word and action they bear witness to the fact that the Holy Ghost is active in them, that they live on the air of heaven (*spiritus*) which in the final analysis, is the only atmosphere in which man can rightly and worthily breathe. They, who represent Christ, and thus the heavenly Father, represent the atmosphere of heaven. They are, therefore, the ambassadors of heaven. Their appearance is a call to set out for heaven.

Because it is the Holy Ghost who establishes the relationship between Christ and the Father and those ambassadors with Christ, because he is the pledge by which the Father is continually shown the love of the Son, and the Son the love of the Father, he is the most precious gift God has to give. In giving him to men, he gives evidence of his will to save. When the Father and the Son give to man the love in which their own happiness rests, they are giving him the highest pledge of their will to save him, of their love for him. They offer their own happiness as a guarantee of the seriousness of their love for men.

Yet complete surrender in faith to Christ, and through Christ to the Father in heaven, is a hazardous undertaking. In this, man's surrender to Christ is like the surrender of one human ego to another. Any meeting between men is hazardous. He who entrusts himself to another, hopes that the other will open his heart to him and take him to his heart. It may happen, however, that the other shows indifference to him, and that he who would give himself is forced to withdraw into himself, disappointed and ashamed. Even if the other opens his heart and accepts him, their encounter cannot be free from disappointment, for no man is able to fulfil the hopes that one who loves him has of him. Every man is a disappointment to every other. It is the task of true love, and also of the lover and the beloved, to suffer and overcome such disappointments. By doing so it proves its power and its genuineness.

Man's encounter with God is also something of a risky undertaking. The man who gives himself to God does of course know, from the divine promises, that God will accept him, but he does not know what to expect from God. God is a mystery always full of surprises for his creatures. One of these surprises is God's sending of sorrow to his own. If a man has a reasonable view of his communion with God, he will, of course, expect God to afflict him with sufferings, for communion with God is established through union with Christ, who was crucified. He who is united with the crucified must expect the cross to make itself felt in his life. Because of the cross, his life will pass in continual unrest. The cross involves the disturbance of wordly abundance and security. The death of Christ does not eliminate, but corroborates the peril and danger to man represented by death. The cross represents an added uncertainty. In the cross it is revealed that the road to the consummation is called Destruction. Everything that does not bring nearer the consummation must die.

Thus God's call to glory involves a call to death and sufferings. From this point of view, suffering is not an act of fate, but an act of God. The path of the man who has set out to glory is ever a way of suffering and death.

Claudel had this fact in his mind when he wrote in *L'Annonce faite à Marie:* 'Alas, the cup of sorrow is deep, and whoever once lays his lip upon it, cannot withdraw it, much as he will!' Similarly, Hölderlin's words—originally intended to relate to the mythical realms of Hölderlin's gods—find their fulfilment in the atmosphere of Christianity: 'I am at peace, for I want nothing better than the gods. Must not everything suffer—yea, and the more excellent it is, the more deeply? Does not holy nature sorrow? Oh, my divinity, I cannot understand how thou art happy. But delight that knows no pain is sleep, and without death there is no life. Shouldst thou be timeless like a child, and slumber, like nothingness, foregoing victory, and not hasten to the end of all things? Truly, pain is worthy to lie in the heart of man, and to be thy confidante, O Nature! For it leads only from one joy to another, and there are no other companions but it.' Thus when God calls man to pain, he calls him to that place in human history from which passage may be made from mortal life to the fulness of life. 'We die to live' (Hölderlin). The more pressingly God calls man to suffering, the more urgently he is calling him to glory. A call to suffering is a call to love. Its voice echoes through the uproar of the torments that have laid hold on the body and soul of man. Thus anyone wanting to devote his love more completely to God, must expect proportionately greater suffering. The sobriety and genuineness of his love are shown in the fact of his accepting such disappointments as God sends to him and requires of him.

We might ask why God did not accomplish salvation in such a way that through Christ, his representative on earth, he could take death and suffering, as well as sin from the world.

The reason for this lies in the fact that suffering and death show for all time that mankind, having fallen into sin and fled from God, cannot in its present state of separation from God, live in a way truly worthy of humanity. Suffering shows that if man rules himself, he cannot lead a full and happy life. All man has is the choice: by renouncing self-glorification, he may live in a truly human way, in obedience to God; or, on the other hand, he may lead a life of grief and care, pain and torment, in rebellion against God. The pain God sends to man is a constantly-renewed proof of this truth. When a man understands the meaning of suffering, it affords him an opportunity to give God glory. He who obediently takes suffering from God's hands knows that life truly worthy of mankind is impossible in a world ruled by sin, a world far from God. He knows that man cannot live far from God, that only God represents true life and light, fulness and abundance for man. He therefore gives God the glory that in sin the world refuses him. In sin, men behave as though they were their own lords. They use the world, themselves, their bodies and minds, their gestures and words, as though they were all their own, and not things entrusted to them by God. They refuse to recognize God as the ruler of the world and of history, of individual things and individual men. If a man accepts suffering with understanding, he gives honour to God, for in suffering he learns that God is all man needs. In suffering he learns, too, that God can dispose of men and the things of the world, that he has the right to withdraw them from man to bring him to recognise his position; and he recognises, too, that God can bind and fetter a man with suffering to give him a true understanding of himself and show him how lost he is. For recognition of God's lordship is the ultimate aim of the world and of history, and the sorrow which man accepts from God affords a good opportunity for man to further the ultimate end of creation. By voluntarily suffering pain, he gives honour to the love which rules him.

This does not answer the question why suffering falls not only on sinners, but also on the righteous. The chief puzzle God presents to believers comes from the fact that he visits them too with afflictions —and often, indeed, with sufferings of peculiar intensity. To experience this is often a great test of faith for those who believe in God. Is it possible to believe in a just God and a just ordering of the world if pain falls indifferently on sinners and the virtuous —and indeed not infrequently spares scoundrels and fells the noble?

In connexion with this, it must be pointed out that the whole human race is a single community. Within this human community certain men are bound together in special ways, in smaller parties, by their natural or super-natural destiny. Thus the single community is made up of smaller subordinate communities. Now, it is not merely the individual, but the human community as a whole, with its internal communities, which is bound to give God the honour due to him, and so fulfil the purpose of the world. God being omnipotent love, due honour is given to him by man's accepting the rule of love and submitting himself to its laws. The responsibility which the human community, and the subordinate human communities, have in the fulfilment of this universal duty

—and thus in the establishment of the dominion of love, which is God—is borne by every individual. But it may happen that this man or that may be slothful or negligent in the fulfilment of the responsibility laid on him, and may become blind to the most important thing in the world. Heavier responsibility then falls on those who can see and are ready to act. The task of giving honour to God, which is binding on the whole community, must be fulfilled under all circumstances if the world is to achieve its purpose and chaos is not to return. If this man or that is disloyal, the responsibility of those who have kept their senses becomes that much greater, in order that God may be glorified. Suffering affords a particularly good opportunity to fulfil this indispensable duty. In suffering, God lays his hand on man, and binds him. This gives a man a chance to say to God: I permit thee to bind me, for I see that thou art the Lord. I recognise thee as sovereign love, which calls man to his own life even whilst calling him to suffering. So then, the acceptance of suffering involves the recognition of God as the Lord, who has the right to do as he will with the life of man.

To this thought should also be added another: that God himself is anxious for the fulfilment of the purpose of creation—the establishment of his dominion, the rule of love. He therefore selects from the world (which is threatening to neglect its own chief purpose) men through whom, as through fitting instruments, he attempts to realise his dominion, men who will subject themselves to whatever his rule brings them, and in suffering will give proof of the sincerity of their loving obedience. Thus it comes about that God's chosen are visited by suffering. Theirs is the highest task, and theirs the highest position in the course of history. It is not to everyone that God can give this important task: he can entrust it only to those who are, as it were, made in the right mould, and offer good surety of the proper fulfilment of the world's task. Hölderlin was conscious of the fact that such a hierarchy exists among men, as he showed when he made Empedocles say: 'Even the death of the great is great. . . . I believe that what happens to a man, happens only to him'. Or again: 'What thou sufferest, no servant suffers, and poorer than other beggars thou wanderest through the land. Not even the most vile are as distressed as your love will be, if the gods once touch it with dishonour'. From this point of view, the suffering God gives men, or allows to come to men, is not torture by someone who is indifferent to them, but trust put in them by someone who loves them.

If the suffering of the man united to God has a definite place in the fulfilment of the purpose of the universe, the chief reason for this lies in the fact of the union with Christ of those who suffer. In the sufferings of Christ, the world's meaning, which had been destroyed by sin, was restored to it, for the Father gave up his own Son unreservedly to the sufferings and death of Christ. When Christ was nailed to the cross, he was so fully subject to the will of the Father that he lost all freedom of movement. In this too, the Father showed himself to be the Lord. Christ accepted the Father's sovereignty and showed it forth in his own life. He allowed himself to be bound unreservedly. The dominion of God proved to be the dominion of love, for whilst fettering Christ, it led him through death to eternal life. Thus by his death, Christ set up the dominion, the Kingdom, of God, who is truth and love.

The death of Christ opened the way from death to life for the whole of mankind. But this path could not be forced on man mechanically: it had to be given him in a way worthy of human freedom. God wanted men to behave not as children, but as adults, who must bear the consequences of their action. He did not, therefore, take from them the death and suffering, brought on them by sin, but he changed their meaning. Such suffering and death were to be the way to life for those men who committed themselves to Christ in faith. This was achieved by relating their sufferings and death to the sufferings and death of Christ.

If we look at the sufferings and death of those who are united to him from the standpoint of Christ, the death of Christ looks like a beginning, which is continued and completed in the sufferings and death of Christians. What Christ did was no more than a beginning, but it was a first move which had within itself the power of further development. As a result of this relationship between the sufferings of Christians and the sufferings of Christ, everyone has the power to contribute something to the fulfilment of the purpose of the world. Suffering is an opportunity to further the dominion of God, the dominion of love, in the world. Suffering and death advance the kingdom of God.

The intimacy of the communion in which the Christian is bound with Christ and through him with the Father leads us to a further question: Can man endure this proximity? As Guardini says, for a life truly worthy of man, he needs to be alone, he needs a place reserved for himself. Could a man bear it if his innermost being, the plane of his deepest life, were constantly, unendingly filled by someone else, if he had to converse with him unendingly and live constantly aware of the other's gaze upon him? Would he not be bound to become nervous and uneasy if he knew he was always being watched by someone else, even on the deepest levels of his being? Such an experience of God was for Nietzsche a ground for rebellion against God.

In the valley of *Schlagentod*, Zarathustra met the odious man: 'I know thee well', he said in a metallic voice. 'Thou art the murderer of God! Let me go! Thou couldst not bear him who saw thee through and through, thou most odious of men! Thou tookest revenge on this witness against thee!' Whereupon the odious man replied: 'Thou seest what manner of mind it was that killed him. Stay! And wert thou to go, impatient one, go not the way I came. The way is bad. . . . And I warn thee too against myself. In myself and what I do, thou perceivest my best, my hardest riddle. But he had to die! He saw with eyes that saw all things; he saw man's depths and foundations, all his hidden offences and hatefulness . . . The God who saw all things—even man—that God had to die! Man could not tolerate that such a witness should live!'

In answering this question, which springs from man's feelings about life, and is especially common among people today, the following points must be taken into consideration: The divine ego, which lives in immediate and most intimate communion with man day and night is different from human personalities. Every human person is in some way alien and unfamiliar to every other. This is true even of those he loves best, for every man is divided from every other man by an unscaleable wall, the wall of his physical being. But God, on the other hand, is not alien and strange to man. As Guardini has said, he is rather the one who calls man into personal existence. The human soul is not only not threatened and endangered by God: it is, rather, founded and re-founded continually by him. The love that looks at a man when God looks at him is a creative love. It creates the human soul by an uninterrupted action: it creates man together with the place that is his, into which no one else can penetrate. Thus through God and with God, man is being continually given his own individuality, his bodily existence. Indeed, he needs God if his life is to reach its highest potential. If it is true that man only awakens to true life in another, if he can gain fulfilment of his life only in love, only in encounter with another, then he can come to fulness of life and being only through God. On the unshakeable life of God, on the intimacy and power of his love, human life bubbles up to its highest peak as though against a rock which itself sets over against man.

Communion with Christ and with the Father is primarily a condition. But this condition demands action. As we have already seen, Christ is present as someone who acts, who does things. Christ exerts an effect in the depths of the human personality. But his action seeks to push upwards out of the depths of the human personality into the realms of human consciousness, in which resolutions and decisions are made. Thus the man who is united to Christ is driven to action. What moves him to action is ultimately not impersonal duty, or impersonal law, but a personal being. This is true even when the man is not conscious of Christ's activity, even when he does not in the least realise that it is a living being, and not an impersonal law, that it is in fact Christ alone, which is driving him to action.

Christ's activity in the man united with him expresses itself in the actions, the activity, of the man. Inactivity would be a contradiction of the activity Christ requires of men. Activity does not mean business, but the loving acceptance of Christ's acts in one's own will and heart. Fichte had realised this relationship when he described human activity as a beatific force. In that kind of activity in which man accepts and exhibits acts of Christ, he shows himself one of the just, one of those who are united with God.

It is an impenetrable mystery how the activity of the human being is not extinguished by the overwhelming efficiency of Christ.

This is the mystery of Christian action. In it, Christ acts through man, and yet the man himself acts. The splendour of human action lies in this, that it is an act of Christ: every human act is an act done with Christ. In the actions of Christians the Father sees the activity of his own beloved Son. In the words of Christians, he hears the words of his own Son.

The acts of Christians are of the same kind as the acts of Christ. Christ's acts were acts of love for the Father in heaven, and for men. Whatever he did in his life—his suffering and death, speaking and remaining silent, sleeping and eating, helping and healing—in everything he gave expression to his love for the Father and for men. Hence human activity, in which the action of Christ displays itself in men, is an act of love.

Love for the Father expresses itself in converse with him—in prayer and unquestioning obedience to his commands. Because the Christian is a partaker of the Lord's glory, his sharing in the life of Christ consists in prayer and obedience to him. Fundamentally prayer is the communication of the human ego with God, with the ego of the divine. This communication is the outward expression of the Christian life. In it this life becomes audible. In it, it is put into words and in so far as the expression of ideas in words is essential to man, it is essential for the Christian life to be expressed in the words of prayer, in converse with God. For, in the words of prayer, union with God expresses and exhibits its spiritual nature, the fact that it is love. Men united with one another, express their union in words. If they do not speak in one another's presence, so that no sign passes from one to the other, their love may be seen to be dead. Similarly, loss of interest and indifference is displayed when man refuses to speak in the presence of the divine ego. Prayer—speech with the divine—is therefore a primary activity of man. Were he to ignore God by refusing to speak with him, his silence would be an ominous thing, as can be seen from men's relationships with one another. For in ignoring him, he ignores the supreme being who, alone, can save him from the last distress.

When those men who are united with God through Christ form a community, a second kind of prayer besides that of dialogue with God becomes possible. This is that form given supreme expression in the liturgy, in which men come together around Christ before God, to speak with one another about God in praise and thanksgiving. This form, too, is an expression of the Christian life, for in it those who believe in Christ express the fact that they are united with God, and hence are no longer delivered into the hands of the powers of this world. Joyfully and confidently, in praise and thanksgiving, they express their freedom. This form, too, is indispensable to anyone who does not want to lead a dull and slow life, who does not want to forego the right of thinking about who he is. It is the appropriate expression of his union with God and with his brothers and sisters.

Both forms of prayer are prayer with Jesus. Every Christian prayer is Christian because it is prayer with Christ and therefore prayer through Christ.

The other outward expression of love, obedience with Christ to the Father, is embodied in the commandments. Man fulfils the law enjoined on him by his union with Christ in the power of love. Duty, commandment, law, the voice of conscience: seen from this point of view none of them loses any of their significance. They are the forms in which Christ's activity, urging men to action, makes itself felt.

God's commandments, and the commandments of the Church are, as we saw at the beginning of this volume, signposts and instructions for the concrete expression of love. In every commandment, God calls to man, telling him how he, as a lover, should behave. Thus, for example, in the fifth commandment, he lays on him the duty of so treating other human beings that the preservation and fulfilment of life are advanced. The fulfilment of the commandment is, then, a concrete expression of love, and nothing more. Man's duty towards love itself comes itself only from love. The command to love can only be given in earnest by love itself. Thus all the commandments given by God are obviously appeals made by love. In them it is shown that the love that calls men in Christ is obligatory for men. One has a true understanding of the law and the commandments only if one remembers that the commandments are modes of love. He who commands is he who loves, and he who loves is he who commands.

At this point the question arises as to whether love will allow itself to be commanded. Love seems to arise from the secret depths of the human heart, and it would not seem that it could be subjected to orders and commands. However, if we have a right understanding of the love referred to here, these objections vanish. For the love that God commands is neither emotional love, nor a natural faculty of the heart. It is not to be compared with good nature. Its antithesis is not a harsh, hard heart. The love required by the commandments is rather a resolution of the will, an attitude, a turning towards others, a readiness, as it were, with regard to others. The opposite of this love is self-love, in which a man closes himself in against others, and hate, in which he tries to eliminate them.

Love has various dimensions: one upwards, towards God; another outwards, towards other men; another downwards, towards the world. In practice, these dimensions are interlaced. Loving God means being available to and present with him. It expresses itself outwardly in the fact that the lover has time for God. In the heat and hurry of our modern way of life, to have time for him shows a great deal of love for him. In giving time, a man shows that he loves whoever it is to whom he gives it. If we love someone, we shall have time for him. Moreover, love also involves listening to God, submitting oneself to his sovereignty, putting the establishment of his sovereignty before everything else; giving honour to him, to the Lord of love, putting concern for the coming of his kingdom first before all else. Anyone who endeavours to do this also becomes able to accomplish the other side of loving: to base his whole life on God, to cleave to him with unbounded confidence, to leave all care and the ultimate responsibility to him, to live from his hand. Implied in this love is hatred and loathing for everything that does not serve God or come from him, the abandonment of all considerations, and breaking of all arrangements which stand in the way of communion with God. Christ names two principal powers against which man must declare war if he will love God: Mammon and the love of glory, of prestige—the attitude, as Stauffer says, of the Pharisees.

The temptations, vexations, abuses, sorrows and afflictions of life on earth are love's crucial ordeals by fire. In them, as Stauffer says, love is revealed as a glowing passion for God—as the devotion of those who remain unshaken by any problem, power or threat, until he whom they love is revealed to them.

He who sets the kingdom of God, of love, before everything else, is aware of the promise that everything he needs will be given to him. To interpret this promise as an assurance of a peaceful, protected, well-provided, or even comfortable life for those who give their love to God would be to misunderstand it completely. The promise contains nothing of this. What it promises, rather, is that he who loves God will be given whatever he needs for the true, unending, eternal life. What he needs for this, he himself does not know. All he knows is God. A man may be of the opinion that he needs success, earthly love, possessions and honour, whereas, in fact, it is precisely when he has these things that he lacks true love. Success and possessions can be a help to one and a hindrance to another in the winning of the true life. God has given those who love him the assurance that he will bestow on them the things that are essential. The fulfilment of this promise may lead God to give man sorrow, or again it may lead to him giving him joy.

Love of God finds concrete expression in the love of one's fellows. Turning to a human being in love is something in which the divine being is ultimately concerned, for in another human being God himself comes to us. The countenance of God looks out at us from beneath the veils of the person of another human being. Hence, the value of the human being is guaranteed by God. Behind man towers the majesty of God, standing surety for him.

Love for another human being fulfils itself on various levels. The first step is when the lover recognises in others the individuality which comes to them from God and is given them by Him. Recognising this in others, he no longer wants to shape them according to his own will, which would involve treating those he loves as beings with individual existence, whom he needs and uses, but not as persons with individual worth and dignity.

The second step in love consists in the help one who loves gives to the needy in body and soul. By so helping them, he fulfils the commandment 'Love thy neighbour as thyself': 'As you would that men should do to you, do you also to them in like manner'. What is specified in this commandment is not primarily the

164

intensity of love, but the manner of loving. It commands us to give to others what we would wish for ourselves.

Love opens our eyes to want, to which the self-seeking man is blind. He overlooks it. Love is sensitive: it always does what must be done. It would fail if it put aside the need of the person who has been set directly in its path by God, the man who is here and now its neighbour, in order to give help to someone further away, for then it would be not love, but universal philanthropy, which feels itself bound to no particular act of mercy. Love does what the moment demands. The love which ignores this immediate demand falls under that condemnation which Christ pronounced over the Pharisees in the parable of the Good Samaritan.

The man who refuses help to the neighbour sent him, refuses it to the Son of God. His refusal to man is a refusal to God. And the judgement of condemnation falls on him.

Love of the brethren stands under the sign of the cross: it is readiness to serve and to give sacrifice, devotion and consideration —to bear with others and suffer with others, to support the weak, and re-establish the fallen. It lives in that community which owes its whole existence to the mercy of God and the sacrificial death of Christ.[1]

It attains its highest expression in love of enemies, for even in an enemy it sees the countenance of God, and in him it sees not the evil, but the divine concealed by the evil. It loves him because he bears the image of Christ.

There is no utopianism in Christ's command to love one's enemies, and accept willingly and sacrificially the enmity of the world; in his commandment to repay oaths with blessing, to do good to those who hate us, or in his giving martyrs the duty of praying for the hostile world that hates God and kills his faithful. He knows this world—and yet he calls for love in the midst of a world of hatred, doing so with a sober objectivity and certitude, with great deliberation. His action is so incredible that his contemporaries preferred to believe that he expelled the devil, the embodiment of hatred, through diabolical powers, than that he overcame him with the power of love.

[1] Stauffer. For Stauffer's theology on the New Testament see J. Schmid: Art. in *Theologische Revue* 44 (1948), pp. 83-7.

The kingdom of God is being established in the world, and the sovereignty of the devil is being smashed by a love that will give not an inch of ground to hate. Every relationship in which one person gives himself to another in love exists within the kingdom of God.

The third dimension of love is that directed towards the world. We shall explain this in a separate chapter.

The love in which the kingdom of God is established and advanced is a part of that love in which Christ gave himself up on the cross. It is therefore part of the sacrificial death of Christ. It mirrors the death of God. Thus it is itself a death—a death to self-seeking and self-glorification. Those who seek anxiously to protect their own personalities may fear that to accept such love would be to lose themselves. In fact, however, they are subject to the promise: 'Whosoever will save his life shall lose it; and whosoever shall lose his life . . . shall save it'.

In self-giving love, man realises his inmost being. As we have already seen, because man comes from God, who is love, he bears in his inmost heart the impress of love. Self-devotion, therefore, is the only mode in which he can really exist and live. Self-love and introspection are a contradiction of the inmost being of man. Such attitudes revenge themselves on those who share them, and lead to spiritual, and often to bodily disturbances, which can be cured not through the healing art of the physician, but only through a change of heart, through conversion. He who is bounded by self-love and hatred is by the same token alone and unblessed. He who devotes himself to self-seeking, devotes himself to joylessness. Conversely, through the surrender of his own personality, man gains the fulfilment of his life. On that account, the effect of the commandment to love to the ultimate limit of earthly possibility—to the point of giving up life itself, does not limit life, but advances it. He who loses his life through love, is in fact not a loser but a gainer. If love partakes of the sacrificial death of Christ, it must also have a share in the redeeming power of the death of Christ. The lover himself enters into the blessing of the death of Christ, for in his offering of himself he reaches the only crossing-point from time to eternity. But he does not reach it alone: he draws all those he has encompassed with his love to this same place, so that they too can make the crossing. Let us try to explain the redemptive power of love from another point of view. He who loves advances the rule of God, who is love. The sovereignty of God means salvation for men. Therefore, the further one advances the kingdom of God in this world through acts of sacrificial love, the greater is one's contribution to the true health of the world. Those who love are therefore the salvation of the world. Ultimately in fact there can be no other way of serving salvation.

The love that redeems the world has made possible an everlasting future. In this world of death, everything is subject to the law of temporality. In his first letter to the Corinthians, St. Paul says that even the highest things of religion are subject to it in their present form. Faith will pass away, because its appearance will be changed. Hope will vanish, for it will be transformed into possession. But love will outlast the world of death. In it the world to come is projected into this passing world. In love, man shares in the indestructible life of God, who is love, and love will therefore survive the collapse of earthly forms of life. Indeed, when earthly forms founder, love will shine forth in its final glory and true worth. During the time of our pilgrimage on earth, it may often seem that love is the weakest and most poverty-stricken thing in this world. In this world, those who are full of self-love can laugh at love's fools. For they, the thoughtless, the powerful, the tyrants, are successful here. But every earthly power, and all earthly success, will pass away with the passing world. Love is indestructible.

CHAPTER EIGHT

THE CHRISTIAN IMAGE OF GOD

I : GOD THE PERSONAL HOLY SECRET

In Christ the God who dwells in inaccessible light has made himself accessible to man. At last man can leave perdition behind him and enter the realms of love, for in Christ love has turned its face to him.

We must now turn our attention to the problem of the nature of God as revealed to us in Christ. What was the reality that entered the world with the coming of Christ? What manner of person was this Christ who broke into human history—broke into it in such a way that never again could it be sufficient in itself, so that its horizon would for ever be a reality not of this world? To answer these questions is to solve the problem of the meaning of our lives, for God is the measure of man. Our picture of man therefore depends on our image of God and our concept of the purpose of human life hinges on our idea of God's nature.

Human philosophy has suggested many answers to the question: 'Who is God?' It has called him The Absolute, The Thought of Thoughts, The Highest Spirit, The Highest Good, Absolute Will, The Idea, The Numinous One, The Holy One. Each of these definitions grasps one facet of God, but in all of them God is understood one-sidedly. Who God is, and what he is, we know through Christ. God is what he revealed himself to be in Christ, and in the revelations he made of himself, preparing the way for Christ in the pre-Christian era. God is the one who speaks and acts in Christ.

In Christ God revealed himself primarily as personal power. He is the Lord who, in a mighty act of will, made the world, time and mankind, and leads men and things to the goals he has set for them. He is essentially and qualitatively different from the world he has created. He is not dependent on, but Lord of, his creation. He can break its rules, put an end to its time, or change the whole world. He has made the sun set at midday and brought darkness to the earth at noontide. The mountains melt under his feet and the earth starts back in confusion before him. The mountains shake and the hills quiver. He knows men: he knows our hearts and minds. He commands and ordains. He is jealous and sensitive. He longs to be loved by those he loves, and is deeply wounded if obstacles are put in the way of his desires, if he is withstood in disobedience. He grows angry and reproves men. He punishes and threatens. He is graceful and merciful. He keeps man in a continual state of anxiety. Continually, he brings men out of themselves when they become introverted and lethargic. He is the great Disturber. At the same time, he is the peace of those who cannot find peace in the world. Because he gives himself to man in love, man can bind himself to him in faith, thanksgiving, petition and penitence. Man can speak to God: he can address him by name.

In conversing with Christ, his contemporaries conducted a deeper conversation: converse with God. Paradoxical as it may seem, yet it is true: he who talks with Christ, talks with God. God has revealed his name to man: his name is Lord. And he listens when they call upon his name. The heathen, who does not know the name of God, cannot speak personally to God. The faithful on the other hand, those who know his name, can call him by name. This is the guarantee of all salvation. The faithful can call him father.

Human hopes are kindled by the personal nature of God: because God is personal, and yet is not entangled with time and the world, as though he were a part of them, we can set our hopes on him, hoping that he will free us from the world, with its afflictions and misery.

Even he who believes in the gods of the myths has confidence in his gods. But they are not distinct from the world. They are woven into the rhythm of nature and are, indeed, nothing but deifications, personifications, of natural powers and processes—of the birth and growth, ripening, fruitfulness and dying of nature, symbols of spring and autumn, of the sun in his course. Despite the great number of names used of the mythical gods in the course of the millennia—in spite of Isis and Osiris, Marduk, Apollo, Dionysus and Balder—no myth has shown a way out of nature; all have but led their devotees deeper into it. They lead their believers to complete incorporation into the rhythm of nature, so that they lose their personalities in the universal life of nature. Those who have sworn by these Gods have sworn by death, and not by life.

More than ever, man is locked in a completely materialised world, that no longer knows anything of God and of gods, but only of technology, machines and atomic bombs. He cannot surmount the insurmountable walls that now enclose him. In the world that is without a personal God all the prayers, all the cries of those who weep, die away unheard and unheeded in the haunted spaces of which science tells, which know nothing of us and are closed to us. They are thrown back from the darkness, a ghastly echo of the cry that made them. Man lives in this world in frigid and desolate loneliness.

In an age when these things were still hidden from most people, Nietzsche saw the ghastly significance of the separation of man from the personal God. Movingly he describes the condition of Godless humankind, when belief in God has died in human hearts: 'Have you not heard of that madman, who lit a lantern in the broad light of morning, ran to the market and cried incessantly: "I am looking for God! I am looking for God!" Many had come together there who did not believe in God, so he aroused a great deal of merriment. "Is he lost then?" said one. "Has he wandered off like a child?" said another. "Or has he hidden himself? Is he frightened of us? Has he gone to sea? Has he emigrated?" And so they shouted and laughed among themselves. The madman jumped in among them and transfixed them with his gaze. "Where is God?" he cried. "I will tell you. We have killed him, you and I. We are all his murderers. But how did we do it? How could we drain the sea? Who gave us the sponge with which to wipe away the whole horizon? What did we do, when we unchained this earth from its sun? Where is it revolving now? Where are we revolving? Away from any sun? Are we not falling for ever? Backwards and sideways and forwards: on every side? Is there still an above and a below? Are we not wandering through unending night? Cannot we feel the breath of empty space? Has it not grown colder? Is not night coming continually, and ever more night? Are we not compelled to light lanterns in the morning? . . . God is dead! God stays dead! And we have killed him! How shall we console ourselves, the most murderous of all murderers? The holiest and mightiest thing that the world used to possess has bled under our daggers. Who shall wash this blood from us? With what water can we cleanse ourselves? What atonement can we make—what holy games must we invent? Is not the enormity of this deed too great for us? Must we not ourselves become god—just to look respectable? There was never a greater deed, and whoever shall be born after us, belongs by this fact to a higher history than any history that came before". At this point the madman fell silent, and looked at his audience. They, too, were silent, and stared at him in consternation. At last he threw his lantern on the ground, so that it flew to pieces, and went out. "I came too early," he said. "My time is not yet. This monstrous thing is still happening —it is still going on. It has not yet come to the ears of men. Thunder and lightning need time, the light of the stars needs time, acts need time, even after they are done, to be seen and heard. This act is still farther from them than the farthest stars: yet they themselves did it!" They still tell how the madman went into various churches on this same day and said his *Requiem aeternam deo*. Brought out of them, and taken to task, his only answer was a continual "What are they then, these churches, but the tombs and monuments of God?" '

When God is engulfed, the light goes out; confidence and trust die. 'Love dies, as soon as the gods fly' (Hölderlin).

The personal God, mighty in history, who bestowed his countenance on us in Christ, encourages us in and binds us to our tasks, disturbs us in the sloth of our hearts, and helps us to overcome sins and failings. He encompasses us with his eyes and heart, with the gaze of his love and the hand of his omnipotence. We feel protected in all the main uncertainties of life, and safe in a love of inconceivable power, warmth and intimacy. Every moment of life, is a moment of encounter with love—with the love which in Christ stretches out its hand to man. Schell described the importance of the personal God to man in these terms: 'The fact that God is personal means that the plan of destiny is not that of an unconscious and indifferent fate, but that it comes to pass through the sympathetic and loving spirit of the Godhead, and indeed comes wholly from it. It is therefore certainly so ordered that it will lead to the perfecting of the human soul in truth, justice and life. The personal God is himself a reply to true prayer, in whose heart lie goodness and truth and who is therefore eternal salvation.'

That there is a personal God is then the ultimate hope of those who believe in Christ. A hope such as this which arises victorious over all apparent hopelessness, cannot exist in a pantheistic world, in which the god crumbles away with the material world. The man who believes in a god who is one with the world, usurps the name which is proper to God alone. His God is no more than a word, extended to cover created things—an idea with which he fastens everything together, a poem, through which he gives the world a religious consecration, and by which he seeks to explain life. It is like a many-coloured blanket spread over the world to veil its hatefulness. His god is noise and smoke, sounding brass and tinkling cymbal. All that remains in this of the true, living God is, as Bernhart says, an outer garment, a costly relic.

Such a god is fostered by the mysteries and despair of history. It is bound up with the coming into being and dying of things, with growing, flowering and ripening, with death and rebirth in nature. It effects nothing by the blooming of flowers, the rushing of the waters, the raging of the elements, the swelling of fruits, the whirring of machines, or by man's search for truth, the intimacy of love, the rise and fall of nations, the awakening and dying of cultures, or in hate, self-seeking and the lies and slanders of men: it effects nothing, for it is rather all these things. It comes and goes with created things. The stone in the road is not merely an indication of a god who is present and at work, but is a part of the god itself. The beating of the heart is no longer merely his work: it is the movement of life itself.

This is especially clear in the most influential form of pantheism, Hegelian pantheism, in which history is the logico-dialectical self-unfolding of god. Divine life and history fade away together. All historical events are phases in the process of god's growing consciousness of himself in time—indeed, of the deification of god.

In this system, the individual loses his personal being and worth; he is merely part of the channel for the temporal realisation of the ideal. This concept burdens god with all the afflictions of the world and of history: good and evil, truth and falsehood, are all in the same way expressions of the divine life, if that life exists only in the process by which the ideal is realised.

About this, Schell rightly says: 'A universal spirit which has no inner being and personality of any kind, which has so little interest in truth and good, which from the moral point of view has been everything in the fullest sense for millennia, which for thousands of years has dwelt in the same way in churches and houses of pleasure, the castles of tyrants and the quarters of slaves, banqueting halls and hospitals, peace conferences and battlefields, and which seeks its satisfaction in all these places—such a spirit would indeed be everlasting characterlessness, but it would be no spirit.' If God were such, every standard of good and evil, truth and falsehood, and the compelling power of moral standards would vanish away. There would be no judge of our consciences. The philosophy of existentialism is in no point essentially different from the pantheistic concept of God. There is indeed talk of transcendency. But it is not asserted of a true and living God, but is rather one facet of the world itself. It is not therefore a true transcendence, but the mystery of the world which lies on the far side of experience. It therefore belongs to the totality of the world.

In Christ, however, God has revealed himself as the Lord, mighty in time and different from the world and from mankind. His revelation of himself was made in such a way that he remained veiled from those who saw the mystery. The God given to man in Christ is different from any god man discovers for himself. He speaks and acts in such a manner that we are continually compelled to say: God is quite different in every way from man. To man, God is an insoluble riddle. This is most painfully evident when we stand before the cross. God's revelation of himself in the cross is so confusing to man, so incredible, that he has to laugh and mock at it, as long as he does not surrender his human and worldly standards.

Because God is different in every way from man, his visitations are incomprehensible and puzzling to man. The plans of God are not transparent: his decisions are incomprehensible. Hence men can find on earth no answer to the questions 'Why?' and 'Wherefore?' that torment him. He can discover nothing. He has to learn that before God, the Mystery, questioning is but vanity, and that in thankfulness and praise lies the true respect for Divine Omniscience.

A vision reported by St. John in his Apocalypse is informative in this connexion. John was shown a vision of heaven. He saw God seated on the throne. God had a book sealed with seven seals. John heard an angel call: 'Who is worthy to open the book and loose the seals thereof?' No one came forward in answer to the angel's question and that made John weep. It was imperative that someone should be found to open the book, for it contained the fate of mankind: in it was revealed the meaning of history, and no man of earth could open the book, for no man of earth could interpret the meaning of history. The earth can give no answer to the questions 'Why?' and 'Wherefore?' And therefore, John wept. These questions would have to remain unanswered, and would therefore always disturb and torment men. John wept in the name of all of us. But he learned that there was yet one who could give the answer so anxiously sought. The angel called to him: 'Weep not! There is one who can loose the seven seals. The Lion of the tribe of Juda, the root of David, hath prevailed to open the book, and to loose the seven seals thereof.' He is the lamb, who was slain, yet lives. Christ can explain the meaning of history, but only he can do so, for he, who was sent by the Father, who is love, gave its meaning to history. He is called the embodiment of the sovereignty of love. In all visitations and disappointments, in all afflictions and sorrows, the meaning of history is realised. Through his death, Christ has forwarded it decisively in this world. He will consummate it at the end of history.

In addition, John heard the heavenly ones through the mouth of the angel voicing songs of praise and thanksgiving for the lamb's ability to open the book—that is, to explain the meaning of history. With so many riddles is the meaning of history burdened, that anyone who can reveal it unveiled and uncovered, is received with thanksgiving and praise.

Only in the worship which faith offers the God of mystery can man find the solutions to the problems presented by the mystery of God.

In the pre-Christian era this point was never made so forcibly as in the Book of Job. To all the complaints and accusations against God that arose from Job in his seemingly hopeless despair, Sophar of Naamah replied: 'Peradventure thou wilt comprehend the steps of God, and wilt find out the Almighty perfectly? He is higher than heaven, and what wilt thou do? He is deeper than hell, and how wilt thou know? The measure of him is longer than the earth, and broader than the sea. If he shall overturn all things, or shall press them together, who shall contradict him?' Eliu said: 'Behold God is great, exceeding our knowledge'. When, despite the warning of his friends and even despite the advice of the angel, Job would not end his accusations against God, God himself spoke out of a storm, and Job, being inwardly defeated, was compelled to bow before God's wonderful incomprehensibleness and confess, not to understanding the ways of God, but to belief in the mystery of God: 'I have spoken unwisely, and things that above measure exceeded my knowledge. Therefore I reprehend myself and do penance in dust and ashes.'

Thus, when confronted with the mystery of the history wrought by God, men can find peace only through confidence in the mystery of God. Paul cried: 'O the depth of the riches and the wisdom and the knowledge of God. How incomprehensible are his judgements and how unsearchable his ways! For who hath known the mind of the Lord? Or who hath been his counsellor?'

The God who gives himself to man in Christ is the sole Lord of history. There is no other God, no God near him or over him or under him. In pre-Christian times, God revealed himself as the only Lord, not in what he said, but in what he did. He made himself a people which was to be ruled by his power. He showed it that he was not one among many gods, that he did not belong to the multiplicity of contentious and power-seeking gods of the Eastern world.

There was a long road to travel before the unity of God was established in history and in the hearts of men. The temptation to follow the gods of polytheism was difficult to conquer, for everywhere men encountered the power of the numinous. They felt it in the murmuring of their own blood, and in the workings of nature —in light and darkness, in birth and death, in the great events of history. They gave it form in their gods. When the heathens were victorious, their victory seemed to be a victory of their gods over the God of Israel. Were they not more powerful? Were not Assur and Marduk more powerful than Jahweh? Was not Astarte preferable to their own austere God? To such temptations the prophets replied: The gods are nothing. They cannot help and they cannot be of any use. God set forth his claim to sovereignty continually and with shattering force. In grief and anger, the prophets reproached those who had become believers in the gods with their breach of faith, called them to obedience to the one God, preached his power and greatness and threatened his judgement.

The disciples of Christ conducted throughout their lives a resolute struggle against the polytheism which they met everywhere—in Athens, in Lystra and in Ephesus. Service of the gods was for them just like godlessness, for the gods did not exist. Service of the gods is denial of the one true God and leads directly to the sovereignty of the diabolic powers. Although polytheism continually threatened even the Christians, the many gods and lords in heaven and earth were no gods to them. They attributed their salvation neither to the emperor in Rome, nor to his procurator in Jerusalem, but to the almighty Christ alone. For them, there was only one true God, who had spoken to the world in Christ. Before the one true God, the Christian might confess no other god, whether it were Mammon or his belly, or the images of the gods, or the dominion of the sum of all things or the supermen called gods.

It can be seen from this last commandment of St. Paul that polytheism is a temptation to men not only where the names of the ancient gods are honoured, but wherever the things of this world are held in reverence. Hence we must ask whether a wide stream of polytheism has not arisen again in modern times in the world which has deserted God. In fact it seems to rule among men today just as mightily as did mythical polytheism over the men of antiquity. In modern polytheism however the gods have other names from those which they had in the old times. Today's polytheism is characterised by the rule of technology and the denial of the presence of God and life in the world and history through the loss of the feeling of the numinous. Thus the gods of the modern age, to whom all are ready to sacrifice their peace, and their sons and daughters, are called money, power, pleasure, prestige, the state, imperialism, militarism and mankind. Opposed to this polytheism, there is everywhere preached the mission of Christ, in which testimony is borne to the one God. He is the Lord even of all those powers to which mankind bows as to gods; of every power, therefore, to which men become slaves if they refuse to submit themselves to the true God. They are the destroyers of the world, whereas the true God is its salvation. But men would rather trust themselves to the powers hostile to the world, because they feel more closely related to them than to the one God.

The God who speaks to men in Christ reveals himself as the holy Lord of history. When we say of him that he is holy, we are thinking both of his moral bearing and of his essential nature, of his natural holiness. His holiness consists in the fact that he is distinct from the creation—distinct from everything that we know by experience. He is the inviolable, unapproachable, yea, threatening and horrifying majesty. And at the same time, he is the alluring power who rejoices, blesses and hallows us. He is justice and grace, righteousness and love. Hence he calls forth in men both fear and love, horror and delight. God's highest revelation of his holiness was made in the death of Christ. If God showed his holiness among sinful men, men would be overwhelmed; before the holy God, sinful man would pass away. On the cross we learn who God is and who man is.

That self-revelation of God, in which Isaias participated, was a harbinger of that revelation of the holiness of God which was made in the death of Christ. When the prophet received God's call, he saw Omnipotence sitting on a high uplifted throne. His train filled the temple. Seraphim stood before him. Each had six wings: with two they covered his face, with two his feet, and with two they held themselves in flight. One called to another: 'Holy, holy is the Lord of Hosts' (the repetition of the cry of Holy denotes intensification). 'The whole earth is full of his glory.' Then fear fell on Isaias, and the 'lintels of the doors were moved'. He felt the antithesis between himself and God. He felt that he would die from fear and awe.

There is a description by St. John of what might be thought of as a continuation of this vision in 'Revelation' of the heavenly liturgy. It is acted out in the realms reserved to God beyond creation. The seraphim offer God their cry of Holy. God is praised as the Omnipotent One who was, and is and is to come. Omnipotence and everlastingness are therefore characteristics of holiness. The Holy One will avenge the blood of the martyrs. If he is still silent, and lets things take their course as though he did not exist, it is only to allow the number of the chosen witnesses to be made up.

The suitable attitude for men in the face of the Holy God is that of worship. It is the natural response to the holiness of God, which was revealed to man in Christ.

To those who believe in the world, this attitude may seem remote from and alien to life. In fact it is in worship that the meaning of life and the salvation of the world are fulfilled and accomplished. If God is, then there is due to his holiness, to him, the Holy One, holiness in person, the highest and unconditional recognition. The recognition of the holiness of God is then man's chief task. The chief purpose of human life consists in giving honour to God, the Holy One, to God, who is Love.

If God is denied honour, if man honours himself or something in the world—money, business, erotic love, the State, power—giving it the honour owed to God, he is perverting the right order of things. This fateful act usually occurs in a hidden place to which the human mind and powers cannot penetrate. But this invisible disorder usually reveals itself quickly in visible symptoms: in economic and social disturbances, in wars and revolutions, in the collapse of families and the downfall of cities.

The successful men, therefore, who, to the superficial gaze, seem practical and skilful in life, and who refuse to worship, are in fact a threat to the order of things: they dig the world's grave. The worshippers who, to those believing in the world, seem impractical and remote from life, are in fact the guardians and watchmen of life. The work of the world carried out apart from God is in fact the destruction of the world. Only worldly work performed in reference to God can in fact shape the world and establish its true order. History shows that where men seek their own honour and glory and forget the honour of God, then honour of men and the glory of the world, too, are lost and destroyed.

Only he who honours can also heal the world. Therefore, Christ has saved the world from ultimate wretchedness, because he gave God, the Holy One, honour, unreservedly, even unto death.

The holiness of God appeared in Christ under the guise of love. God in Christ gave himself to sinful man, so as to execute judgement on him and thereby lead him out of his sterile and wretched life, out of his misery and despair. Love has the right of justice, but its justice is the judgement of mercy. This is clear from the fact that God sent his Son to death to reveal and embody his holiness in the world, and at the same time to uncover the abyss into which the sinner has fallen, to lead the sinner through death to everlasting life.

But, of course the love of God is different from the love we all know by experience. It does not seek any good for man whatsoever, except his ultimate salvation. And for that very reason it keeps him in a state of unrest, giving him a push onwards every now and then, so that he will not fall in love with the glories of this world, but will continue on his way to the final ego, God himself. If it did not goad him on constantly in this way it would not be true and pure love, for it would not direct him towards ultimate perfection. This explains why suffering has a part to play in the love of God. Suffering is one form of God's love—of the love which cannot tolerate man's being self-sufficiently satisfied with the things of this world. The love of God displays its standards in human history in suffering. Chief among its emblems has been the cross. All other sufferings are reflections of this, the chief sign of the love of God.

Because the love which is God is different from the love in which men give themselves to one another, we need to be called to belief and confidence in it. At the last supper, Christ called on his disciples not to lose confidence in the love of God in the midst of the world of affliction and hate. The love of God, he said, would be theirs for ever, although things in the foreground of human history might suggest a completely different picture. In his last discourse he bade his disciples persist in love—that is, suffer themselves to be loved by God and trust in his love despite anything that might suggest his love was an illusion (cf. John 15, 9). This divine command extends to the whole of human time. The Lord's appeal to us is that we should trust in him and let the love of the Father come to us.

Men need such a call, not only because the love of God may seem illusory and like a fairy-tale in view of the boundless suffering in the world, but also because the Father's love can be dangerous as far as life in the world is concerned, for it offers sorrow and pain to those to whom it comes. But anyone who obeys the Lord's command, and allows himself to be loved by the Father, will live to see the fulfilment of the promise that God—love himself—will be his eternal reward. He looks forward to a time when he will be ruled entirely by love and thus will receive blessing.

On the other hand, anyone who rejects the love of God faces the prospect of hell. Of this Bernanos wrote that the most unfortunate man alive still has the ability to love, even if he believes he no longer has love for anyone—but that hell is the state of loving no more. To love no more does not sound very important, for to the living person, loving no more means loving less, or loving in a different way. But, Bernanos asks, what if this faculty, which seems inseparable from our nature, and indeed seems to be our nature itself—for understanding itself is a kind of love—were to wholly and completely vanish away? No more to love: no more to understand, no more to live—what an incomprehensible mystery! 'It is a very general mistake to talk about these rejected creatures as though they were still somewhat like us, as though they still had something of our constant mobility, although they are fixed outside time, outside change for all eternity. Even if God were to take us by the hand and lead us to one of these painful monstrosities, in what language would we talk with it, even if it had once been our most loyal friend? If a living man, our likeness, even the least of all, the most worthless of the worthless, were cast into the burning abyss, I should want to share his loss, and should try to save him from his executioner. To share his loss! . . . The misery, the inconceivable misery of these dead ashes who were once men is that they no longer possess anything in which anyone can share.'

Those who during their earthly pilgrimage will not let themselves be loved by God and, as a result, let themselves be filled not by love but by self-seeking and hatred, bear within themselves the seeds of this condition. But on the other hand those who let themselves be ruled by God, and are therefore filled with love and are ruled by it, bear within themselves the seeds of that condition in which they will converse for ever with love, who is God. The love with which mankind will converse lovingly for ever has been revealed in the world, and given to the world, by Christ. As long as worldly time endures, its countenance is veiled, so that men of goodwill, the faithful, those who love, can see it, but the others, men of evil will, the unbelievers, those who hate, cannot do so. It will reveal its face when earthly forms pass away. From that moment on, nothing will be more mighty in the community of men than the love that shone forth in person from the cross of Christ.

CHAPTER NINE

THE CHRISTIAN IMAGE OF GOD

II : GOD THE HOLY TRINITY

God, the Lord of human history, who in Christ shows his countenace to the world, is a person, and hence mankind can enter into converse with him. In Christ, God calls man, to bring him out of his perdition —but it is man's responsibility to answer that call, to let himself be called by the love revealed in Christ.

In the Old Testament, God revealed himself as the one God, besides whom there are no others. The Holy Scriptures of the Old Testament testify to the advances made by the rule of the one God before the *logos* of God entered human history, but under the old covenant no clear information was revealed about the inner life of God. It was first necessary to establish the fact that God is one both in a world teeming with divinities, and in human hearts tempted to polytheism. When this had been done, God could reveal the threefold nature of his inner life without the risk of men misunderstanding him and thinking that he was talking of three Gods. Christ bore witness to himself as the Son of the Father in heaven, and by so doing he both showed us his own divine personality, and at the same time revealed the personality of the Father. In his last discourse, he promised that, for the period between his death and second coming, he would send his invisible representative, the Holy Ghost, so that his followers in the world would not be deserted and alone. Hence he who believes in the God revealed by Christ, and suffers himself to be baptized into him, is baptized in the names of the Father, the Son and the Holy Ghost.

Thus the single personal God exists in a tri-personal form. The tri-personality is the fundamental distinguishing mark of the God revealed in Christ, differentiating him essentially and completely from all other divine figures. The tri-personality of God is the expression of the fulness of divine life. It would be completely wrong to see in the tri-personality only an inducement to the higher reaches of faith. The threefold personality was not revealed so that we might have an opportunity of bowing our intellects, submitting them most humbly to God. It is rather a sign of the uncreated, ever-flowing life of God himself.

We have already remarked the difference between nature and person. This differentiation throws a valuable light on the tri-personality of God. Whereas our nature—our spirits, bodies, faculties of learning, will-power—are sufficient only to enable us individually to lead a miserable and limited life, the life and being of God is of such abundance, so overflowing with ability to know and love, that it cannot creatively display itself in the living, knowing and loving of a single person. It requires a threefold ego. Thus the tri-personality of God is a sign of life at its highest and richest potential. Whereas, for instance, our physical eyes have a power of vision sufficient only for one ego, the spirit of God has power of vision sufficient for three. If only one person gained knowledge by its use, God's power of vision would not be fully employed. The same is true of the other divine faculties, both in willing and loving. But, on the other hand, three persons use God's power, life-potential and faculties of knowing and loving to the full. There is no impersonal zone in God, but rather, in the sphere of the divine being, existence, life, knowledge and will are taken to the highest possible peak of personal existence.

We call the three divine persons Father, Son and Holy Ghost. Although we use the words Father and Son, we must notice at once that sexual differentiation has no place in the reality of God. The Christian concept of God differs from every other in that sexuality is quite foreign to it. For each mythical god there is usually a mythical godess. In the true God—who created sexual differentiation—there is no kind of sexual differentiation. If we use the word Father, we use it to express creativeness, and mean by it the Generator, Guardian and Preserver of life. When we use the word Son, we use it to express the fact that there is in God an ego that has received its whole being and whole existence from another.

The three divine persons exist in the closest relationship with one another. There is continually being carried on an exchange of life between them. Indeed, it is in this exchange that their life consists.

The Father, the first of the divine persons, is characterized by the fact that everything that is proper to him—his divine being in all its depth and breadth, his knowledge and will, his life and thought—he gives unreservedly to the Son. He has no mistrust towards the Son, fearing that he will perhaps push him out of the realm of existence which is his, as an earthly father might fear that he might be ousted by his son, the coming generation. On the contrary, the Father delights in giving his Son everything he can bestow on him. He holds back nothing for himself. So full is he of the joy of giving, that he lives wholly and completely in it, that he spends himself in it. Unlike any earthly giver, he has the power to realise his desire to give completely. Everything that exists is at his disposal and he holds this whole reality, which could not be further enriched, in such a way that he can offer it to the Son. We must go further: the Father spends himself utterly in giving. He is the concept of giving itself. His whole being is the embodiment of the idea of self-surrender. In giving he brings forth the Son. The Son is brought forth so that the Father may give him the whole of his divine being. Speaking analogically, we call this giving, the Generation of the Son.

The Son, on his side, takes joyfully from the Father what the Father gives him. He does not make claims and demands on the Father, as an earthly son might do. Nor in self-glory and pride does he refuse to have anything to do with the Father's gesture of generosity, as an earthly son, a man who prided himself on directing his own life, might do. He takes what the Father gives him in genuine thankfulness. No one could receive more than he receives, for what he receives is personal existence, personal ego, and hence the whole of what constitutes the life of God. More than this it would be impossible to receive. The Son's whole being is that of one who receives. Indeed, just as the Father is the pure concept of giving, so the Son is the pure concept of receiving. The Father and the Son, therefore, possess one and the same divine being, one and the same divine knowledge, one and the same divine love.

The one possesses the being of God as a giver, the other as a receiver. Only in the acts of giving and receiving are they different from one another. The difference is that of I and Thou. The I of the Father and the Thou of the Son therefore perform the act of knowing through one and the same almighty, all-piercing and all-comprehending divine faculty of knowing. The I of the Father and the Thou of the Son perform the act of loving through one and the same comprehensive divine faculty of loving, which imbues the whole of reality. Father and Son exist through one and the same faculty for absolute existence.

We should remember that to personal being there appertains a double movement: that of existing in oneself, and that of turning to others. Existing in oneself is accomplished in a continual act. A man exists in himself because he continually enters into himself. In just the same way, his turning towards others is accomplished in a continual movement. He turns to another, by opening himself to another and serving the other.

In this two-dimensional personality there is involved a task which, as we saw earlier, man cannot completely carry out: the task of giving himself without losing himself, and of preserving himself, without turning in completely on himself. One has to find that narrow ledge along which it is possible to walk safely between the abysses of self-destruction and abandonment on the one hand, and introspection on the other. During his life of pilgrimage on earth, man cannot succeed in finding this narrow ledge. The perfect solution to the problem set before man is possible only in the life after death—where it will, of course, not be solved by man's own endeavours, but by God. During time, man is always on the point of falling into one of the abysses. When he gives himself to another in such a way that his self-surrender becomes self-prostitution and destruction, he is falling victim to an animal existence. When, on the other hand, he gives himself, while at the same time remaining bound up in himself he is falling victim to individualism. Thus the road of time runs for ever between the Scylla of soulless existence in the mass, and the Charybdis of individualism. Now the pendulum swings to the one side, now to the other. History proceeds in a continual swinging between these extremes.

But what is fundamentally insoluble to man is fulfilled perfectly in the reality which is God. The three divine persons exist beyond the power of the forces that reduce man to the level of the mass, and beyond the power of individualistic introspection, for each of them exists only in devotion to the others. Each of them gives himself in his relationship with the others without thereby destroying himself.

Whilst we men are implicated in a net of relationships, which are in fact not relationships, the personalities of the divine persons really consist in their relationships with one another. The relationships into which we men are woven have various depths. They may be of a purely external kind, such as for example spatial or temporal relationships, that is, existence at the same place and time as another person. They can penetrate further into our personalities, as, for example, in the relationships of children to parents. They may reach that depth at which one person gives himself in true love to another. But however deeply the relationship may penetrate into the ego, the inner kernel of the human ego, because it subsists in itself, is always separate and withdrawn. Hence relationships always take place on the edge of the ego. The divine relationships on the other hand are of such power that not only is the heart of the ego given by each of the persons to each of the others, but I and Thou are built up together.

The divine persons are relationships whose power is in themselves, and which exist in themselves. Every divine person is therefore individual only in his giving of himself, his movement towards the others. The Father is therefore not only Giver, but also Gift. The Son is not only Receiver, but he is Reception.

None of the persons can think I, without also thinking Thou. If, only for an instant, any of them were to stop thinking Thou and considering Thou, in that instant his own ego would vanish away. Existence as a person for each depends on his orientation towards the others. The existence of one person is therefore in the fullest sense existence with others.

What we have learned about the life of the divine Persons from the relationship between the Father and the Son, is made clear by the relationship of the Holy Ghost to the other two divine Persons. The Holy Ghost is brought forth from the Father and the Son in their giving of themselves to one another. In the Father's giving of himself to the Son, and the Son's to the Father, there springs into being from the mightiness of their giving, a third divine Person. He not only comes forth, he is the Coming Forth itself. In him, there is shown directly to the Father the Son's readiness to let himself be given everything by him. In the Holy Ghost, there is shown directly to the Son the complete and unreserved willingness of the Father to give him everything. Thus the Holy Ghost is the pledge of the intensity of the exchange between the Father and the Son. Thus they experience their union in its most potent form.

The exchange of life between the Father and the Son is the basis of the bliss of God. If happiness pertains to relationships with others, then God cannot be without happiness. In the human sphere, the consciousness of the ego grows in its encounter with others, and in this encounter it finds its joy and happiness. It is the same with God—although the similarity is of course veiled in a greater unsimilarity. Each of the divine Persons finds his existence and his joy in the personalities of the other two. But the divine Person does not awaken from a previous state of slumber as a result of his encounters with the others. Rather, he is continually awakening in this relationship, because his personality depends on the personality of the others. If God was not tri-personal, he would lack that happiness which in the creaturely sphere seems to us to be the highest happiness: he could not awaken to himself and to his own joy in creation. If he could not continually carry on within his own being the intensive exchange of life which springs from the encounter between I and Thou, an animated and sharply defined life would be impossible to him. Then the Godhead would lead a miserable existence. And those pantheistic ideas, according to which God is an unconscious indifferent force or an unconscious idea which finds its first clear expression in human consciousness, would be right. Then, too, Monism, according to which God needs man and the world if he is to be himself, would be justified. Effective refutation of these Monistic and Naturalistic ideas of God is offered only by belief in a God who is tri-personal. Such belief, indeed, refutes all pantheistic concepts absolutely.

If the three divine Persons have divine consciousness only in their encounter with one another, and if they are happy in that, we should not expect ever to see their happiness diminish, or to see them grow weary of one another, as one human being can sometimes grow tired of another. Even where men are united in the most intimate love, they need, from time to time, separation from each other in order to maintain their union at an intensity which everyday living would shatter. The reason for this is that what one human can give another is exhaustible, by reason of the limited nature of man, and therefore one human being may not be able to see anything new in another, or take anything new from him, if the other has given him too much and has given it continuously. They then become bored with one another. It is therefore essential for the continuance of the community that the self-giving of the one to the other be limited by distance. But such dangers do not menace the divine exchange, for what one Person has to give to the others is, because of the limitlessness of the divine life, inexhaustible—the more so because as a consequence of the indestructibility and everlasting quality of his divine life each Person is eternally fresh and vigorous. The being of God is ever-flowering. Hence each of the divine Persons continually receives from each of the others fulness of life in the eternal bloom of youth, fulness so perfect as to be incapable of any enrichment.

From the fact that God is tri-personal, it appears that the reality that stands behind all visible and experienced realities is tri-personal in form. The whole visible and perceptible reality is God's self-expression of the divine being. It is a mirror of God. Although this mirror may be spoilt by sin, so that it becomes impossible to see what is reflected in it clearly and perfectly, the world is still in some measure a reflexion of God. The whole of the created world is therefore built up in threes. The eye of faith—that is, the vision of those who have been given sight by Christ—therefore takes in everywhere in creation signs and tokens of the tri-personal mode of God's existence. It is visible in created things to varying degrees. The observant spectator will notice that a place is marked by spoor of God, just as a hunter in the forest sees from the tracks of game, what animals have passed that way. In another place, the threefold personality of God is reflected like a human countenance in a glass. Thus, for example, the careful observer can see a trace of the exchange of life between the three Persons in many biological phenomena. The theologians of the early church found it in the trinity of root, stem and branch. The modern biologist may see it in the circulation of sap from roots to tree-top, and back. The anthropologist and psychologist can find the image of the tri-personal God in the trinity of knowledge, will and love, or that of memory, reason and will.

Such trinities in creation and those like them, which become visible to us in the light of trinitarian belief, also in their turn open a new approach to the mystery of the tri-personal life of God. They cannot of course lay bare the inmost depths of the mystery. If every personal being is an impenetrable mystery, the tri-personal nature of God is a mystery, doubly and triply impenetrable. Without Christ's act of raising the veil, we should not have known about it. We cannot comprehend its content but must be content to look at the mystery and grope our way towards it, with the analogical ideas and words at our disposal. What we have already said, however, is enough to show that the mystery lies beyond the scope of reason, but does not contradict it. When rationalism imputes unreasonableness to trinitarian belief—as when, for instance, it maintains that the dogma of the Trinity affirms that one is the same as three—its assertion shows a misunderstanding based on superficialities. For belief in the Trinity teaches that the one being of God is possessed of a three-fold ego. It is prerequisite to the understanding of such a definition to grasp the difference between nature and person.

The three-fold personality of the divine life also makes it possible to understand why three grades of divinities appear in all religious systems. The Christian doctrine of the three Persons is not just a particular case of the universal belief in divine trinities. This belief is rather a consequence of the fact that divine reality does exist in three Persons. From the beliefs of non-Christian religions in divine trinities, we can see that there is a presentiment, as it were, in the human mind of the ultimate reality which lies beyond all things. The difference between the non-Christian trinities and the divine reality in three Persons revealed to us by Christ, is the difference between dream and reality. The trinities dreamed of by believers outside the sphere of Christian revelation always include three gods which come together in an organic unity. The three-fold personality revealed by Christ, on the other hand, shows us how one God exists in the mode of three persons. Unity and trinity are thereby bound together in the closest intimacy. God's being, God's spirit and God's knowledge are one: God's ego, which possesses this divine being, and through which God's powers are employed, is three.

As we saw above, the blessedness of God consists in the exchange of life between the three divine Persons. Because the life in three Persons, which is the life of God, cannot be imperilled, the happiness of God can also not be endangered either by enervation or by the menace of self-love. In faith in the three-fold personality of God we have, therefore, the assurance that there somewhere exists absolute, indestructible bliss. The believer can look out from the world of hate, unhappiness, melancholy, unfulfilled and unfulfillable self-love to the realm of bliss. Only if, and because, there is such a realm of bliss, can the human hope of bliss be anything but an illusion. What man thinks he sees beyond the world of hate and misery is no *fata morgana*, but absolute reality. Only because there is a happy God, can we hope to come to a state of fulfilment. Indeed, only because man, the creature, originated from the realms of bliss, can he continue, despite all disappointments, to carry in his heart belief in happiness. Because God, who is bliss in person, is also the Creator of the universe, the reflected splendour of joy lies on the cosmos, on history, and even on every individual man. Great as may be the melancholy in the world man has corrupted, and even if it is perceptible everywhere man's gaze falls, the blessedness of God yet shines through all earthly decay. All earthly joy is some kind of distant presentiment of the absolute blessedness of God. Even carnal pleasure, to which the name joy cannot be applied, is still in a way an echo of the bliss of God's tri-personal exchange of life. It is a caricature of it. Even hell is a caricature of the divine bliss, for even he who is damned does not lack all pleasure, even if he lacks all joy, for he lives in the pleasure of self-chosen and firmly-maintained, absolute autonomy, of Godless self-glorification.

If the divine bliss is the reason why the yearning for joy lives on indestructible in every human heart, this yearning can only find its ultimate fulfilment in God. Christ demonstrated this, when he consoled his disciples at the moment of his parting with them by the promise that he would give them his joy. The joy he gives them is a part of that joy which lives in him as a result of his exchange of life with the Father and the Holy Spirit. In him, joy is an ever-flowing stream, and he shares this stream of joy with his disciples. But, during this life, his faithful share in his own joy only incompletely. But he promises them that their joy will one day be full. It will attain its full intensity after the collapse of earthly life.

The divine exchange of life between the three persons and the bliss which springs from it will be more easily understood by us, if we remember that God is love. We shall then see the Father, who gives the whole of his divine being to the Son, as self-giving love.

As we have already seen, God is not love in that form in which one person lays hold on another to use him for his own ends. He is love in that form in which the lover gives himself to the beloved in order to fulfil the life of the beloved. We must now pursue this point further. The fact that God is self-giving love, and that the divine exchange of life is an exchange of love, may help us to come to a deeper understanding of the fact that he is most happy, in fact: happiness in person. If love means happiness and God is love in person, then he is happiness in person. Hence, to meet God, in so far as it means meeting love in person, at the same time implies meeting happiness in person. During his short earthly pilgrimage, immediate encounter with happiness in person is not possible for man. But it is promised for the life after death. Encounter with love and the happiness which is based on it will be ours in heaven.

This shows, furthermore, that community is essential for man. It is essential for man to be related to others in a community. For he originated in the love of God, which is accomplished in the coming together of Persons. He is therefore destined for encounter with others. Hence a man can come to the fulfilment of his being only through encounter with others.

Furthermore, it becomes clear that everything in creation forms a great unity: all things stand together in an indestructible relationship. But the singleness of creation differentiates it from the tri-personal being of God, in so far as this latter unity of being in trinity means that there is relationship in God, whilst the singleness of creation contains within itself multiplicity of substances and unity of relationship.

The word love itself can help us penetrate still deeper the significance of the relationship in which the three divine Persons stand to one another. Holy Scripture gives us no clear explanation of the mode of divine generation and procession. But it gives us various indications which theologians have pursued in the course of the ages. On the basis of these theological attempts at explanation, we can make certain other statements about the divine exchange of life. We must not forget however that it is a question here of tentative attempts, in which men have tried to pierce the impenetrable mystery of God. If we would define divine procession and generation yet more precisely and distinctly, we must realize that God is love and truth: that he is the true love, and truth enkindled by love; that to him knowledge and love are the same thing—and indeed, that he is knowledge and love in person.

From many indications in Holy Scripture, the relationship of the Father to the Son seems to be maintained through an act of knowing, and that of the Son to the Holy Ghost through an act of love. The first is indicated by the title *Logos*: the second is an assertion about the mode of existence of the Holy Ghost which has been generally held since St. Augustine.

We would express the generation and personal character of the Son as follows: the Father understands and comprehends the whole of reality. He comprehends both his own divine existence, and at the same time, all the possible ways in which he might reveal himself in a final way. With this all-seeing, all-comprehending gaze, he looks on heaven and earth. There is nowhere anything else to know, because nowhere does anything else exist. What the Father learns from this all-piercing gaze, he fashions into a deep and comprehensive thought. In spite of its bottomless depth and infinite breadth, this thought is of great clarity and sharp definition. The Father shapes and fashions his knowledge into a thought of absolute fulness and breadth. In it, he puts his own divine existence and, at the same time, the life of creation. In it he discusses with himself both his divine glory and the glory of the universe, as a

193

man might discuss with himself, in his thought, what was present in his mind. We could therefore call the comprehensive, deep thought fashioned by the Father, the Word which the Father exchanges with himself: the Father's *Logos*.

Two characteristics differentiate this Word from any word spoken by man. It is not, like human words, poor of content and temporary in duration. In our words we can never give more than an abstract of our thought and feeling, and this abstract can only be a weak outline. Indeed, even those men who are skilled at fashioning thoughts—the poets and artists of genius—realise that they cannot put into words what is within them in pictures and thoughts. The pain that dwells in human conversation is this: that we cannot express our thoughts and our love adequately in words. In our words, there can never be more than a scanty fraction of what is in our minds and hearts. Human speech is therefore never more than an indication of the invisible and inaudible world of man's inner being. Human speech demands of the listener that he take careful note of the reality which it expresses, but which it cannot completely contain. If he is not capable of that, he cannot grasp the underlying reality that human speech is intended to express. The most perfect human speech must remain empty for him.

In contrast to this, the divine Word is of unlimited richness. In it, the whole fulness of reality is expressed, so that there is no longer any unexpressed, underlying reality. The divine Word is therefore more profound than the most profound human utterance. Indeed, it reaches down to the bottomless depths of the divine being.

The second way in which human words are incomplete is in the shortness of their life. Human words are fugitive: they come and go. They are spoken, and they blow away like the wind. Among the many which are not worthy of enduring life and which therefore, rightly fade away, there are of course also some which are forceful: and among these again are some that are worthy of perpetuation because they are worthwhile and valuable in themselves. Thus it may be that a human word moves and changes him who hears it, in his inmost being. It can happen that words will change a whole epoch, and open an horizon to a new picture of the world and knowledge of life. Such words are powerful in history, and work beyond the moment at which they were spoken. But even in the case of such historically powerful words, what endures is not the sound and form of the word, but the power of the word.

In contrast to this, the divine Word exists absolutely: it is not susceptible to mortality, for it shares in the life of God. Indeed, its life is the absolute life of the Father. Hence, the Word in which the Father expressed the universe and God, existed before all time, and it will outlast all time: it is an eternal Word. It is spoken by the Father for ever. It exists in unlimited potentiality, because it is formed by the Father in an unending process. It sounds therefore in all spheres and all times. If we cannot perceive it, that is because we do not possess the faculty necessary to do so. The ears needed to hear this word will one day be given us. In the life beyond time, God himself will bestow on us that faculty of hearing by which we shall be able to perceive the eternal Word of the Father.

We must go one step further: the Word spoken by the Father is not only of unlimited meaning and indestructible life; it is personal. This Word has a face so that one can see it and enter into converse with it. The Father's Word can itself address another. It is the divine Son.

In spite of the profound difference between human speech and the divine Word, human speech can help us to reach a deepened understanding of the divine Word. Man's greatness is expressed in words. In the dignity of human words there shines forth the majesty of that Word which is the Son of God.

The dignity of human speech is praised by O. Miller in his book *Der Individualismus als Schicksal* in these words:

Word: first symbol of humanity; first-born of wisdom; first gift of mind wed to body; mystery and revelation, soul and body! Unfathomable is thy conception: painful and propitious thy birth: blooming thy fresh youth: powerful and creative thy maturity: withered and shadowy thine old age.

Thou art the victor and loosener of all the creature's dumbness; thou loosest the spirit from its congealing loneliness; thou breathest life into dead things; out of the phenomena of the visible world, thou bringest their essence to view; thou givest essences reality and individuality; thou callest men by their names, and things by their natures. Thou art the laughter of the soul and the crystal tears of its.

sadness. Thou art the reflexion of its delight and the dark shadow of its sorrow.

Winged art thou, and flighted like Psyche; thou hast the speed of the angel, and the power of distant illumination of the sunbeam. Thou piercest time, space, millennia and continents; thou dost divide and unite the nations, and when an age grows grey, or a people dies away, thou preservest its spirit in thy costly urn. And when the divine reality broke into that of the world, thou camest in the storm of the divine Spirit and in flaming tongues to men, with whom the new age of the world began and the spring of God's kingdom began to bloom. Nothing among perceptible things has power such as thine: thou art strong as a lion, supple as a gazelle, thou hast the watchfulness of the eagle, and the attacking power of the sparrow-hawk. Thou art sweeter than honey, and more bitter than wormwood. Thou art beguiling and deluding, as intoxicating as love and wine. Thou art clear as the holy, calm waters, thou dost animate what thou wilt animate, dost kill what thou wilt kill. Thou art like the feathered arrow sped from the bow of Apollo, thou strikest things and men to the heart and killest them like that divine couple, the flourishing children of Niobe.

Thou canst cut through darkness like lightning and canst rumble like thunder. Thou art, the Epistle to the Hebrews saith, the lofty speech of the Holy Ghost, 'living and effectual and more piercing than any two-edged sword', piercing to soul and spirit, marrow and joints, dividing them one from another.

Of all art, thou art the noblest, the handiwork of God, thin and strong as the lonely Acanthian pillars, and graceful as the flow of line in the marble portraits of Myrthenhain; thou hast the hymnic ring of the Semitic Psalmist; thou sleepest, sweet euphony, in the golden string of a Grecian lyre; thou art the honey of the holy bee on the lips of Pindar and Apollo, the speech of the gods in words of Plato; in the Grecian spirit thou dost encompass the Mediterranean, and in the Roman faculty for ruling, the *orbis terrarum*. Like a translucent ruby dish art thou, full of dark wine; and like the crystal cup, full of limpid water; like a mourning urn on the mound of the dead, and like the evergreen ivy which encircles the stump of a pillar, as does a loving wife grown grey the shoulder of her husband.

Thou hoverest over the moving waves of rhythm, and over the undulations of melody; thou art the ineffable music, and the secret sound from the remote reaches of the invisible world. Thou, the first gift of the mother soul, the messenger of yearning, the interpreter of young love, the holy message of eternity breathed in on us the dying; the holy inviolable chalice of our faith and paten of our prayer.

From the fact that the Son is the Word shaped and spoken by the Father, it becomes possible for us to define more precisely the mutual self-devotion binding Father and Son together. The Father's relationship to the Son is that of Speaker. Indeed, he is not only he who speaks, but the act of speaking itself—utterance in person. Conversely, we can see the Son's devotion to the Father as the act of responding: he is the Word that submits to the Father, and hence is also response. The Son is one who replies: indeed, he is not only one who responds, he is the act of response itself. Hence the life of the Father and the Son is such that the one is speech, the other response, in person.

What the Father says to the Son is the most elevated and profound thing that one person can say to another: it is the mystery of God and of the universe. What the Son receives is the most blessed and richest thing that one person can receive from another. The Father keeps no secrets from the Son. The Son's interest in what the Father says to him extends to the inmost depths of his being. His interest in what the Father says is such because his life depends upon it. Were the Father to choose to reserve to himself any part of the mystery of reality, he would, by doing so, bring death on himself. Were the Son to be uninterested in any part of what the Father mediates to him, his lack of interest would mean death for him.

Because God is love, the converse between Father and Son is a converse of love. The Word the Father speaks is a Word of love, of unfathomable profundity and incomprehensible fulness. The response the Son makes, is, because he is love, a loving response. It is the ultimate reality, beyond which there is nothing: the converse of love; indeed, absolute loving converse.

If we so define the ultimate reality—that is, as the act of a converse of love—we do not by so doing lessen the reality of God. In the human sphere such converse might be weak and incomplete. But the converse of love that we call God is of a mightiness and richness that is absolute, for the acts of speaking and responding are, in God, of infinite potency. What exists here is divine fulness of life in the mode of speaking and responding: the absolute being of God. Scholastic theology expressed this in the formula: each of the divine Persons is identical with the divine being.

As we have seen in the blessed converse carried on between Father and Son, there is described not only divine, but also cosmic, reality. Their converse covers the world as a whole, things individually, and especially the destiny of man. The thoughts of the Father about things and about people are described in this eternal divine conversation. Herein lies the eternal meaning of the world, the meaning of the individual things in it, the meaning of individual men and of human history. Towering above all meaninglessness is the eternal purpose that the Father has given shape in his Son.

Faith in the eternal Word of God therefore, involves faith in the eternal meaning of the world and of people in themselves; and belief too, that no one and nothing is superfluous, because everything is discussed between the Father and the Son. Faith in the eternal significance of the universe and of men, which is guaranteed in the converse of love between the Father and the Son, contains within itself the power to overcome the paradox of the universe. He who lives in this faith can force his way through all meaninglessness and reach the mystery of the eternal purpose of the world. Thickly veiled as this may be during the history of the world and the life of the individual, the believer knows that it does exist: he lives in consciousness of the fact that its meaning will one day be revealed. In that phase of life which begins after the collapse of earthly forms, God himself will explain to men the eternal meaning of the world, and of their lives, by permitting them to share in that converse he conducts with the Son.

If the ultimate reality is converse between the Father and the Son —the act of conversing itself—the splendour of heaven must be reflected in human conversation, in the speech of men. Human conversation is an echo of the converse which is Father and Son: a reverberation of the heavenly converse. The divine converse can be heard through human conversation. Human speech is therefore a thing of very great worth, coming not from the earth, but from heaven. The higher that which is said stands in the ranks of human speech, the more the divine Word will be heard in it.

From the fact that human speech is an echo of the converse between Father and Son, its significance for life in community is obvious. Human speech is an expression, and, at the same time the food of unity. In human speech the orientation of one person to another is made plain, and gains new force. Thus speech is a sign of love. How could it be otherwise? The converse conducted between Father and Son is itself a converse of love. Hence human speech, if it is conducted in the right way, is also a converse of love. When men speak in love, the eternal converse of love echoes in time.

This being the nature of human speech, it is clear why words can produce happiness.

But man, being free, can corrupt the meaning of speech. He can bring chaos to conversation in just the same way in which he has brought chaos into the world: by rebelling against God, by selfish use of the world that God has created. In his self-glory, man does not allow the converse of love, which is God, to sound through his words: he allows them to contain only his own self-glorification. In his godless self-will, man uses speech not as though it were a gift of God, but as though it were his own possession absolutely. He uses it as he likes, as an instrument either of love or of hatred. Words of hatred and lying, self-love and tyranny conceal the true significance of human speech.

In his work of redemption Christ also sought to liberate human speech from its state of distortion and emptiness. From the fact that as the Son of God took human destiny on himself, so the eternal Word of the Father took human destiny on himself, it follows that his work for human speech was intended to be of decisive significance. In the Incarnation, which followed many preparatory utterances, the Father spoke his eternal Word into human history. Thus we can see in Christ the eternal Word of the Father in visible form. We can perceive it in the human words which Christ spoke. The eternal Word of God rings through every word spoken by the Lord.

What we can perceive of the eternal converse of God are those excerpts from it that the Father intends for us. When the eternal *Logos* took human destiny on himself, he also took human speech. In all his earthly conversations, the eternal Word of God was poured into a human vessel. What was done in the Incarnation— namely, that the Son of God emptied himself, taking the weakness of man—was done especially in Christ's conversation on earth. The eternal Word of God emptied itself in the weakness of human speech. Human speech, the human word, which man, in his self-glory, has cut off from God, has been led back by Christ to the sphere of the divine. It has therefore regained its true meaning, so that it is again an echo of the eternal converse of God, and reveals this converse in time. This was effected by the return of man to God.

Christ did not bring man back to the Father in a mechanical way, but in such a way that human freedom suffered no disrespect at his hands. He brought back human nature to God in his own Person, and called on all the rest of humanity to unite itself with his human nature in faith and the sacraments, and so follow the way to the Father. It is man's responsibility to hear the Lord's call and follow him obediently. As it is the responsibility of any man called by Christ to see that Christ's work of redemption is successful in him, he is also responsible for seeing that human speech is brought back to God. It is returned to him in so far as the man returns to him.

For the duration of cosmic history, Christ produced certain words which are continually in the course of returning to the Father—namely, the words of preaching and the sacraments. In them, the words of grace spoken in time, in which the eternal converse of love is made audible in part to us, are spread further through time and space. In the words of preaching and the sacraments, the converse of love echoes in every age.

Those who believe in Christ are therefore responsible for seeing that the converse of love conducted between the Father and the Son, is traceable and perceptible in their everyday speech. This involves two things: that human conversation should be truth and not lies, and that it should be of love and not of hate. Only the word of truth and the word of love are echoes of the heavenly converse between Father and Son.

The most profound reason why human speech must echo truth and love is that it is the nature of human speech to be the echo of the converse of God. Only when it serves truth and love does it fulfil its real purpose—that the eternal converse of God should shine through it, and the sovereignty of love thus be advanced. When on the other hand, it is an instrument of lies and hatred, it contradicts the inmost meaning of human speech: it advances the rule of lies and hatred, and thus makes its contribution to the reversal of the true order of the world. That true order can thrive only under the rule of God, of truth and love.

This tendency to act against God and man is inherent in every word of lying and hatred. But in the age inaugurated by Christ, hating or lying words are an essentially greater and more violent contradiction of the true meaning of human speech than they would have been in pre-Christian times. Just as sins, because they are those of the Christian age, are more sinful than they were in the pre-Christian ages, so also is the divorce of human speech from God a more terrible perversion of speech in the ages inaugurated by Christ, than was misuse of speech in pre-Christian times. Human words divorced from God, and therefore words of hatred and lying, have a diabolical character in the Christian era. They are the instruments by which Satan, the lord of lies and tyranny, advances his rule. In such speech, Satan usurps that gift, the faculty of speech, in which the humanity of man is revealed. He usurps it for the victory of hell.

This perversion reaches its climax when, through his earthly servants, he masks words of lying and hatred with a facade of truth and love. Just as hell imitates everything divine, even to the sacrificial death of Christ, in order to deceive men, so in the words of hatred and lying, masked as words of truth and love, it imitates the true speech of truth and love, so that he who hears will be misled.

The distortion of human speech is not always diabolic in origin. It may also consist in the fact that without directly serving lying and hatred, it serves emptiness. This happens when although lies and hatred are not echoed in human speech, neither are truth and love, when, in fact, nothing is echoed by it because it is an empty vessel, an empty husk. Such vain, such nihilistic, words are signs of nihilistic people. By emptiness here we mean what is generated when man concentrates on his own inner being, and has therefore withdrawn from the external reality. This is what Hölderlin was referring to when he made Rhea say of Empedocles: 'I don't understand this man. Does he, like us, also have his empty days, when he feels old and insignificant to himself? And does he, too, know human sorrow?' Nihilistic emptiness of speech comes from nihilism of spirit, before which no horizon lies open but that of nothingness, and which therefore finally fills its words with nothing, and hence cannot fill them. Such words are ordered boredom. Emptiness reached its highest point in loss of speech—not in that dumbness which occurs because the fulness of spirit and heart cannot be expressed in words, but rather that which occurs because there is nothing that can be expressed in words. Decay of speech, chaos in utterance, reveals man's nihilism.

Of course, even chaotic speech cannot completely hide the fact that its home is in the converse of the Father with the Son. Even on it there still lies the glitter of heaven.

Although empty speech is not the tool of hell as words of hatred and lying are, it does come close to being so. For ultimately every perversion of the divine comes from Hell. In Holy Scripture it is made plain that dumbness, the illness which is least consistent with human dignity, is a work of Satan.

Just as everything truly human can thrive only in nearness to God, so too, human conversation, the echo of heaven, can only prosper in the vicinity of the Divine.

The converse of love between Father and Son stands before us in a new—in its ultimate—profundity, when we draw the Holy Ghost into the action in which the Father and the Son are engaged. The Father's love for the Son, and the Son's for the Father is of unsurpassable power and intimacy. In the words of love which he speaks to the Son, the Father breathes towards the Son the breath of love. In the same way, the Son breathes the breath of love to the Father. The breath of love which each receives from the other, is not a fleeting motion, a wave, which arises and sinks again. Just like the Word the Father speaks, it has life and personality. We call the Holy Ghost the living and personal breath of love which blows to the Father from the Son's heart, and to the Son from the heart of the Father.

The union between the Father and the Son attains its highest intensity and clarity in the Holy Ghost. What we saw before is now even clearer: because he is the breath of love who flows backwards and forwards between the Father and the Son, the Holy Ghost is the token and pledge of their union of love. He is the sign of love because he is love itself. From what he sees on the face of this personal love, the Father can always be certain that the love of the Son is his. From him, the Son knows continually that the Father's love is his. From him the Father learns continually —by his constant reception of him—that the Son is giving himself to him unreservedly. Likewise, the Son knows through receiving him uninterruptedly, that the Father is giving himself to him unrestrictedly. The Holy Ghost is the sign of their unreserved and mutual devotion.

We shall comprehend this even more clearly if we remember that both for the Father and for the Son, it is a life-and-death matter to bring forth the Holy Ghost. Just as the Father would fade into nothingness if he were but for one moment to cease giving himself to the Son—this would be a contradiction in itself, but for the sake of explanation we must express the idea in these terms—just as the Son, too, would sink into nothingness if for one moment he neglected to give himself to the Father, both Father and Son would cease to exist if they ceased only for a moment putting forth the token of their loving union, the Holy Ghost. Their own existence depends on that of the Holy Ghost. Without the breath of life which they breathe to one another, the converse of love could not exist, and the Father and the Son could therefore not exist.

If we ask the same questions about the love in which the Father and the Son give themselves to one another as we asked about the Word generated by the Father, we shall receive the same answers: In their love for one another there is contained the whole reality of heaven and earth, the glory of God and of the world.

The love of the Father and the Son for the universe is taken from this wealth of love. It is the basis of the existence of things outside God. If we ask why God brought the world into being, we can receive only one answer: he did so from love; or, more precisely, from love for himself. The love of God is not a dreamer's love, but the love of a sober and far-seeing being, and therefore it values itself at its true worth. God's love for himself is expressed in the Father's love for the Son, and the Son's for the Father. He consummates this love for himself in such a way that he can see his glory in finite reproductions of itself. To make this quite clear, we must of course add, that God does not receive any increase in perfection from the world, and can receive none, because he is absolute blessedness. Why he nevertheless consummates his love for himself in such a way that he produces the world is an impenetrable mystery. The question as to why God made the world cannot, in fact, be finally answered. All we can know is that God is so delighted by his own glory that he was pleased to make a finite replica of it, although to do so did not in any way increase his bliss.

If then, we look closely at the tri-personal nature of the divine love, the picture we see is as follows:

The Father loves the Son so intensely and intimately that he ponders every possible way of giving him joy and happiness. The same is true of the Son: he is devoted to the Father so intimately and intensely that he is determined to give him all the joy he can. The same is true of the relationship of the Father and the Son to the Holy Ghost, and of the Holy Ghost to the Father and the Son. In this determination of the divine Persons to give each other every possible kind of joy and happiness, they contrived the plan of creation. The Father conceived the plan of giving the Son a new source of joy in a finite replica of his own divine glory. The Son assented to the Father's plan for the universe, in order to give the Father a new ground for joy. And so it was too with the Holy Ghost.

Although therefore, we cannot know the ultimate reason for the existence of the universe, because we cannot answer the question why God consummated his love for himself in the form of love for the world, we can say that the reciprocal love of the divine Persons for one another is the basis of the existence of the cosmos. If love is the most profound basis for the existence of the world, the world must, in its inmost heart, be shaped by love. This throws new light on the fact that everything in the cosmos is permanently related to everything else, and that created things together form a unity. For they are all manifestations of the love of God.

Of course, if we look at the world in the actual form it has today, it will not give us the impression of being the work and manifestation of love. Rather, it will look as though cruelty and tyranny, love of destruction, and a bias towards nihilism rule in it. The reason for this is that the world no longer possesses that form which God gave it, but has been corrupted by man. We shall look at this more closely subsequently. Because the world no longer has any appearance of being a manifestation of love, man feels lost and neglected in it. If it still had its original form, he would find it a place of abundance and friendliness. Because of the corruption man has brought into it, the world can no longer be seen as an expression of the creative love of God, and therefore man is afflicted with melancholy in the world.

But for those who have eyes to see it, the world still possesses enough connexion with God, to be able to point for men the way to him, and to keep the yearning for God alive in them. But at the same time they will realise that the world itself cannot fulfil the yearnings which it awakens and keeps alive in men. So the man who is in the world, is constantly being led out of it, by these yearnings. He lives in the fear that that which in him calls for fulfilment can never find it. There is truth in Hölderlin's saying about life in the world: 'Oh eternal secret! What we are and seek, we cannot find: what we find, we are not.' At the same time, the world enkindles in those who live in it the hope that there is fulfilment beyond the earth. This hope preserves them from despair in the face of melancholy and sadness.

In particular, the fact that love is the basis of the creation of the world, reveals to us the inmost heart of the being of man. As we have already seen, because this is love, man therefore fulfils his being only when he lives according to love. Hate is a contradiction of the innermost being of man. Thus it is understandable that anyone who hates must also be unhappy, as he is living in contradiction of his own being, and experiences this as internal disunion. The contradiction of the inmost heart of the being of man which is represented in hate, can culminate in the destruction of man's essence.

If human love finds its most profound basis in the God-given nature of man, human love must be an expression of the love of God, and is therefore of potentially infinite profundity and, at the same time, has an imperishable compulsive force.

Of course the nature of human love is concealed during the time of man's earthly pilgrimage. His love will reveal its inner potency and glory only when it can be a perfect mirror of the love of God, in that consummation which we call heaven.

CHAPTER TEN

CHRISTIANITY AND THE WORLD

Man lives in the world and under its ordinances. He has, therefore, many inseverable connexions with the world. Hence, it is only to be expected that the change effected in man by Christ will be influential in the world. It would, of course, be a complete mis- understanding of Christianity—which in Christ makes us a part of the revelation of God—if we were to think of it as a measure taken by God for the direct improvement of the world, for the establishment of a certain political, social and economic order for the formation of a culture, for the education of the human race, or for any other cultural reason. Christianity has of course, a wide and profound importance for the ordering of the world. But it was not instituted primarily for the sake of any particular given order of things. As we saw earlier, the inmost meaning of Christianity is concerned with the sovereignty of God. God acts in human history in order to realise his sovereignty in the world. Christ's work on earth served this end, and the establishment of the rule of God will mean salvation for men. By subjecting himself to the rule of God—and hence of truth and love in reality—a man enters into communion with God, with fulness of life and being, and by so doing earns indestructible life and salvation for himself.

But although the Christian revelation is not directly concerned with the ordering of earthly things, it brings a message which is of great—indeed, of decisive—importance for proper understanding of the world and the life of man in the world.

The most profitable step to take for the elucidation of this would seem to be to take as a guide that expression which we have already used for the elucidation of human life: 'The Word was made flesh' (John 1, 14). The divine *Logos*, the Son of God, assumed human nature, with both mortality and man's limited powers. That is, he took on himself a product of this world: stuff from the stuff of this world, dust from the dust of creation. By doing so, he gave his approbation not only to man, to the human body, but also to the universe. So the world received endorsement from God, and the seal of approval was set once for all on what God did at the beginning of the world.

The world was made by God. It is not based on itself, but was called into being by God, and is therefore dependent at every level. It exists because it is held in being by God.

Such an interpretation of the world conflicts with the modern attitude to it. Hazard, Guardini, Friedrich v. Weizsäcker and other authors have investigated the origin and development of this feeling about the world. The picture of the world which for the middle ages was sharply defined and limited, grew ever larger through discoveries and inventions, and its boundaries were pushed back continually until for man the world finally came to fill the whole of imaginable reality. Thus the world became everything, and it became impossible to see anything outside or beyond it.

So then there was no room for God. The divine and the numinous were attributes of the world itself. The world was deified. A similar process took place to that which we saw at the birth of the ancient myths.

It was possible for man to deify the world because the world bore the stamp of the divine on account of the fact that it did indeed come from God. It had a numinous dimension. It was a veiled and concealed revelation of God. In the modern concept of the world, the world's numinous aspect was divorced from God and made independent.

In the later course of this development, the consciousness and presentiment of the numinous aspect of everything was lost to man. He learned more and more to envisage everything from the merely material point of view. Positivism was satisfied with seeing things and their relationships with one another. The world lost its dimension in depth.

In contrast to this, the world is shown in Holy Scripture to be a creation of God. God expressed himself in words creative of the world, its life and its order. The world is therefore his image, whether taken as a whole, or in its individual phenomena. Things have a symbolic character, and therefore the things which surround us in our everyday life are such that they can bring us to God.

It is a profound mystery why God permitted his word to be distorted by man. The creation no longer mirrors God in its original purity, but is instead a broken mirror. We are able to ignore God, as though he were not there, and thus the symbolical nature of things has received a severe blow. Things have become ambiguous: what originally mirrored God, who is holiness and love, can now also mirror evil. (This phenomenon we call the ambivalent nature of mythical images).

We cannot fully explain the mystery of sin. But we can say that God has such a high opinion of human freedom that he does not control it at all, and does not even prevent it from operating when its effects will be fatal. Such an attitude in God may seem foolish to us when it persists even whilst the world is being perverted. But God has prepared a remedy. He saw a way to redeem the world. It would have to be a way of tears and affliction, but it was a way. When the world was perverted by men, God entered the world a second time: the divine *Logos* took into unity of life with himself material from among that with which God had made the world. Since the incarnation, the world has been united in the closest intimacy with the life of God, and this God-given approbation of the world will never be withdrawn.

Just as in the Incarnation the *Logos* united with himself dust from the dust of this world, so he also took man's destiny on himself for the sake of the world. His work on earth was to be the redemption not only of men, but also of the earth, and even of the cosmos itself.

The time and trouble God expended on the world shows clearly that the world is of indestructible worth. That God should twice have come into the world, is a guarantee to us of its unending value. Its right to exist is based on its value to him. The world is worthy of existence.

Yet because the universe bears the stamp of the divine, it can be a fatal temptation to man. The glory of the world leads him to expect from it what only God can give. When man tried to live a godless life in self-glory, he turned to the things of the world as though they were God, to share their glory. Thus he accomplished his revolution against God in and with the world, and the world was drawn into his flight from God. When he set himself free from God, he also in a sense divorced the world from God. Thus man's decision was of great significance for the world. To the world divorce from God meant distortion. In fleeing from God and trying to escape his sovereignty, man submitted himself to the rule of the devil, and brought the world under this same rule. This was possible because his relationship with the world was many-sided and intimate, and because through this relationship he was the lord of creation. The world had to serve him: he used its service in breathing, eating and drinking. In letting it serve him, and thereby honouring what God had laid down for it, he preserved the order of things. Hence his actions are of decisive importance for creation: they are of pan-cosmic significance. Even sin has this importance.

The rule of the devil brings ruin to man and the world: as the bringer of chaos, he digs the grave of the right order of the universe. When the world was given up to his rule, it was surrendered to futility. And so through the devil, the destroyer of the world, who confuses everything, a new and fatal state of affairs arose.

As we saw earlier, man, through his rebellion against God, has subjected himself to death. The futility to which the world has been surrendered is a part of man's submission to death. By this we do not, of course, mean to say that death did not rule on earth before the sin of man—that the plants, for instance, did not wither, nor animals die. It would be fantastic to think of the world before sin as a world free from death: even before man's sin, the plants served animals for food, and animals ate one another.

So then, mortality did not enter the world through the sin of man, but rather, through sin mortality has become a sting, a torment, the agony of meaninglessness. Premature and senseless decay show the chaotic state of the world.

The effect of the divorce of the world from God through human sin should therefore be understood thus:

Without human sin the world would be a parable of the eternal life. Everywhere man would be reminded of that fulness of life which God intended for him. He would receive from the world what he needed for his earthly life and then, satiated with life, he would be given life in its final form through a divine transformation.

But now the world, perverted by human sin, is on every level a parable of human mortality. Nothing reminds man of the immortal, eternal life. It is a mirror of his own mortality, and Death is an ever-present reflexion of himself, hung before the man who lives in the world. When he sees it, his inadequacy is brought home to him—he is reminded that he is himself consecrated to death. It reflects the image of one marked by death. The world, then, offers him no support for his hope of everlasting life—which, therefore, cannot have been kindled by the world. Indeed, the universal manifestation of death enters a constant protest against his hope of an indestructible life. Anyone choosing to retain it, must therefore hold it fast against his daily experience of life.

As the world is not a parable of eternal life, it certainly cannot impart eternal life. It serves mortal life and passing works of temporary duration. Even the most permanent thing is irremediably stricken with mortality. Death was history's first Great Power, and nothing or no one on earth can contest its primacy. There is no power on earth which can avert the curse of mortality.

The new state of things brought into the world by sin was therefore altered by God himself in another visit to the world. The Incarnation of the *Logos* of God meant that Christ, whilst accepting human destiny, also took on himself the destiny of this world. In his death, he took on himself the law of temporality which binds the whole universe and by doing so he on the one hand confirmed the law of mortality for ever. There is no hope that the world will ever escape from its condemnation to mortality, for it stands under the sign of the cross, the sign of the death in this world of God himself. But on the other hand, through the death of Christ there was brought into being a mode of life completely new and hitherto unknown to earthly matter. It was manifested in the transfigured body of Christ. In the resurrection that physical matter which until then had been exclusively the bearer and instrument of death became the herald and instrument of eternal life. Matter was so changed that it was capable of carrying within itself the energies of the divine life, and allowing them to shine through it. And so the body of the risen Christ participated in a completely new way in the indestructible life and fulness of the being of God. What was done in the flesh of Christ is of significance for the whole of creation, just as the death of sinful man was important for the whole of creation. The risen Christ was the first-born not only of men, but also of the universe. The whole universe is on the way to that condition which was seen in the glorified Christ, to a state of glorification. In the glorification, the whole creation will be given immortality. This will be done through the brilliance and fire of God himself shining and glowing through the cosmos.

We call this future state of the world the new heaven and the new earth. It will not come into being within the human time-scale, within development of the cosmos comprehensible to and explainable by science, but rather in the age beyond time and the cosmos. The way the world will have to travel to reach its final condition is that of destruction—of the complete collapse of its present mode of existence and being.

The promise of such a future state for the world throws new light on the ultimate meaning of God's approbation of the world. That the world is of value is shown very clearly in the fact that God will give the world a new form when he enters it for the third and last time.

Thus we see the whole course of the world suspended between the death and resurrection of Christ on the one hand, and its own complete collapse and total transfiguration to its indestructible form on the other.

The containment of the universe between two such fundamental events gives it a definite character, the beginning and end of which can be expressed in the two words, death and rebirth, or decay and re-creation. These concepts describe not only the new beginning made by Christ and the last end, but the whole course of the world's history. And they describe, too, man's relationship, especially the believer's relationship, to the world and his own duty in the world. The Christian attitude to the world is defined both by the sign of the cross, and hence of death, and by the ultimate form to be attained by the world.

In the sacraments Christ himself instituted models which show the double nature of everything happening in the world before the last times. The sacraments are signs both of death and of re-creation, for in them both the death and resurrection of Christ are operative. In them, too, both the complete collapse of the world and the final form to be assumed by the cosmos are anticipated. They re-echo the death and resurrection of Christ and, at the same time, herald the end of the world and its glorification. In the sacraments the power of the death of Christ is made present in such a way that it can exert an effect on man, giving a death-blow to his earthly, sinful, mortal life, his 'life according to the flesh' as St. Paul so often called it. In this death-blow we may also see the final collapse of the world already at work. Just as in them the death of Christ is made operative in a wider field, so too in them the end of the world is foreshadowed within time. But also operative in the sacraments is the power of the resurrection of Christ. The seed of the glorified life of Christ is sown in those who receive the sacraments, so that St. Paul could say of them that they are transplanted into heaven. Just as the resurrection of Christ acts on the present from the past, so the coming transformation of the world is operative in the present.

Past and future operate, however, not only in those who receive the sacraments: they reveal their potency even in the sacramental signs themselves. For the sacramental signs are so deeply marked both with the death of Christ and the end of the world, that they lose their merely natural mode of being. This is most clear in the case of the bread and wine of the Eucharist. The substance of the bread and wine—that is, what makes bread of bread and wine of wine, that inner nature, because of which bread is bread, not a stone, or a piece of wood, because of which wine is wine, not water or blood—is changed into the substance of the body and blood of Christ, into that essence which makes the body of Christ itself, different from everything else in creation, and the blood no mere worldly fluid, but the pure blood of Christ. The bread and wine, then, undergo a kind of death, if it may be so called. In any case, the terrestrial, the purely natural being of bread and wine passes away. Their place is taken by the substance of the glorified body and blood of Christ.

In this change the efficacy of the death, and the new life won through death, is particularly clear. In the passing away of the natural substance of bread and wine, the transforming power of the death of Christ and the end of the world are powerfully revealed.

213

At the same time, the Eucharistic bread and wine powerfully show forth both the resurrection and glorification from the past, and the new creation from the future. Thus the Eucharist is a thing in which past and future join hands. In the eucharistic acts, the future is anticipated.

The faithful Christian—the man whose eyes have been opened to the mystery of the world by Christ, and thus the man who can see properly—sees in the Eucharist, as through a veil, a reflexion of the ultimate form of the world. In the Eucharist he sees sketched the final form of the life of the cosmos. Thus in the Eucharist there is foreshadowed what the future will bring not only for this or that element in the world, but for the whole universe.

We should not of course, over-emphasize the parabolic nature of the Eucharist: the new creation will not bring about the changing of the world into the body and blood of Christ. The similarity lies in the fact that there will be a change to a glorified mode of existence. The giving of its final form to the world will involve the perfecting of what was begun in the resurrection of Christ.

Within the epoch bounded on the one side by the death and resurrection of Christ, and on the other by the decay and re-creation of the universe, in which past and future are bound together in one by the sacraments, Christ has to complete his task in the world. What then is his task?

First, we must make it clear that God did not create the universe in its ultimate perfection. Rather, he entrusted the perfecting of the world to men, in so far as its perfecting is possible during its temporal existence. God commanded man to shape the earth and to subject it to himself. This double commandment is recorded for us in the first book of Holy Scripture, where we read: 'Increase and multiply, and fill the earth, and subdue it, and rule over the fishes of the sea, and the fowls of the air, and all living creatures that move upon the earth. And God said: Behold I have given you every herb bearing seed upon the earth, and all trees that have within themselves seed of their own kind, to be your meat' (Gen. 1, 28 f).

These words from Genesis imply that man is bound by God himself to earthly tasks, to serve and love the world. If he were to try to avoid serving the world, he would be rebelling against God.

Flight from the world would be flight from God. When in modern times we are called on to 'remain true to the earth' (Nietzsche), there is support for this summons in Holy Writ itself. Our Christianity is not spiritualism. But if this summons comes from a merely human will it has no authority in comparison with a command received by the faithful Christian from the mouth of God himself. Every commandment of man has about it something of the doubtful quality and inconsistency to which everything human is subject. But on the other hand, any command issuing from the will of God is unquestionably valid and binding. Any man who knows that he is bound by God to the service of the earth feels a much stronger obligation than anyone whose whole faith is in the world.

God gave this command before sin came into the world. The trouble man takes in the world—his work for civilization, and his political activity (the most efficacious ways of changing the world)— is not therefore, a consequence of sin. To assert that it is would be contrary to Scripture.

But man began to obey God's command only after the Fall. His shaping of the world is therefore carried on in the atmosphere of his sinful nature, which has its part in all his endeavours to shape the world.

Furthermore, in the face of an obligation like this, it is not fitting to wonder whether the passing world is worth the time and trouble. This thought might arise in view of the transitoriness of all earthly things. Not only what man produces in his daily toil, what is won from the day, but even work valuable in civilization, cannot withstand the power of mortality. But the fact that God himself considers it worthwhile to enter the world three times, with great expenditure of time and trouble, is enough to confirm once for all that the world repays human trouble and effort. Any doubt as to whether the world is worthwhile, must yield to the fact that God himself entered the world. Earthly forms will only pass away as far as their temporal existence is concerned: their inner essence is immortal. They will all have their place in their eternal forms in the new heaven and the new earth.

The divine command to serve the world contains the corollary command to man, to make himself, and to remain, lord of the earth.

Man would be disobeying this order if he let the world make itself his lord. When, therefore, the form which man imposes on the earth leads him to become the slave of creative things, he displays not only lack of aptitude, but also disobedience.

Man becomes the slave of things when he becomes a rebel against God. Enslavement to the world, enslavement to technology for example, is a revealing sign that man is in rebellion against God. The rebel against God becomes the slave of the world, of money, of the State, of machines. As recent events have shown, if man will not submit to the sovereignty of God, he has no choice but to live as the slave of the world. He can but tolerate the rule of God if he will not accept the bondage of the world. There is no escape from this dilemma.

But this shows that technology is not in itself destructive or diabolical. It is rather a stage or step in man's endeavour to subdue the world to himself. But whether it operates favourably or unfavourably for him depends on the use he makes of it. Here again, things depend on man being conscious of his own responsibility.

Yet man's tendency to put advances in technology at the service of hate, rather than at the service of love, cannot be denied. Human morality, and human love, have not advanced as quickly as scientific knowledge and its expression in technology. Intellect has cut itself free from the heart, and has run on ahead so that it has become irresponsible. Destructive as the headless heart may be, it has not the same opportunities for destruction as the heartless intellect. It is not man's duty to limit or deny technology, but to bring it under the charge of love.

This task is made much more difficult by the fact that, on account of man's yearning for power, technical achievements are a great temptation to him. He is tempted to use them in gaining and in protecting power, without reference to standards of morality. Even the fulfilment of his divine task of ruling the world through forms of technology quite legitimate in themselves, presents man with the danger of falling victim to an atheistic search for personal autonomy. Indeed, the further he advances in technology, the deeper he falls into the mistake of thinking that he can help himself without the help of God. Hence every advance in technology demands that man become yet more responsible.

In the enslavement of him who rebels against God, who demands to rule himself, and therefore lives under the tyranny of things, there is advanced that enslavement of man to the world which he himself brought about by his first sin, by his first attempt, that is, to lead an autonomous life, free from God. The world avenges itself, as it were, on man, for God entrusted man with his creation, leaving it to him to form and shape it, and when he does not fulfil this commandment, and uses what was entrusted to him as though it were his own possession, the world turns on him.

From this it is clearly shown how the tasks which God has laid on man in this world should be performed. The basic prerequisite is that he should recognize God as the Lord of the world: that he subject all his endeavours in the world to the overlordship of God the Creator. Unreserved recognition of God's position as Lord of the world, we call adoration. It should be man's first concern in the process of shaping the world.

The worship of God is not the honouring of a despot, but the giving of honour to love in person. It must, therefore, itself include love. Worshipping love, and hence loving God, is the basis on which, if it is to be profitably done, man must apply himself to the world and serve it.

Homo faber, working man, must at the same time be *homo orans et amans*, if his attempts to shape the world are not to be more destructive than constructive.

Such an attitude requires the overcoming of man's lust for power and human hate. That is possible only for those who are willing to share in the cross of Golgotha. Only where the cross is set up, is the world really advanced. Without the cross, there is only pseudo-progress, the illusive nature of which is evidenced time and again by history. At first sight it may appear that the attitude of worshipping love, and loving worship, is of but little importance for the shaping of the world—indeed, that such attitudes would be alien to the world and to life. But in fact it is this attitude which determines whether man's service of the world is constructive or destructive, fruitful or negative. Those who hate, or seek power, use the things of the world as instruments for their hatred and love of power, and thereby misuse them. They use them to satisfy their own egos, seeing in them welcome aids to the annihilation of those whom they hate or who stand in the way of their drive for power. In their hands they are instruments of annihilation. Using created things, they bring chaos and death to the world.

On the other hand, in the hands of those who love, of those who feel bound unreservedly to love through the worship of God, the things of this world are the instruments of life. In their hands, the things of this world are means of giving life to others, and as a consequence they are profitable and beneficial.

We can look at this from yet another point of view. Whatever man does, he does to, and with, the things of this world. He cannot do any purely spiritual act. He must bring the things of this world even into his spiritual activities. In his hate and his pursuit of lies, man takes the things of this world into the movement by which he himself moves away from God. But just as remoteness from God means perdition for man, so it also means loss for the things of this world. Destruction rules the world governed by the hatred and self-seeking of man. On the other hand, if man puts himself on the way to God in love, he takes with him the world in which he lives. To turn towards God is to turn towards order, and just as in moving towards God man becomes a partaker of salvation, so also in moving towards God, this world is healed. So then, order and well-being rule in a world governed by the love of God. Man can only fulfil his duty of serving the world, if he performs his service to the world in an attitude of adoring love towards God. If he rebels against God, his rebellion is an action which affects not only his relationship to God, but goes beyond this and has an effect on the world. Refusal to worship involves destroying the world. Every individual human being fulfils his responsibility towards the world by filling with his love that portion of the world which is entrusted to him, over which he has control, in which he can act. For by this means—but in a mysterious way—that piece of the world over which he has sovereignty is led back to God, and thus shares in salvation.

In so doing, man continues what Christ began, but did not complete during his life on earth. In so acting in the world, man furthers the work of Christ, advancing the sovereignty of God established by Christ on earth. Whatever a believer in Christ accomplishes on earth with respect to the world, is of precursory significance for the world's final condition. Just as on the one hand it advances what Christ began, so on the other it foreshadows what the whole earth will one day be. This is true even of those transitory services which man performs, as long as they are performed in love. Such service of the world means devotion to the world, and, at the same time, renunciation of it: devotion at a distance; distance in devotion.

Whoever so serves the world, in distant love for it, is safe from the temptation to see in the world the ultimate and highest good. He cannot confuse the world with God. He does not give the world the honour that should be God's. He does not deify the world, earthly power, earthly pleasure or earthly possessions. He does not fall into the new polytheism. He sees shining through the world, as through a window, the ultimate and highest good, the being of God, and this alone he worships. He comes to that place whither the human heart feels itself continually drawn in worship.

A relationship such as this to the world, in which man sees the world as the penultimate reality, does not lead to indifference to the world. Those who believe in God will, rather, take the world seriously as part of God's creation. He can love it more intensively than can the believer in the world, because he loves it with the almighty power of the divine love, whilst the believer in the world loves it merely with the power of earthly love. He therefore handles the things of this world carefully and lovingly. But he does not, of course, treat it as seriously as does the believer in the world. He does not treat it as though it were the last reality. To do so would seem to him to show a misguided earnestness and a pitiful foolishness. The believer in God is therefore protected in his devotion to the world, both from Buddhist contempt for the things of earth, and from their deification in our own age.

Although the Christian is prepared to abandon the world because he does not see it as the ultimate reality, yet his attitude is essentially different from that taken by the Buddhist. The Buddhist flies from it because he sees it as something not worthy of love, but as something which can only be an obstacle to his salvation. The Christian, on the other hand, stands apart from the world, but loves it. He does not confuse it with God, nor does he fall into the godless belief that blessedness is to be found in the world. But nevertheless he gives it his love from a distance because, for him, it is an expression of the love of God himself. He does not fall into the error of that false piety which scorns the world.

The love of God is his standard for the loves he gives the world, and he is therefore prepared to relinquish the things he loves, if God takes them out of his hands. Because he loves things, he experiences pain in surrendering them, but he is ready to sacrifice the things of the world when God requires it. His love for the world is based on his hopes regarding the future form the world will take. He knows that the world is full of pain, but he is filled with joy, for he knows that its pains are the birth-pangs of a new and splendid universe. He prays that it may soon receive its glorious form, may soon be clothed in it: 'The form of this world passes away, and the glory of the Lord will be revealed'.

Sometimes a believer will be so convinced of the precursory and penultimate character of the world, that he will withdraw wholly from it, in order to embrace the glory of God, and the world's ultimate form, in a physical way, in the Religious life. Such a way of life is born, not of rejection, but of strong approbation of the world. Those who so live, embrace the world with their love in order to bring it to God. By so doing they make their contribution towards the full establishment of the rule of God in the world, towards the world's glorification, and hence towards the post-historical mode of the creation. But at the same time, they also do something for it in the form it has in history, for the more protection the world has against the powers of destruction, the nearer it is to God. Those who love are saviours.

Because Christ's faithful see the world as a created thing, and because they acknowledge its connexion with Christ, they make it the purpose of their service of the world to let God and Christ shine forth in it. In all their endeavours to shape the world, they seek to make it a window on the lordship of God. This involves taking pains on behalf of the world, and the things in it which God has made, endeavouring to realize its inner purpose, and revealing it in their work in it. It is, therefore, their task to perceive the relationship between the things of the world and Christ, and to embody it in their work.

By doing so, they give the world their own likeness, for their likeness is an image of God. Their attempts to serve the world also reveal the relationship of created things to mankind. It is because man gives the world his own form that it seems familiar and friendly to him. In it he finds an echo of himself. Thus for example, the place in which he lives is much more to him than a mere shelter: it is rather an expression of his personality and a place of safety. Gradually, as he shapes it, the whole world becomes man's home. But this end is attainable only if the endeavours he makes to shape it to himself also serve to establish the image of God and Christ—and thus of love and truth—in it.

But if on the other hand, the shape he gives the world hides the characteristics of God and Christ, of truth and love, if he turns it to the service of hate and self-love, it becomes for him an insecure and alien place. In a world where God cannot live, man cannot live either. For where God is not to be found there is no real place for man. Thus, if the dwellings of men are destroyed, this is a sign of a state of things in creation in which man has twisted to his own purposes that which God has entrusted to him.

There is still one question to be considered: are there any special forms of social, cultural, economic or political life which the believer in Christ should promote if he would shape the world in accordance with the pattern of worshipping love? In other words, are there certain forms of which we can say that they, and only they, reflect the Christian revelation? The answer to this question is no. It can, of course, be said that there are certain ways of life which definitely contradict the mandate given by God to man. Among these are those forms of civilization in the widest sense, in which no place is given to the dignity of man, which destroy human freedom, and in which man can live only as a machine, or as a cog in a machine—those forms which make humanity an ant-heap. Such forms leave no room for human dignity because they refuse a place to God, the guarantor of human worth. Hence it can be said of many forms of civilization that they contradict the true form of the world.

But on the other hand, it is not true to say that there are particular forms of life in which the essence of Christianity is creatively revealed in an unequivocal way. There is no social, economic or political order, there is no cultural order, of which we can say that it is the Christian social order, or the Christian culture, as we can say of certain cultures that they are Greek or Roman. The reason for this lies in the fact that Christianity is not an institution for the furtherance of a particular culture, but was instituted for the establishment of the rule of God, and through this, the salvation of men.

How the world should be shaped so that the rule of God may be most effectively shown forth in it, and man's salvation, dignity and power best be guaranteed through the establishment in it of God's rule, is a problem left for man to solve. Our judgement on this question must depend on our estimate of actual natural conditions. It is therefore subject to human fallibility, and hence it may happen that differences will appear, even among those who are working earnestly for the establishment of the rule of God and for human salvation. They may differ about the best form for the world, the best form for the state, or the best economic or social orders. Indeed, they may have completely contrary opinions.

It may also happen that the form which in any given order, based on prevailing conditions, has been of service in the advancement of the rule of God, and therefore of human salvation, will, because of a change of conditions, become an obstacle to the rule of God and the salvation of man. The day comes when things which were once of great value become obsolete. It may prove impossible for those who have borne the weight of, and guarded the earlier order, to understand this, for their old order seems to them to have been tried and proven, whereas, the new order growing out of it may still be very far from having been tested. But such tensions as these can be fruitful if those who experience them are moved only by concern to advance truth and love.

It would be fatal to identify any given form of civilization, or of social, economic or political life with Christianity, and to wish, therefore, to preserve it beyond its natural life-span by an appeal to Christianity. No cultural endeavour can be more than an attempt to promote the rule of God and the salvation of men in this world, or, rather an effort at shaping the world so that it may become an expression of the rule of God, and an instrument of the salvation of man.

Human endeavours can never be anything but attempts and beginnings. The real, final form of the world cannot be achieved during the course of its present life. Yet it will one day come. Christ's promise makes the believer certain of this. The final form of the world will, however, be given it only in the post-cosmic period, yet every attempt to shape the world economically, politically, artistically, or scientifically, is one step taken on the way to its final form. But the final form itself can only be given it by God, in an act transforming the world.

Because any earthly attempt to shape the world can only be a first step, every form man gives the world and life in the world, is condemned to death. Even the most permanent earthly works are branded with symbols of mortality. The most fundamental reason for this is that everything in the universe is subject both to the active power of the cross, which, reaching from the past, lays holds on the things of the earth to leave its mark of death on them, and also to the power of the future, from which the end of all things reaches into the present, drawing everything into its whirlpool. Thus, there can be no everlasting work for civilization and nothing in the world lasts for ever.

The question then arises as to whether in this situation man is not bound to fall victim to despair. But great as the temptation may be for every man, he who falls victim to it rebels against the commandment of God. It is the responsibility of the believer in Christ to see that the world and life, economy, society, state, culture, art and science have the best form possible, and that the countenance of Christ, and not the mask of Satan, shines forth in every sphere of man's activity. He must endure the strain of having to exert all his powers in works which are consecrated to destruction. He will find himself able to do so if he turns his gaze on the creative power of God, which is ever capable of renewing the earth and the peoples of it, and which is primarily directed to bringing about the world's ultimate future.

Despite his constant experience of decay, and the continual threat and danger to all his work, he is saved from despair by the knowledge that the development of human history is not subject, as organisms are, to unalterable laws, and that whatever he does will one day attain its final perfection. He trusts God's promise that nothing of value will be completely lost. Everything done in human history will be given a new form by God in the new heaven and the new earth. Indeed, the forms of the new heaven and the new earth depend partly on the endeavours the individual makes to shape the world. All the pain and love which man expends on the world have their effect in the kingdom of God. Their effect is twofold: direct and indirect, indirect in that through love, the rule of love is advanced, and direct because everything of objective worth will be given by God a new form, hitherto unknown to us. Its earthly decay is the way it must take to its changed and eternal existence in the Kingdom of God, which will be perfected after the passing of the world. What Thompson made God say to the man who fled from him, is true of all human activities:

> All which I took from thee I did but take,
> Not for thy harm,
> But just that thou might'st seek it in My arms.
> All which thy child's mistake
> Fancies as lost, I have stored for thee at home:
> Rise, clasp My hand and come!

Thus, he can look calmly on the world's rubble-heaps and will not become a Nihilist because of them. Everything that he does is illuminated by the glow of the future. In all his cultural accomplishments he signalizes an indestructible future. Whatever he does has meaning, has purpose for the final outcome of the life of the earth. In his fleeting work, subject irremediably to ephemerality, he foretells the world's future form, the form in which the world will no longer be subject to mortality. In all his work done in pain and love, man sets forth the sign of things to come. The night of mortality, in which all the works he can do are but temporary, is therefore made bright for him with the immortal light of the promised things to come. Everything he does is, in its inmost significance, immortal.

CHAPTER ELEVEN

CHRISTIANITY AND THE CHURCH

We have seen that the heart of Christianity is Christ: everything else is grouped around this central point. The life and work of Christ were the revelation of the love of God. Christ's task is the establishment of the rule of God, of truth and love, of the kingdom of God. It is through this that man gains salvation. The goal is a new heaven and a new earth. The means are words and signs. The way is death. We can therefore say that heart, purpose, goal, object and way are all the glorified Christ.

When he had performed his work in the world, Christ left it again, for such, as Hölderlin says, was what was demanded of him by 'the spirit and ripening time'. But at the time of his departure, his work was not completed. He had, rather, only made a start, although, of course, it was a start different from all other beginnings, a start containing within itself imperishable power for the effecting of the ultimate end. The task which Christ received from the Father will be completed when the whole world is changed to the likeness of the glorified Christ. The way to this is Christ's way: the way of the cross and death. The means to it are the means he himself used: those of speech and signs.

The words Christ spoke during his life shall never fall silent. The signs he established shall never vanish away. For in them, the rule of God is advanced towards its final form, and through them, the redemption of mankind and the universe is effected. Christ was concerned to see that the words of love should be spoken for ever, and that the signs of love should be displayed for ever throughout the whole of history. He empowered not individuals but a society to speak them and set them forth, and commissioned it to spread his words and signs abroad. It is the Church's task to preserve the words and signs, the work of Christ in every generation between his ascension and his coming again, to explain them and make them comprehensible. Its task is one of representation, re-presentation.

Christ concerned himself with the formation of this society throughout the whole of his life. But certain of his actions during his life are especially indicative of his concern, from the outset, to build a society to carry on his work through the ages. Such acts were the vocation of certain men to discipleship, the selection of the Twelve, the mission of the Apostles, the giving of special powers to the Apostle Peter, and above all the institution of the eucharistic sacrificial meal. The Church is built on the foundations of Christ and the Apostles. The Apostles preached what they had heard from Christ and understood in the Holy Ghost. What they preached was the fulness of revelation. Their preaching was done in words and in writing. They were the mediators, as it were, of those things which the heavenly Father wanted to give men through Christ. They saw the revelation from within. Through what they said and what they wrote, they confided to coming generations what must be evidence until the end of the ages. The Church transmits what it received from the Apostles from generation to generation. It cannot abandon its apostolic foundation without surrendering its essential nature. It can never reform apostolic teaching: it can only make it comprehensible. If it were to do more, it would stop being what Christ meant it to be when he instituted it: the guardian and witness of his revelation.

The community Christ established is different from every other community. It has no biological foundation. It is not based on cultural interests. It does not stem from the powers and needs of the earth. It is, rather, a foundation from heaven. The Spirit which informs it and gives it life is not a human spirit, but the Holy Ghost. Christ made him his invisible representative in the community he established. From that day forward, the Holy Ghost, the stream of love flowing between the Father and the Son, has poured forth from the body of the glorified Christ into the community of those who believe in Christ. The Holy Ghost is the heart and soul of the community founded by Christ. It is he who makes the community of believers what it is, just as man is confirmed in his nature by his soul. He is the heavenly atmosphere in which the community of the faithful breathes.

In the Holy Ghost, Christ himself remains for ever present in the community of his disciples, as he promised he would do when he took leave of the world. At that time, he told his disciples he would come again: he came in the resurrection and will come in power and glory at the end of the world. But in the meantime, he comes continually to his own through the Holy Ghost. Thus in the Holy Ghost he remains with the Church until the consummation of the ages.

In the Holy Ghost, he is united in the closest intimacy with the community of those who are true to him, for the Holy Ghost, the eternal stream of love between the Father and the Son, is an omnipotent bond of love between Christ and the community at one with him. This is why Paul could call the Church the body of Christ. The Church is the community of those men united by Christ in the Holy Ghost.

The community given life by the Holy Ghost and ruled by him, reveals the fact that it is different from every terrestrial community even in its name. For the Greek word *ekklesia* means, in terrestrial usage, the assembly of the people, the assembly of the citizens summoned and called into being by the herald. But in Christian usage the word means the people called out and gathered together from all the world, from all the nations, peoples and tongues, by God through Christ. The summons comes from God: it comes from heaven, not from earth. It is God who in free and graceful condescension calls and summons men to himself. His call is not empty sound, but has power and life. It is an act of God, through which men are brought out of their sinful decadence into the life of God. The Church is the heir and successor to the Old Testament people of God. We have said what most needs to be said about this. The Old Testament people of God were not willing to take the step forward in revelation represented by Christ; they wanted to persevere in their old ways. By so doing, they proved themselves an instrument hereafter useless to God in the establishment of his rule. God, who can make children of Abraham from stones, therefore brought into being through Christ a new people of God which took over the task which had hitherto bound the

Old Testament people of God; namely, that of serving God as an instrument for the establishment of his sovereignty in the new age inaugurated by Christ, and in the ways established and defined by Christ. Just as in having to make present the past, and the work and words of Christ, the people of God has a duty of representation in the horizontal plane, so also it has a task of re-presentation in the vertical plane, in that it has to reveal God in his self-revelation and glory. Because it has this task of re-presentation, there is no contradiction in her appearing outwardly great, provided that she does not detach herself from her duty, which is to reveal God, not men. The glory of God shows its might much more powerfully in pervading creation and shining forth in it, than it would do in stopping short on the edge of creation. The glory of creation is a revelation of the *gloria Dei* because it can exist only through God's glory and from it.

As God's instrument, the New Testament people of God is his representative with plenary powers. It is God's supreme ambassador in history. It is therefore authorized and indeed bound to exercise sovereignty in the name of God. Christ has established definite organs for this task: the Pope and the bishops are officials instituted among the people of God, by God himself.

On account of its inner relationship with Christ, the people of God is also the body of Christ. Christ is the head, and the people belonging to him are his members.

If the Holy Ghost is the soul and heart of the Church, then the innermost being of the Church is love. It is therefore a community of love, for the Holy Ghost is the revelation of love within the divine being itself. He is the breath of love which the Father breathes to the Son and the Son to the Father. He is the seal of that love which encompasses both the Father and the Son. Love is therefore the deepest mystery of the Church. The Church is a federation of love. It is not a federation made by men in which those connected with one another chance to find themselves involved, but a community made and governed by the love of God. His love is the soul, law, and fundamental nature of the Church, which is an expression of that ardour which unites the Father and the Son, and is itself a turning towards the Father and the Son.

This love is not of that kind which turns in on itself and takes things into its own possession, but of that which gives and sacrifices itself. The love of God proves itself to be what it is, by making us partakers of his glory. This will be easier to understand if we remember that the love of God is shown forth in the life and death of the Son sacrificed on the cross, and that the Holy Ghost is present in the Church as the invisible representative of the incarnate Son of God.

If the innermost being of the Church is love, its expressions of its being—its actions—must be done in love. Thus every act which is an expression of this love is in conformity with the Church, and any act which is not in keeping with it, contradicts the inner being of the Church. Lust for power and tyranny, self-love and pride, contradict the innermost nature of the Church. The only actions in keeping with the Church are those to which the members of the Church are moved by love, those acts of its members which are governed and moved by personal love, in which they give themselves in selfless devotion to the community and to those who belong to it. The more fully they devote themselves to acts of love inspired by the Holy Ghost, the more perfectly they realize the nature of the Church by their actions. Thus the inner being of the Church is the more perfectly expressed in their lives.

From what we have said so far, it is clear that the only possible concrete form of Christianity is the Church, for Christ lives and works in the community of the Church and through it alone. He does indeed lay his hand on men who do not belong to the Church— but he lays his hand on them through it. Thus the only community of men of which the heart is Christ is the Church. Only if we take the word Christianity in a vague and indefinite sense can we call institutions outside the Church Christian. They are so, in so far as they are led in some way by the spirit of Christ. A man becomes a Christian when he is accepted into the community of the Church, into the community of Christ, which is based on the Lord's life, and depends for its life on the operation of the Holy Spirit sent by him.

Admittance into the Church is effected in baptism. Only through baptism can a man become a member of the community which gives concrete form to the life of Christianity. Conversely, all the baptized belong to it, although their titles and effectiveness may differ. Speaking very generally, every baptized person who accepts the Lord's work in its entirety belongs to the Church.

This would seem to be the teaching of the much debated section of the encyclical *Mystici Corporis Christi* on membership of the Church. In the loosest sense anyone belongs to the Church who gives basic approval to Christ, although he may select certain parts from the fulness of his life and work and ignore or reject others.

We might, with Mörsdorf, clarify the different modes of belonging to the Church by making a differentiation between ontological and functional membership. All the baptized are ontological members, but only those who belong to the group which recognizes all Christ's revelation, also possess functional membership. The opportunity to work effectively in the Church is denied the others.

It is also clear that Christianity can only exist in the form of a Church. If all the baptized form a community in Christ, there is not and cannot be more than one Church, neither with the same, nor different, bases of authority. If, despite this, we speak of Christian Churches, we are compelled to do so in order to describe a state of affairs which exists on other grounds than that of the revelation of Christ. Groups have come into being within the one Church which are opposed and even hostile to one another. The situation is comparable to that in a family with many children, where mutually hostile groups may be formed, some of which support the father, whilst others cut themselves loose from him. They do not cease to belong to the family even if they do not recognize that they have their father's characteristics and have inherited his blood. They cannot free themselves from their inheritance. Yet they do not take part fully in the life of the family. In just the same way, all the baptized belong to the family of the brethren and sistren of Christ, even if they are separated from the main body of the community outwardly expressed in the bishops and the papacy, and do not take part in the life of the community. Catholic Canon Law recognizes the fact that all the baptized belong to the one Church of Christ, for in principle it is binding on all the baptized in the West.

Secession from the Church, as we have said, does not produce separate bodies with the same, or with different, commissions. Separation from the father of the family is always unjustified and destructive of the true order of things, even if his lack of love, his injustice, or his lack of care for the children is responsible for their leaving him. (To say this is not to judge the guilt or innocence of those who cut themselves off. Guilty or not, they are objectively in the wrong). But the community is not destroyed, although it may be unbalanced or distorted. When we speak of several churches we are demonstrating the fact of this objective disorder. We are recognizing a state of affairs which is anomalous. If anyone were to forget the irregular nature of this state of affairs and maintain that it was justified, he would, in his acceptance of this division, be in conflict with the revelation, which was of one Church.

But there is no way of avoiding talking about more than one Christian Church, when we are speaking of the attitude of Christians to the things of the world: to the State, culture, science or art. For then we are not speaking of the one body of the faithful united in baptism, the basis of whose union is Christ, but of groups with different organizations, and represented by individuals who are members of them. Talk of different confessions and Christian Churches is therefore based on the considerations and needs of the world and politics rather than on those of theology. Fundamentally and in fact, Christianity lives as a single Church, the community of the baptized.

There is, then, not several Churches, but one Church. The single Church is not a body made up of different or complementary component churches. It is a unified whole, and is built up of members co-ordinate with one another. The multiplicity and diversity of the parts, and the unity of their co-ordination are aspects of the whole. Unity and multiplicity support one another and depend on one another. The Church is unity in diversity, and multiplicity in unity. Its unity is both visible and invisible.

All those who belong to the people of God have the task of carrying on the Lord's work down the ages, and furthering the sovereignty of God which he established, until, through the intervention of God himself, it reaches its perfection. Every individual is therefore responsible for seeing that this, the Church's chief task in time, is accomplished, and that by this means the rule of truth and love is spread further afield. It is the duty of everyone to make his contribution to this. Everyone's contribution is different, and is his alone. No one is dispensable, no one superfluous. In the last resort it is Christ—or, rather, the Father in heaven himself—who advances his sovereignty, the rule of love, through the community of those who belong to the Church. They are therefore the instruments, the servants of God. They share in Christ's teaching work, and his priestly acts.

The task which is to be fulfilled is of significance for the whole of human history and for the whole cosmos, for through the establishment and consolidation of the sovereignty of God, God's creation will be brought back to him and so saved. The establishment of the rule of love meant that there had come into being a realm of safety, where alone mankind can truly live. Just as remoteness from God occasions perdition and destruction, so closeness to God means salvation and redemption. Those who set forward love and truth in the world bring the world a step nearer that state in which alone security and salvation are to be found. Thus God's servants are the saviours of the world. All this shows the weight of the responsibility which lies on every member of the community of Christ, and shows, too, that even the most limited contribution to the advance of truth and love is of universal consequence. Indeed, whoever serves truth and love installs in creation forces which will direct things to come. Every generation can be either a help or a burden to the future. Even those who have been taken out of time, and have come to final perfection—the Saints—make an essential contribution to the fulfilment of the Church's task. They accomplish it through their prayers and their love. For through their prayers and love they remain in communion with the Church militant, and so further the advance of the sovereignty of God.

In this, a special rôle is played by Mary. Not only was she the door through which the Son of God entered human history: she is now the door which admits to grace. Indeed, in her everything has reached that final consummation to which the risen Christ has opened the way for all creation: she has already been given physical glorification. Thus, in her we can see the form that will be attained by those who are touched by the dynamic of the risen Christ.

The weight of the Church's task means that the faithful are kept in a state of continual activity. They can never be satisfied with the present state of the world. They can never fall victim to *amor fati* love of things as they are. They can therefore never be self-satisfied with regard to things as they are. For they are driven on by their task of advancing truth and love, which is God, and driving back the powers of chaos, the powers of hate and of lies. They see how much the actual condition of the world differs from that true character which it should possess. They are therefore fully aware that 'enough is not enough . . . enough does not and can never suffice'. But they are driven on, not by a fearful haste, but by that unrest which liberates man from slackness and sloth. They do not need to submerge themselves in business, for they are certain of final success. They know that they are the instruments of God, who will, beyond any doubt, carry out his design despite all apparent set-backs. Violently as they are driven on by this unrest, yet they do not fall into blind activity. Their aim is not to do things for the sake of doing things, but to do only those things which will be of service to truth and love. They do not live by the principle that something should be done rather than nothing at all, but are ruled by the consideration that only right may be done.

It is their confidence in the final success of their efforts—which is guaranteed by God, which makes them able to bear the knowledge that they make only slow progress in their task. Despite this, they do not fall into pessimism or despair. They can bear the knowledge that the Church seems to fail continually, and that the task of advancing truth and love in the world must be begun again by every generation because they know that truth and love cannot be inherited from one generation to the next, like some factor in biological life. Every generation is, rather, called on to decide anew for truth and against lies, for love and against hate. Hence no generation finds the task easier than the last: the work must always be begun afresh.

Big and important as the task of Christians is, the aids at their disposal are limited. They cannot use power to help them, as do the powers of this world in establishing and advancing their sovereignty. The community of Christ has at its disposal in its great and crucial task, only what Christ had at hand: words and signs, the words of witnesses, and the signs of the Sacraments and of life.

The faithful are called to bear witness to Christ throughout the centuries, and by so doing, to bear witness to the truth and love manifested in him, before a world beset by lies and hatred. This witness they bear in the face of a world which resists Christ.

At the same time, they bear witness to Christ among themselves: children to their parents, and parents to children, the elder to the younger generation. Witness to him is given in every word of love and truth, for every word of truth and love is disturbing to mankind, which is tempted by lying and hatred and subject to the power of untruthfulness and tyranny. In a world of lying and hatred, expressions of love and truth are striking. They are, as it were, an echo from a completely different world, and they therefore make men prick up their ears. They stimulate the question: Where does it come from? They bring love and truth—which is God—to the notice of men. If such words of love and truth were not spoken, God would be completely hidden by lies and hatred, so that men could no longer see him.

Truth and love are also advanced in man's actions, in the example he gives. Deeds of love make God credible. In the world of failure, of torment and torture, the human heart is constantly beset by the questions: Can this world really be the creation of God? Can there be a God, the world being as it is? If there is a God, is he not a cruel tyrant? It is such questions as these which burden belief in God. But the love of God shines as through a window in those men who perform acts of love in their lives, so that his existence again becomes credible. Such acts answer the distressing question as to whether there is a God. If love is made perceptible in the midst of the uproar of hate, the voice of God is made audible in it.

The sacramental signs are excellent evidence for God in the world, and are therefore superb means of promoting the rule of God. In them the acts of Christ, and especially his dying and resurrection, are made present in a mysterious way. In the midst of this world of signs there stands the Eucharist, for in it the death, and in an indirect way, the resurrection of Christ are made present with particular potency. As we saw above, in his death and resurrection Christ established the rule of God once for all, and therefore through the re-presentation of these events, the rule of God is advanced in a particularly effective manner. As to advance the rule of God is to fulfil the most fundamental and profound need in the world, and is of significance for the redemption of the world, the community of Christ celebrates the Eucharist with symbols of joy.

The whole Christian community is responsible for the Eucharistic celebration, through and in which, the whole Church fulfils the task laid upon it. Those who have been ordained have a special task which is theirs alone. In the encyclical about the Church as the Body of Christ, we read on this point:

> For it was the will of Christ the Lord, that the wonderful, priceless union between us and our divine head should be made visible to the faithful in a special way through the eucharistic sacrifice. At that sacrifice priests in fact represent not only the figure of our Saviour, but also the whole mystical body, and the individual faithful. But even so the faithful themselves do offer the unspotted sacrifice, which is made present on the altar by the word of the priest alone; offering it through the hands of this same priest in prayerful communion with him, to the eternal Father, as an acceptable sacrifice of praise and propitiation for the benefit of the whole Church.

The community of those who celebrate the Eucharist enters into the death of Christ, and by so doing, allows the rule of God to burst forth in it with greater intensity; and at the same time, in every eucharistic celebration, it draws the whole of history and the whole cosmos more fully under the rule of God.

A sign of a special kind is that of the sacrament of penance. In it too, the rule of God is advanced in this world, for in it also, the death and resurrection of Christ are operative, as judgement and pardon. In the sacrament of penance, God is, as it were, the holy Lord Justice over sinful man. But his judgement is a judgement of mercy, and his lordship a lordship of love. In penance, anyone who has failed as a member of God's people, and has acted sinfully, as though he did not belong to Christ, but as though he belonged much more to the world, is so changed that he again becomes a living member of the people of God. The sacrament of penance proves that through the merciful power of God man is ever capable of renewal, that he can at any time be released from his godless past to a present in communion with God, and a future of union with God for all eternity.

And of this sign of judgement, too, it can be said that, from one point of view, the whole community of the Church is its minister. In the early Church this found expression in the public nature of the arrangements for penance. Of course, at all times different individuals performed different functions. Those endowed with special priestly ordination have a special and indispensable part to play in it, which we shall look at more closely below.

If the whole community of the Church is an instrument of God for the establishment of his sovereignty through the words of witness and the sign of the sacraments, then the whole community must also be a manifestation of the rule of God in the world. Just as it is responsible for seeing that through its words and actions the rule of God in the world is advanced, so it is also responsible for seeing that in its words and actions the rule of God is made visible in the world, so that it can be seen by those of good will. This responsibility lies on every individual and on the community as a whole. No one can leave it to others.

The community of Christ is a federation of love. Let us go one step further: it is an ordered federation of love, an ordered community. But order involves higher and lower ranks. There is therefore a hierarchy among the members of the Christian community, as such Biblical comparisons as temple, house, nation and body would suggest. The community of Christ is the nation of God: the community of those who are called together out of all the nations of the earth into a new, ordered unity. It is a body, in which the members of the body come together in a single whole, in which each acts according to its nature, and each makes a contribution to the existence and life of the whole body.

The hierarchy which exists in the Church among its individual members was in its essential features ordained by Christ himself, but it is also in part the result of a natural historical development.

Many of the members of the community of Christ are invested with special duties and are given special authorization for them. They therefore also have special obligations, among them the warrant and duty which is given to all—that of establishing the rule of God in this world—and in them this is both strengthened and modified.

What all receive because of their baptism, takes a special form in them. Christ instituted a special process for this: that of ordination. Those who are ordained—that is, those from among the baptized who are consecrated to special duties, and endowed with special powers—have functions to fulfil within the community as a whole which no one else can fulfil. Through their warrant and commission, they serve the good order of the whole. Their special powers are not given them for themselves, but for all. They are unmistakably different from the other members of the community. The special and general priesthoods must not be confused with one another. The special priesthood must not be swallowed up in the second. Those members of the Church who are marked off by a special consecration to the priesthood, possess their powers as members of the community. They are therefore completely dependent on it, on its existence and life. They are, as it were, the supporting framework of the whole building.

The forms in which they exercise their warrant and commission are the same as those through which the community as a whole performs the duty laid on it. They are the words of preaching and the sign of the sacraments. But in their mouths the words of preaching have a different significance from that which they have in the mouths of other members of the Christian community. For those of the baptized who are ordained are bound in every phase of their lives to the utterance of these words. Their whole purpose in life is, essentially, to serve the word and set forth the sign of the sacraments. The other members of the community therefore have to go to them to receive the word and the sign. It is their duty to accept this service.

The words of preaching and the signs of the sacraments are effective because the Holy Ghost (and through him, Christ himself) works in them.

The teaching and actions of those of the baptized who are ordained are the service they perform for the community. But what a service! Its significance is greater than that of any other service which one man can do for another, for their service is done in relation not to the passing life of the earth, but to the only life of importance—to the eternal.

In their service, the Church guarantees that the Scripture is

237

the word of God and interprets it reliably and authoritatively. Without such a guarantee, human uncertainty and arbitrary interpretation would prevail. In their service the Church gives ever clearer expression to the individual parts of the treasury of faith entrusted to her—the Dogmas.

Those who are allotted to this service set before men the glory of God. They are therefore worthy of great honour and distinction. Indeed, there can be no other honour or distinction given within the Church.

Because their service is crucial in salvation and perdition, those who perform it may be tempted to pass sentence regarding the salvation of any particular individual, thus assuming their superiority over him, and falling victim to the lust for power. Christ warned his disciples very emphatically to beware of such temptations as these. He explained to them that it was the custom of the lords of the earth to oppress those they ruled, but that the task of his disciples was to serve men, giving them that service which he himself gave them in his death. In his first Catholic Epistle, St. Peter, too, opposes such temptations with great energy.

Christ himself acts through the words and signs of the Church. Or more precisely: In the words and signs of the community of the Church, the Father in heaven acts through Christ and in the Holy Ghost. This fact gives the words and signs through which the Church advances the kingdom of God in this world a binding force. The obligatory character of love, which in the words and sacramental signs of the Church takes possession of men, is given expression in the Church in the laws and commandments. The rules and regulations we meet with in the Church are in no way contradictory to love. They are, rather, a manifestation of it. They are a result of the fact that the Church is an ordered community. The ruling Church is not therefore something to be contrasted with the loving Church, but rather the whole legal organization, and the whole corpus of the law, as well as the individual regulations and orders, are to be thought of as manifestations of compulsive love at work in the Church. Order is the guardian of love. Jurisdiction and organization are the indispensable vessels of love: without them love would be threatened by anarchy.

As Mörsdorf says, the Church is commissioned and empowered by

God to establish sovereign laws, through which men may be compelled to enter into and remain in the kingdom of God. Their ultimate purpose is the service of salvation and nothing else. When, for instance in the sacrament of penance, the Church, by an act of power, puts sinners out of her community, and then in an act of pardon accepts them back into her community, this whole proceeding is, ultimately, one of brotherly service. The legal Church is not, therefore, something which works against the service of men, but rather, as Pope Pius XII said, it serves them. The office of shepherd may reasonably take its place in the Church beside those of teaching and the priesthood. Just as the teaching and priestly offices are in fact extensions of the teaching and priestly functions of Christ, so too the pastorate is an extension of his kingly dignity.

Thus we see that the particular priesthood serves order in the community of the Church. It is the service of order which is responsible for the fact that there are different levels in the particular priesthood. Among those who were to be endowed with the special priesthood Christ instituted a hierarchy. The Church is a hierarchical community. The steps in the hierarchy have to do with ordination in the Church, and the administration and jursidiction of the Church.

The former of these is concerned with the administration of the sacraments, and hence with partaking of Christ's priestly office; the latter with sharing in Christ's pastorate. The teaching office in the Church fills a middle place. The hierarchy has three stages: Diaconate, Presbyterate and Episcopate.

The power of jurisdiction is given to that stage which includes the papacy and the episcopate. Whilst the bishops in general are the successors of the apostles, and thus every individual bishop shares in the authority of the episcopate as a whole, the Pope is the successor of one particular apostle: St. Peter. The fulness of the jurisdictional power is given to the Pope. He is the bishop of the bishops. But he has no power of ordination transcending that of the episcopate. The power of jurisdiction belongs to the bishop, and the power of ordination is also reserved to him.

Thus, at the summit is the Pope. The papacy has indeed undergone far-reaching development in the course of history. But in essence, it was instituted by Christ himself. The development has concerned the form of the papacy. What the French theologian Sertillanges said of the development of the Church in general, is true of the papacy in particular: 'In the beginning the Church was a single ripe seed, which began to germinate and grow after its own fashion. Seen in this way and from this point of view, it was then already wholly what it is today: just as the chicken and the egg are the same thing, or the oak and the acorn. For out of the one, just as out of the others, there developed conformably with its nature only what could develop from it: namely, what before its development was already present in it.'

Christ inaugurated the papacy. The Holy Ghost he sent works according to the needs of the times in the development of what Christ himself founded. It is with it as with all living things: at the time it first came into the world, the papacy was like a child, which in a few weeks grows more than it grows later in ten years. The fact that a child grows in this way shows that there is in the child a something that we can only describe with the indefinable word life. What is life? No one knows. But we do know one thing: we cannot explain the life of the child by saying that it is provided with everything necessary for growth: the right temperature, good air, a good nurse, food, room to take its first step, and then a wide field in which to jump and play. Life is something quite apart from all this. It is the power to assimilate from embryo on. It is the development of a definite limited seed, which can grow only in the direction inherent in it, and develop in a fixed way, and which already contains within itself everything essential to what it will become. This is the true explanation of life. If Christianity had not contained within itself what was necessary for its life and growth, it would not have grown. God prepared everything beforehand, shaping it according to the ordinary pattern of things, so that there is nothing that can be called miraculous. In a word, divine prescience was at work here. But granted that God did all this, and that history was—profanely speaking—the ideal environment for such a flowering, there still remains the problem of identifying the seed of life in the Church. What sort of power is it that can call a group of fishermen together, and, as Sertillanges said, invest their words with life and superhuman success? It could, of course, only be the personalized power of God, the Holy Ghost, who acts through and in the members of the Church.

The highest pastoral jurisdiction in the Church is given to the Pope. With this office it is given to him to perform the highest service for the community. When the Pope calls himself Servant of the Servants of God (*Servus servorum Dei*), his words are not empty rhetoric, but a statement of the true state of the matter. For those who receive his service, there is an absolute obligation to allow themselves to be subject to him, to accept his service obediently.

The most important expression of the pope's leadership of the Church is papal infallibility. Although it was first stated in its full form by the Church at the Vatican Council in the year 1869, belief in it has existed from the beginning, although for a long time in an undeveloped form. By the infallibility of the Pope we mean that if the Pope testifies to and acknowledges the revelation preached by Christ, and intends to bind the whole Church once for all by his definition of it, he is, through the help of the Holy Ghost promised him, incapable of error, whether it be in establishing the true sense of a fact of faith, or in refuting error. Thus, infallibility does not extend to sermons or other such oral or written publications, or to private semi-official or official writings, although they have a high authority, and, indeed, a strong binding force. But what is included among them, according to the opinions of theologians are those fields of reason and historical knowledge which are so closely connected with revelation that it stands or falls with them.

Infallibility is indeed proper to the Pope in his own person, but he is assured of it, not for his own sake, but for the sake of the community of the Church. In his infallibility is anchored that of the Church, the community itself. In the Pope's confession of the revelation, which binds all believers in Christ, there is accomplished the obedience of the Church to Christ. In his faithful obedience, the whole Church believes and obeys the Lord's words. In his words, therefore, witness is borne to Christ by the Holy Ghost who works through the Church, and the witness of the Holy Ghost that Christ promised is embodied in the infallible words of the Pope. His infallibility, therefore, is not based on human power, gifts or conscience, but on the Holy Ghost. Infallible pronouncements on the faith by the Pope are usually occasioned by an attack on revelation, or some particular truth of it. If the Church as a whole, rather than some particular member of it, is threatened by the anti-Christian self-glorying of the human spirit, and the revelation of God confided to us by Christ is in danger, the whole Church gathers together in the person of the Pope and through him resists the attack and the danger. Such things happen but rarely. We might agree with those theologians who hold that, except for the definition of the dogma of the bodily assumption of our Lady into heaven, no formal infallible decision has been taken since the Council of the Vatican (1869-70), despite the great number of papal pronouncements binding on conscience. If the revelation of God, to which the Church professes through the Pope, is the embodiment of his love, the assent the whole Church gives to it must be a response of love and devotion. When, therefore, the Pope binds men by his decisions, he binds them to submission to the love of God embodied in the revelation, binding them to bow to the truth in person as revealed in Christ—that is, to the reality of God shown us by Christ. The power and right so to commit men is given him by Christ's decree. In his 'utterances of power' Christ himself binds consciences.

The infallibility of the Pope is of great social significance. That there should be in this world of error and uncertainty a place from which truth can be learned with infallible certitude is a special grace of God. If no such opportunity were afforded men, they could not avoid uncertainty and error even on the most final and crucial questions. Papal infallibility is a sure guarantee that, high as the waves of error and uncertainty may rise in the world, there will be one place in it from where we may learn decisively what the truth in its perfection is. Only because the Church itself has a guarantee of its infallibility in the Pope can it take the risk of having dealings with the fallen world. If it had not this guarantee, its dealings with the world would be very dangerous to its certitude and to the fulness of the faith. The faith might be swamped by the ideas of the age. But if, in order to avoid this danger, the Church refused to have dealings with the world of error and falsehood, it could not fulfil its task of kindling in the darkness the light of God, by the help of which alone, mankind is able to make its hard and bitter way through history.

We cannot believe that the Holy Ghost who works through the Church would lead the truth to victory without establishing such an infallible human authority. For just as the invisible power of God is displayed and embodied in visible form in the Church, so too the Holy Spirit's witness to Christ must be embodied and displayed in visible signs, in audible, binding words. If the witness to Christ was not embodied in this binding form in the Church, the Church would become the site of endless, wearing and destructive quarrels, and there would be no guarantee and certainty that the word of God was being rightly understood. It would be subject to the researches and criticism of individuals and the decisive and typical forces in the sphere of faith would not be love and devotion, but scientific experimentation and critical acumen. It is therefore a mercy that God preserves an infallible authority.

On the other hand, the human mind is by no means cramped by this authority, whether in its infallible form or in its binding but not infallible form. The sphere of profane research is still its own. Even theology can move in its sphere conformably with the laws inherent in it. The obligations laid on man by the teaching office of the Church are pointers to the truth. They are obligations to the truth—and to this the experimentalist and research worker is naturally bound. History shows, of course, that they may overstep the mark, but that is the result of human weakness, with which everything on earth is clothed. As the witness of the Holy Ghost cannot float in empty space and must, therefore, be expressed in human words, it is expressed with the weakness of human utterance. But the Holy Ghost, the guardian and protector of the revelation, wards off error from the Church so energetically that the whole Church can never fall away from the pure faith, and the teaching of the whole body of bishops, which is the manifestation of the Church, and the Pope's confession of Christ, which he makes in the name of the whole Church as the visible representative of Christ, can never fall into error. Human weakness is, as it were, the price which must be paid in pain and sorrow if the central truths are to be pronounced and heard in human words. History, as it proceeds, helps to ensure that such weaknesses are continually overcome.

The whole community, which finds its pinnacle and unity in the Pope, is divided into component communities, with the bishops at their head. The bishops are the successors of the apostles. They are appointed by the Holy Spirit to tend the flock of God. They are responsible for seeing, and empowered to see, that the kingdom of God is established, and hence salvation mediated, in one part of the whole Church, in a diocese. They exercise the plenitude of their power in their sharing in the papal fulness of authority. The office of bishop also being an expression of the apostolate and therefore ultimately springing from Christ himself, the bishop is also the representative and microcosm of the diocese. So that he may be so, he possesses a special authority. In accordance with the will of Christ, he is empowered primarily to administer the sacrament of ordination and so, as the spiritual father of the diocese, spread farther afield the stream of the divine life. In so doing, he confers on others of the baptized the inner, ontological power of securing and advancing God's rule in the world by the administration of the sacraments, and so giving God's life to men. The whole body of the bishops represents the Church. It is made a representative of the whole body not by a decision of the will of the Church community as a whole, but by the will of Christ. Hence, the members of a diocese embodied in its bishop will do justice to their membership in the love of Christ, only by submitting themselves to the bishop. This means that they must take their places in the community represented in the bishop.

But the sub-division goes still further, for the office of bishop is divided 'not by tapering off upwards, but by differentiation downwards, in consequence of the coalescence of individual communities in their inner needs in the presbyterate.' It was in the cities that Christianity put down its first roots in the ancient pagan world. From there, it spread out into the country. At first, country dwellers came regularly to the services in the town, and gathered around the bishop to celebrate the Eucharist with him. But as their number grew larger, and as the gospel spread far afield, embracing ever more distant peoples, the need for them to have their own celebrations became ever greater. The bishops therefore sent out assistants, first for individual celebrations, but soon, as the country communities took firmer shape, to stay in them more or less permanently. These assistants had, in so far as they had been ordained and possessed the ability to celebrate the

Eucharist, essentially the same qualification as the bishop who sent them. But their sphere of duty was precisely defined and restricted. In the exercise of the plenitude of their powers, they were subject to, and restricted by, the will of the bishop. In the course of time, after many changes, the parish, with the parish priest at its head, grew out of these beginnings. In the parish and the parish priest, every individual member of the Church sees a concrete expression of the fact that the Church is a community.

The parish priest makes visible, and guarantees the unity of the faithful bound together in a parish. He partakes of the spiritual fatherhood of the bishop, in so far that by his mandate, in union with him and subjection to him, he breaks the bread of teaching and life, in that by preaching and administering the sacraments he advances the kingdom of God in the parish and so effuses salvation. In coming together with one another in the parish, the individual members of the parish are made members of the diocese as a whole, and of the Church which embraces all divisions in her oneness. Separation from the parish, therefore, means separation from the communion of the Church as a whole. Those who belong to a parish are the children of that parish: they are those who, at the font, were born into supernatural life, and who gather around the same sacrificial table to receive the bread prepared and offered by the father of the family—who ultimately, and in a hidden way, is Christ himself, and hence the Father of heaven. The life of the community is inseparable from the house in which the community meets together to celebrate the death of Christ, in which, at the font, new life is brought forth, and in which the word of God is preached. The parish church is therefore the focus of the local community of God, comprised of the parish by virtue of its local incorporation and ecclesiastical administration.

Around it are grouped the houses, the homes of Christians. The whole district belongs to it. Because of this ownership the faithful know that their claim to eternal salvation will be made good. It is the place where they can put into operation their readiness to be sacrificed with Christ, where they can exercise their share in his priesthood. From it they are sent out continually into the world, to shape it according to the spirit of Christ.

Because the church is the place where they meet Christ, in the words of preaching and in the signs of the sacraments, it is indispensable to their salvation, and without it salvation is impossible. At first sight, the claim that the Church alone can give salvation may seem presumptuous and intolerant. But in fact, and in its true sense, it is a mission given to the Church by the saving will of God. The doctrine that only the Church can save is a statement of fact, and is directed against no one in particular. Its principal concern is not to say who is travelling the road to salvation, but to describe the way by which they will reach it. Whoever reaches salvation, reaches it through the Church. For he reaches it through Christ; there is no other way to the Father. But Christ works through the Church, and even those who know nothing of Christ and the Church—and indeed, even those who through no fault of their own reject the Church—can, if they are of good will, share in salvation through Christ. Their position is that of foundlings, who, despite all the perils that face them, remain alive, but do not know whom they are to thank for life. Christ, working in the Church, is therefore the only way to the Father. He who is led through Christ to the Father therefore belongs in a fashion to the community of those who believe in Christ, even if he has not been initiated into it in baptism.

The Church fulfils its task in the circumstances of every age, and hence is necessarily involved in the struggles and tensions, antitheses and contradictions through which history passes. But its place in history is of a special kind, for it is not directly related to the pattern of earthly events, although it is concerned indirectly with them as we saw in the chapter on the relationship between Christianity and the world. It is directly concerned with the regeneration and reformation of human hearts, with freeing them from self-glorification, and leading them to the life of Christ. In the Church, man is called and bound by the love of God. Man's self-glorying and autonomy take up arms against the Church. The man who glories in himself arms himself against the Church just as he arms himself against Christ. He rejects the Church's claims, and feels himself the more justified in his resistance, the less the Church, in her outward weakness and powerlessness, inadequacy and imperfection, can justify her claim to a divine nature. He is scandalized by her, and his rejection may go as far as hate and persecution.

It was hatred of Christ that led to his death. Hatred of his body the Church will continue until she and her members are apparently annihilated. The Church cannot oppose the external power crushing her with external might. From the external point of view she is helpless. Christ prophesied her fate:

Behold, I send you as sheep in the midst of wolves. Be ye therefore wise as serpents and simple as doves. But beware of men. For they will deliver you up in councils and they will scourge you in their synagogues. And you shall be brought before governors and before kings for my sake, for a testimony to them and to the Gentiles. But, when they shall deliver you up, take no thought how or what to speak; for it shall be given you in that hour what to speak (Matt. 10, 16-19).

At first the apostles may not have comprehended the whole scope of these words, but they must have realized their seriousness when they were literally fulfilled among them: then they learned that the servant is indeed not greater than the Lord.

Christ disturbed the world, disturbed even those elements in it which were purely worldly, and the world won back its peace from him by annihilating him. It has the same grounds for action against the Church, for the Church re-presents Christ's work in every age:

If the world hate you, know ye that it hath hated me before you. If you had been of the world, the world would love its own; but because you are not of the world, but I have chosen you out of the world, therefore the world hateth you. Remember my word that I said to you: the servant is not greater than his master. If they have persecuted me, they will also persecute you. If they have kept my word, they will keep yours also. But all these things they will do to you for my name's sake; because they know not him that sent me (John 15, 18-21).

Thus the Church will always be afflicted. Because it is in communion with Christ, it cannot avoid sharing Christ's destiny. Christ has indeed been ennobled—but only after passing through death.

247

And the Church is still in the course of this passage. Its way leads to the cross. The Church passes through death in all her children. The redemption of individual men is not effected through Christ's opening a door, through which they are drawn up into heaven, but by their laying hold on Christ, and with him walking in some way the way of death he himself walked.

In his death, Christ defeated the powers of evil. His death was a victory. And so too, in the cross the Church overcomes evil and sin. It is in her cross that her glory is brought forth. Thus it is not those ages of outward peace and unchallenged possession which are really richest in glory for the Church, but those of persecution and death. This being so, we can understand St. Paul's confidence:

> But we have this treasure in earthen vessels, that the excellency may be of the power of God and not of us. In all things we suffer tribulation; but are not distressed. We are straitened; but are not destitute. We suffer persecution; but are not forsaken. We are cast down; but we perish not. Always bearing about in our body the mortification of Jesus, that the life also of Jesus may be made manifest in our bodies. For we who live are always delivered unto death for Jesus' sake, that the living power of Jesus may be made manifest in our mortal flesh. So then death worketh in us; but life in you (II Cor. 4, 7-12).

> Giving no offence to any man, that our ministry be not blamed; but in all things let us exhibit ourselves as the ministers of God, in much patience, in tribulation, in necessities, in distresses, in stripes, in prisons, in seditions, in labours, in watchings, in fastings, in chastity, in knowledge, in long-suffering, in sweetness, in the Holy Ghost, in charity unfeigned, in the word of truth, in the power of God; by the armour of justice on the right hand and on the left; by honour and dishonour; by evil report and good report; as deceivers and yet true; as unknown and yet known; as dying and, behold, we live; as chastised and not killed; as sorrowful, yet always rejoicing; as needy, yet enriching many; as having nothing and possessing all things (II Cor. 6, 3-10).

The various threats and dangers the Church suffers from within and without may continually cast a shadow on her life, but they can never destroy it, either in the purity of its incarnate being, or in its historical existence. It will never stop being the apostolic Church; it will never fall into myth and gnosticism. It is the weakest and most powerless of creatures, in so far as it is given wholly into the hands of free men, with their self-glorying and self-will. But, as Newman pointed out, the less it has depended on sword and bow, chariot and horse and the arms of man, the less worldly it has been, the more purely it has carried out its own tasks: the more defenceless it has been at any given time, the more it has provoked the proud and mighty. But it is at the same time the most independent and mightiest of creatures, as it is the body of the risen Christ, and is ruled and supported by the powers of his glorious body, which is free from the grip of earth. Because Christ—or rather, the Holy Ghost, whom he sent—is the basis of its life it is indestructible. The Holy Ghost is its impregnable personalized power of resisting sin. Even when to some degree sin overcomes the Church, it can never wholly govern it. The Holy Ghost, holiness in person, works in it, and it is therefore in its inmost heart forever holy, and from its holy heart, holiness streams out over its members. It will never be without saints, whether they are recognized or not. Valiant faith and sacrificing love will never disappear from it.

Thus the indestructible holiness and natural invulnerability of the Church spring from its nature, because it is a community formed and informed by holiness in person. This is the ultimate foundation of the Lord's promise that the gates of hell shall not prevail against it. This promise has two facets: it promises first that the Church will have to struggle continually with the powers of darkness; and secondly that it will not be defeated in the final battle. The promise does not offer it the prospect of victory and triumph, power and glory in this age. All that it says is that it will not be overthrown by the diabolic powers. Great wounds and dangerous crises are not out of keeping with this promise.

The hope which Christians have regarding the Church's insuperability is not supported by outward signs of security, but by the knowledge that the Holy Ghost is its heart. This is something which cannot be proved by argument, or reason. It is faith that gives us the certitude of it, and brings us to a deepening knowledge of it. And hence, in the midst of all dangers, the Church exhibits a calm self-confidence: it knows that it is supported by the power of God himself. This final and absolute certitude is not the product of undisturbed peace or possession, but of indestructibility of inner life. Indeed, if important members of the body are sick, it is not unusual—as history shows—for God, for the sake of its life, to arouse storms which break over the Church from without 'beating down everything rotten and decayed, and creating new seeds of light and air'.

God afflicts the Church with the tempests and storms of time so that it will never forget that it is a pilgrim here, whose duty is to advance the sovereignty of God and so fill the world with the life of Christ. God hammers and chisels at it so that it will remain a useful tool. For the sake of its task, the Church will not die whilst mankind needs to be hallowed and redeemed.

CHAPTER TWELVE

THE CONSUMMATION

Inexorably, world history moves towards its end. And within world history, the history of salvation, too, moves on to its end and its perfection. But world history and the history of salvation are not the same thing. World history has a meaning and value of its own, apart from the history of salvation. But it is only of limited duration, and is the vessel of the history of salvation, within which and ever transcending it, the history of salvation is accomplished. The history of salvation is the inmost and most profound level of world history, but it has laws and methods which are different from those of world history. Its essential difference is shown by the fact that it takes a course of its own which has no direct relationship with world history, or the foundation and development of states, great as its indirect influence in this may be. Its methods consist in the preaching of the words, and the administration of the sacramental signs. Its aim is the transformation of the world through death and recreation. These things will be accomplished in creation when Christ comes for the second time. This ultimate state is the goal of every happening from the first moment of creation onwards.

Sin disturbed the foundation of creation, but Christ altered things again. Through the death and resurrection of the Lord, the world made a sudden advance towards its final state. Through the death of Christ, the world in its present form, the old era, received a death-blow from which it can never recover. Its final collapse is only a question of time. The events of Good Friday have the power and tendency to draw everything down into destruction, until the present form of things is entirely lost.

But just as Good Friday was not the last event in the life of Christ, but led to Easter Day, so the purpose of the complete destruction of the world is not mere destruction, but the making of a new heaven and a new earth. Death, however, was an unavoidable prerequisite to the resurrection and glorious life of Christ, and in just the same way the death of the world in its present form will be an absolutely necessary preparation for the formation of the new heaven and the new earth. Just as human history from the death of Christ onwards proceeds in a series of deaths and collapses apparently interdependent on one another, until the final and complete collapse is reached, so too, in joyful events, it is moving towards the new creation.

But the nearer the complete transformation of the world comes, the stronger will be the blows falling on the present world order. This is not difficult to understand, for the closer the world approaches to its final form, the nearer it comes to God. The approach to God within time signifies, however, a crisis. This is shown most clearly in the cross, for in the cross the holiness of God was so brilliantly revealed to men that they could no longer tolerate it, and what was done to the Lord himself in his death will, in the end, be done to the whole of creation, for to reach its final form the cosmos must pass through a crisis resulting from its approach to God. Then there will be achieved that consummation which was begun in the cross and resurrection. The perfected world, the new heaven and the new earth, will show the absolute sovereignty of God. When God, personal love and truth, establishes himself as the absolute ruler of the world, the world in its present form will collapse utterly. For its present form has not the capacity to assimilate the unveiled energy of the divine life. Complete establishment of the rule of God—the kingdom of God—is the final purpose and meaning of the world and of history. Christ laid the foundations of the rule of God in such a decisive way that his victory is no longer in doubt, but the sovereignty of God as established by him is veiled until the end of the world, so that it is not impossible to gain the impression from human history that it is not God, his truth and love, but man, his lies and hatred, who is the lord of history. World events might suggest that it is Satan, the Lord of evil and tyranny, who is shaping history through his earthly servants. For the human capacity for sin, human self-love and brutality, is not weaker but stronger in the era inaugurated by Christ. History is not moving in a straight line of moral and religious progress to a state where all will be faith and love, so that at his second coming Christ will be able to enter a house made perfectly ready for him. Rather, as he himself prophesied, the revolt against God is becoming ever stronger and more calamitous.

The reason why human self-love is becoming more pronounced is that in the age inaugurated by Christ, man has to exert more power and determination if he will rebel against God. For in Christ God has mounted a sharp attack on man so that man, if he is still unwilling to submit to him, has to defend himself more strongly against him. As Guardini has said, the sin of those who know Christ is an adult sin, whereas the sins of those who lived before Christ were, so to speak, the sins of children, of minors.

Revolt and rebellion against God attain their fateful climax in the anti-christ, who seeks to establish a tyrannical, anti-christian kingdom with the help of a high and brilliant scientific and artistic civilization. He makes promises of the most wonderful kind to man. Our contemporaries, with their longing for power, offer him particularly fine opportunities: he offers them the glories of the earth —but he also takes into account their religious needs. He does not deny religious belief, but links it with the world and with himself. He maintains that he is the true redeemer. In the endless struggle between the worship of God and the worship of man, he seeks to establish his worship. He demands the adoration that should be given God. And in fact men are so bedazzled by his success that they fall down and worship him. St. John the Apostle would be horrified to hear the complete perversion of the appeal which Old Testament believers raised to God: 'Who is God but the Lord: and who is strong but our God?' They twist it into: 'Who is God but the Beast: and who is strong but our Beast?'

Thus the decisive struggle of the time of the end, will not be that of faith against disbelief, but of faith against faith: faith in Christ against faith in the world. Those who believe in the world are marked with a sign. Only one small party has remained faithful, and does not bear the sign. Outside it, some are dead, some imprisoned and some under economic boycott.

The work of anti-christ will be so successful that men will have the impression that his sovereignty is established once and for all. St. John explains the basis of the worldly success of anti-christ: he is encompassed by the power of hell; he is the representative on earth of him who from the beginning has been the accepted lord of the atheistic world. But in fact his sovereignty is only illusory, and he digs the grave of the world he rules. He leads human history into a cul-de-sac from which there is no escape. Economic, political and social life collapse. All that remains is a great heap of rubble. Under the powerful image of the collapse of the city of Babylon, the symbol of all godlessness and ungodly behaviour, John describes the fall of all creation. But mankind is not converted even when the judgement of God falls on it: when God can no longer be ignored, it hurls its curses in the face of heaven.

When godlessness has reached its highest point, and when man's position has become completely hopeless, and when the full number of the saints and martyrs has been made up, Christ will step out from his concealment. John sees him in the image of a triumphant rider on a white horse, riding out of the heavenly city, with banners of light and victory, into the world which anti-christ has destroyed. At that moment, the world dominion of the powers in opposition to God will collapse like a house of cards. The powers of evil, lying and hatred, pride and tyranny which during the course of human history have boasted so mightily, will be unmasked in their powerlessness and cast out of the community of men. Never again will they be able to disturb it. Christ will free from all their afflictions those who have remained faithful. His entry into the world will be different from his first entry into it: it will be made in the full light of day, so that no one can overlook him and ignore him. He will be greeted with jubilation by his faithful, but with horror by those of anti-christ.

At his second coming in to the world, Christ will disclose the meaning of human history as a whole, and of isolated events in it. He will be the embodiment of the sovereignty of God. Then there will be revealed the kind of contribution mankind as a whole and every individual event, every cultural and economic work, every philosophical, economic, industrial and political institution and standard, every religious idea, made to the advancement of the sovereignty of God. There will be revealed the importance of the doings of individual men and of nations and the meaning of wars and revolutions, of plagues and epidemics, of struggles between state and Church and groups within the Church, of sects and heresies. Measured by this final standard, much that has seemed great and mighty will be shown to be small and unimportant, much that seemed worthless will be seen to be of far-reaching significance. Hollow appearances will be smashed. What was misunderstood will be brought into the full light of understanding. What seemed injurious may be seen to have been advantageous; what seemed to be healthy, may be seen to be pernicious. The goodness and truth which have developed in hatred and falsehood, and the true and the good that coincided with falsehood and evil will all be revealed. The significance of the sins God allowed, the errors he did not prevent, the bitter fate that fell on believers throughout the whole of history—all will stand revealed. At that moment, all the meaninglessness with which God was accused within human history will vanish away. Belief in the last judgement makes it possible for us to believe in the midst of chaos that life is ultimately meaningful.

The second coming of Christ will herald the ultimate victory of truth and love, when it will be shown that truth and love alone are viable and full of life, because they alone are worthy of life. During the course of history they seem powerless: at the end, it will be shown that they alone are capable of existing eternally. Everything that has run contrary to them will in the end be exposed as powerless. From the last day, truth, love and power will coincide. The absolute worthiness of truth and love will be revealed in their absolute viability.

In the midst of all the afflictions and torments of history, the faithful look with hope and confidence, love and yearning, for the second coming of Christ. In the certainty that the Lord will come, they make ready to traverse the last bloody section of the road of history. It is in the light of his coming that the faithful find it possible in the midst of the perils of life to obey the command of their Lord: Fear not! The expectation of the Lord's coming has left its mark on their inmost being. We might almost define the Church as the community of those who love the coming of the Lord, the community of those who trust confidently in the coming of Christ. In the celebration of the Eucharist, the Church celebrates the coming of Christ, for in it she looks forward to that future time when he shall appear whose death and resurrection she celebrates in her mysteries. This is why her celebration of the Eucharist will continue till that very hour when he comes again. When the last celebration of the Eucharist permitted by God is completed, Christ will appear and the kingdom of God will be established in its final form (I Cor. 15, 24). We are told little in Holy Scripture about his appearing. Our experience tells us almost nothing. It is a mystery; its antetype and foundation are the risen Christ. Just as the Holy Ghost has glorified the Lord's body, so he will glorify heaven and earth. The difference between the present form of the world and the form it will be given might be compared to that between the butterfly and the caterpillar. The repulsive form of the slowly creeping caterpillar gives no hint of the fact that out of it there will come the many-coloured butterfly, with its winged magnificence and free and airy motion. No more can we see from the present state of the world what will one day come out of it. In the perfected world, the physical matter of the world will be completely changed. This transformation will be so far-reaching, that matter will be able to assimilate the infinite energies of the divine life, and will become a mirror of the might of truth and love.

Although it cannot explain these things, modern natural science can give us some small insight into them. If it is the nature of matter to be not small particles, but waves, and if again light consists in wave movements, we might conclude that in their inner nature, things are in some sense composed of light. This would explain why light has been held in high honour in every age, and why it is of decisive importance for the appearance of the world. The change which God will bring about in matter will be such that the inner nature of matter will no longer have to be revealed by a great number of experiments and investigations but will be directly visible.

Again, the fact that matter consists in light is an echo of the fact that God is light: matter is bathed in the radiance of God. Light, and the radiance of God himself will be spread abroad by Christ over the whole of creation. It will pour out from the glorified body of Christ into all the confines of creation. The light of God will stream out from the glorious countenance of the Lord over the whole cosmos and interpenetrate it on every level, so that it will be brighter than the brightest day. A beam from the other world broke into ours and was seen radiating from the countenance of Christ by the disciples on the Mount of Transfiguration. This beam will become the sun of the new cosmos for ever, namely the truth and love flowing, intense with life, from Christ. At this decisive moment God himself will be immediately present in the new world: in the new heaven and on the new earth, so that his light and splendour can blaze forth over the whole cosmos and break on all the corners and ends of the world. In the new heaven and on the new earth, mankind will live in communion with God.

God's presence in the world will mean that man's primal affliction will be done away, for his oldest want is his need for the hidden God, and all other needs are symptoms of this one. The most balefully significant fact of history is man's remoteness from God. In the new heaven and on the new earth sin will have no place, because God will be immediately present in them. Within history, God permits man to be afflicted by one fear and want after another. But as Stauffer has said, he will one day free him from his last want: his need of God. Then the centre of the disturbance itself will have been removed, and the countless manifestations of distress will vanish away: the weeping of children, grief of mothers, the toil of the work of man, the distress of the hungry and sick, the uproar of war, the groans of all living things, and the torment of this world shall come to an end. And above all, the curse of temporality, the mortality of this world will pass away and, in the presence of God, man will be accorded fulness of life and abundance.

In Holy Scripture this is all shown symbolically in the image of the city. The Holy City comes down from heaven so that the whole earth is made a dwelling-place for man. What men expect from a city—but what no earthly city can give them—what they, with the pride of Titans, expect to effect with the power of their own arms, hearts and spirits: fulness, richness of life, security and plenitude of being; these will be given to those who allow God to give it to them from heaven, in the time beyond time. In that city it will be possible to live fully (cf. John 14, 1-3). Nothing like it is possible in time, for the cities of this world collapse: they pass away because the whole of the present cosmos is subject to the law of temporality, and man, full of self-glory, draws the world ever deeper into perdition through his flight from God. In their collapse their inmost structure is revealed: death is built into everything built on the earth. And therefore they cannot fulfil the yearnings man feels with regard to his city, his nation, and security of life. The earth cannot satisfy man's hunger for life. And yet it will one day be quieted, though not from earth, but from heaven, when God himself suffers man to partake of his own fulness of life and being. In the new heaven and on the new earth, everything on earth worth preserving will be physically preserved, although its form will be changed. Nothing will be lost.

Just as the image of the city shows the fulness of life and security of being in the new heaven and on the new earth, so the image of the bride symbolizes union with God. The city, which comes down to earth from heaven and makes the whole earth a home for man, has—according to the evidence of St. John's Apocalypse —the form of 'a bride adorned for her husband'. The world to come will therefore be characterized by the loving union of creation with God. It cannot be brought into being by any effort on the part of creation, but only through God's devotion for the world. When God gives himself to it, it will be able to share in his glory. Heaven and earth will be flooded with the brilliance of his countenance. The new city will radiate with the glory of God.

In view of these facts about the future form of the world, it becomes comprehensible why those who long for it pray: May the fashion of this world pass away: may the kingdom come! This prayer suggests, not flight from the world, but the highest degree of love for it. Those who so pray are not dreamers, but sober and far-seeing people. Like those whose faith is in the world, they are dissatisfied with its present state; like them, they set their hopes on the future. But they do not expect the perfect fulfilment of their hopes at any particular time within history. This differentiates them from those who dream of a paradisial state on earth, such as is dreamed of by those who strive for messianic collectivism. Those who set their ultimate hopes on the coming of the Lord are sensible enough to see that the establishment of an earthly paradise will be a costly thing: costly in executions, murderous wars, destructive revolutions. The millennial hopes of men will not be fulfilled within history. God, who himself enkindled these yearnings in human hearts, did not promise that they would be perfectly fulfilled whilst the world endured. Even the prophecies of the millennial kingdom contained in St. John's Apocalypse, are not promises of this kind. What is promised is the chaining of Satan, but not the removal of all sins and afflictions. According to prophecy, there will come within the age inaugurated by Christ a period during which Satan will not be able to afflict those who believe in Christ. It is possible to connect with this promise the thought that in this period men will not torture one another in the way in which they have been doing in self-love and hatred, incompetence and hopelessness. Thus the hopes of sober and far-seeing men are fixed on the future: on a radically different future beyond the collapse of the present world. From it they expect the satisfaction of all their needs. This is guaranteed by God, as also is the fact that he will establish his rule—the rule of truth and love, in its perfection on this earth. When this state is reached, God will be all in all. Because he is love and truth, this will mean that love and truth will be everything.

The complete realization of the rule of truth and love will mean complete salvation for men. Men will be wholly saved when they live in omnipotent truth and love.

God has planned this salvation primarily for mankind as such —for the human community; and for individuals through the community. Just as during the time of our earthly pilgrimage, it is not individuals as such, but the community of the Church, and through that the individuals who belong to it, which is the bearer and instrument of the rule of God in the hidden form which it has in time, so in the consummation it will be the human community which will support the revealed sovereignty of God. The image of the heavenly city also shows that it will be in the midst of the human community that God will make his dwelling.

With the perfecting of the human community, the material cosmos will attain its consummation. God establishes his rule in the material sphere through mankind. The material world outside mankind lays hold on the light and splendour of God through mankind. This is the clearest proof of the fact that man is made lord of the cosmos by God, that his fate is the fate of the world. In condemning himself to annihilation, man the creature would condemn the created world to nothingness. Through man, it will share in glory, if he himself is made a partaker of glory. Therefore it looks with anxious expectation to mankind its lord. It has a great longing for perfection, which St. Paul pictures as a sigh. But it cannot attain what it strains for: it never gets beyond the first step. All natural developments are first steps of this kind, which never attain their perfect fulfilment. What creation strives for so vigorously will be given it only when man is given what he yearns for, for only then will the hour of deliverance strike for the world of matter. And this shows very clearly that according to the Christian revelation the course of the cosmos is subject to the course of human history. This again throws into great prominence the difference between it and non-Christian concepts. Whereas for instance, according to Greek thinking, the history of man is a phase in the rhythm of nature, according to Christian revelation the course of nature is related to human history.

But although God's first concern is the perfection of the community, he is not indifferent to individuals. As we have seen, the individual has his own irreplaceable worth, and his salvation cannot be sacrificed to anything else. But he attains it only as a member of the community, and it will be accorded him only when he enters the communion of the perfect.

We might also raise the question as to what form the life and existence of individuals will take when the world assumes its final form. If the rule of God will be established unreservedly in all creation, it will also be established in individual human beings. The rule of love and truth will blaze forth so violently in everyone that each person will become a perfect mirror for truth and love. Every individual will therefore gleam and glow with the truth and love which pour into him and burst forth from him. Here too we can say that truth and love will stream forth from the glorified body of God, down through every individual human being. Thus everyone will be a perfect image of Christ. Man—the perfect man in heaven—will be, as it were, a revelation of Christ, and everyone will echo him in a slightly different way. The image of Christ—

which St. Paul is always calling on his readers to show forth—will then be displayed in everyone in its perfection. And thus everyone will see in everyone else the pure token of his kinship with Christ.

This new life will comprehend both body and soul. It is not merely the soul alone that will be glorified, but the whole man corporeally. Such a belief in bodily resurrection is peculiar to Christianity and is not to be found outside of it. In other religions we meet those who scorn the body or deify the body, those who deny bodily processes, and those who worship them. In modern times, Nietzsche has proclaimed that the body is all, that man is nothing but body. Those who oppose the concept of spirit—the pupils of materialism, naturalism and racism—greeted his message with welcoming ears and hearts. The Christian doctrine about the body is a refutation both of those ultra-spiritualists who despise the body as an enemy, and also of those who despise the spirit, confining all life to the body. The body will share in the glorification of the cosmos. At the resurrection of the dead, the soul will for a second time impress its rule on the body, and so take it up into unity of being with itself.

This fact is guaranteed to us by revelation. How it will be done is of course an impenetrable mystery for us. It is therefore controversial whether at the resurrection of the dead the soul will re-assume the matter which formed its human body during its earthly nature, in order to impress its law upon it, or whether no part of the earthly body will be used in the matter employed by it in the future. The soul will rise in its own body whatever matter from this world it informs or shapes, for in that it will be used by the soul, it will be the soul's own body. We may prove that man rises with his own body from the fact that the material of the body is changed even during earthly life, and yet a man remains the same person, although there remains in the old man no particle of the matter that formed the body of the child.

The body which the spirit will build in the power of God on the last day will be completely changed. What is true of the transformation of the cosmos is also true of the transformation of the body. We know that the body will be different, but that it will nevertheless be formed from the matter of this world. The change in it will be so far-reaching that it will be capable of assimilating the energies of the divine life. As Pinsk says, if the divine life were to flow into a body that had not undergone this transformation, the body would certainly break down, just as an electric light bulb fails if a current too strong for it flows through it. The wholly transformed body will glow with the light and love of God, and God's light and ardour will flow into it through the soul. The glorified body will be a perfect expression of the spirit: the spirit informed by God, gleaming and glowing with God. It will prove itself to be light and ardour, for in it will be fulfilled that which, in the earthly body, can be only imperfectly accomplished: it will be the manifestation and expression of the spirit. Thus the bodies of those who have been made perfect will be the perfect expression of their God-united souls and the perfect body shall be glorified. Mankind was redeemed by Christ not from the body but for and in the body.

Death is a prerequisite to the perfect body. Men can only enter into the perfect rule of God through a death in which they share in the death of Christ, in which therefore the death of Christ is displayed and expressed. Death is the radical and irrevocable end of life in its present form, and the beginning of a new kind of life.

When terrestrial life breaks down entirely, men enter the life of God and learn what they are in the sight of God. Then God recalls to them everything they have been in their lives, so that they see the whole of their lives with perfect clarity. God himself is the measure by which those who are so enlightened measure and evaluate themselves. We call this process the personal judgement after death. If up to that time a man has clung to self-seeking and stuck in the rut of the human self, he will need a wide-scale and painful recasting before being able to be wholly accepted into the kingdom of love. This reformation must pierce into the deepest layers of the personality, until everything contrary to God has been driven out. We call this process purgation. It is God who gives man this chance of life after death.

The process of cleansing is hidden by impenetrable veils. We have no certain information about either its form or its duration. We can however say that death does not completely cut men's connections with the material world, those who have died will live in an entirely different way from that in which they lived in time. Every man makes his mark, whether good or bad, on the world, so that later generations encounter it. We can assume that those who die feel sorrow or rejoice in the world they have left behind them. Hence, for those who are undergoing cleansing, the world may be a ground for affliction and pain. This shows why those who live in the state of purgation remain especially closely connected with that part of the world in which their life was spent, either for their consolation or their punishment. With the permission of God, they can exert an influence on earthly affairs, or even make their presence perceptible in a manner corresponding to their worthiness or unworthiness. As their purgation proceeds, so also that piece of the world connected with them is hallowed, and freed from that unholiness with which they stamped it in their earthly life. Since grace does not destroy nature, but exalts and perfects it, so the communion of those who in life were bound by natural bonds, survives especially strongly. Indeed, it increases in purity and intensity. Thus, in prayer and sacrifice, an exchange of helpful love is possible.

To understand the fact of a cleansing after death is impossible if one thinks of pardon as only a declaration of innocence and not as an inner transformation and hallowing. If we see it only as a declaration of innocence, nothing is cleansed, for nothing can be cleansed, as man would remain eternally and forever a sinner regarded as innocent, but in fact still a sinner.

He who is fully cleansed—that is, anyone fully cleansed from self-love and the marks it leaves—will be taken by God into his glorious life, and into the community of the angels and those made perfect whom Christ took with him as his retinue at his entry into the glory of the Father, whose number has since that time been increased continually, and has now grown to a vast multitude. But our partaking in the glorious life of God will reach its final and highest form only in the resurrection of the dead, when the souls will assume bodies. Until then they lack their final form. We might say that before that time, it is in a state of pre-perfection. Great as the joy of this state of pre-perfection is, the soul in it lacks its fulness, for it is bodiless. Therefore those who are living in heavenly perfection, still live in some measure in expectation— not in the unrest and uncertainty common to those who wait, but in the blessed certitude that a still higher life lies before them.

Let us now turn to a consideration of this pre-perfection, as we have called it. In Holy Scripture, it is called the life of heaven. When we speak of heaven in this sense we are not speaking of a definite place, but of a condition—that of union with God. There is no place of which one can say: 'Here is heaven'. Those made perfect are indeed, before the resurrection of the dead, in some way bound to space, although they are not—as they were during their life of pilgrimage—subject to the laws of time and space. But all attempts to localize heaven must fail, for they are meaningless.

To enter heaven means therefore the same thing as to come to God: to be made a partaker in the life of the divine community. Union with God is gained through encounter with Christ. As we said earlier, the Christ-life is characterized by the fact that those living it live both 'in' Christ and Christ 'in' them. Union with Christ is a mystery, and only in faith are we certain of it. Communion with Christ in pre-perfection is different from communion with Christ in the life of pilgrimage, for it is visible communion. Those who are in heaven see the glorified Christ directly. When man leaves the material world and enters the kingdom of God, he enters the unveiled countenance of him on whom he has set all his hopes during his life on earth, without ever having seen him face to face.

Encounter with Christ in the realms of heaven means for man, the fulfilment of his yearning for union with others in two ways: it is the fulfilment of his desire for union with another, and of his need to reverence another. As we have seen several times, men are intended to live in communion with other beings. But no earthly person can satisfy man's inner yearnings, and the hunger of the heart cannot be stilled in this life. During his life on earth, man is condemned to live in yearning. But when the human ego encounters the ego of the Lord, it can unite with his ego in an intimacy surpassing all our experience, so that not only are the heart and soul accorded all they desire, but all our expectations are unimaginably surpassed.

But at the same time those united with Christ see him on high. For Christ is greater than any human ego. And thereby love's need to look up in reverence to the beloved is fulfilled. How strong this need may be in human hearts, is shown by the fact that the lover is always tempted to deify the beloved, and is disappointed and upset when the beloved falls short of the ideal picture the lover has of the beloved. The lover's longing for the beloved to be greater than he is himself is so fulfilled in encounter with Christ that there is no need for further deification, for Christ's nature is that of God. Thus men can look up to him, as to God, with unconditional reverence, without having to expect disappointment from this encounter, as from an earthly one. Encounter with Christ is at the same time reverent gazing and loving adoration of the Lord. In St. John's Apocalypse, these two aspects of heavenly encounter with Christ are depicted under the image of the heavenly liturgy. According to this image, those who dwell in heaven praise the Lord continually in cries of greeting and thanksgiving. In that liturgy there is offered the perfection of the greeting so often offered to the Lord by the community in celebrating the Eucharist: the *Kyrie eleison* in which, in the midst of the world of a multitude of lords and gods, the community acknowledges him as its only lord.

But the glorified Christ is not all: just as during life on earth Christ is the way to the Father, so to those made perfect in heaven he is still the 'way'. The way invites them to walk on it and pursue it to its end. Christ takes them by the hand, as it were, and leads them before the face of the Father. Only when one stands before the Father's face has one reached that place where one should finally be, for only here does one really reach that dwelling for which the heart forever yearns. Only then does one enter the mansion Christ prepares for his followers. Over and above this the soul can go nowhere, for there is nowhere else to go. When it stands before the face of the Father, it is looking into the face of living love and truth in person.

Thus man's basic longing is finally and completely fulfilled. Poets, thinkers, worshippers and philosophers of every age have dreamed of gazing on the face of God. To be able to gaze on the face of God strikes man as the grace above all graces, impelling him to truth and love, because his whole being is orientated towards God. During the time of his bitter pilgrimage, a glimpse of God's countenance could free him from all earthly afflictions. It would show him the answers to all the questions which distress him. Constantly, throughout history, the prayer arises: 'O God, permit me to see thy face'. It was Moses' only—and greatest—request. But he was asking too much, for it is impossible for man to see the face of God whilst he lives a pilgrim on earth. He has no faculty of vision as far as this is concerned.

If God were to remove the veil that hides his form from man, and enter in his unveiled glory into the human mind, man would be blinded by the light of God, and scorched by his ardour. No one can see God and continue to live. Moses' requests could not be granted during terrestrial time. And yet his petition has never been stilled. Job sacrificed everything to be able to see God. The Psalmist wanted to watch before the likeness of the Lord, and to be filled by gazing on his holiness. Philip repeated his petition: 'Lord, show us the Father; and it is enough for us'. The day is coming when God will heed the prayer of the centuries, and we shall see him face to face. And it will be enough for us.

To gaze on God in this way is possible only for those in heaven because they have received a new kind of vision from God himself. They can endure the ardour of God only because they have received from God himself a new faculty for love, which we call *lumen gloriae*. God touches their spirits, their understanding and their faculty for love, and changes them in such a way that the human spirit becomes capable of assimilating the light and fire of God without breaking down. Indeed, in heaven man can accept truth and love which are God, not only without collapsing, but with the help of the divine power of seeing and loving given him by God he can also find in them his greatest joy.

What does a man see when he sees God? To be able to answer this question we need to know what God is. But God is an incomprehensible mystery. Hence the state we call heaven, in which we have a vision of God, is also an incomprehensible mystery. We do not know what we shall see.

Even for those who are in heaven, the heavenly life remains a mystery. For even for them, God himself remains a mystery. Even in the state we call heaven, man cannot pierce the mystery of God. He can look on the unveiled mystery of God, but he cannot penetrate to its most profound depths.

Some faint notion of what we may see when we gaze on the mystery of God can be gained by looking at the world and realizing that it is a reflexion of the glory of God—the hem of his garment. All the glories of nature—from the blooming of spring to the magnificence of summer, the maturity of autumn and the immaculate beauty of winter—all the wonders of human civilization—all these are a reflexion of what we shall see when we look on God.

But the crucial point is that those in heaven, when they look on God, look not on a cold dumb splendour, but into a living eye— the eye of truth and love in person. They are permitted this vision only because love and truth in person unveils his face to them, and at the same time so transforms them that they become able to withstand his look. Thus, gazing on God is an exchange with God: it is to partake of the tri-personal life of God.

Holy Scripture illustrates the exchange of life between the perfected man and God in the image of the heavenly banquet. According to this concept he who is made perfect sits opposite God as though at table with him. To sit opposite God in the heavenly banquet is not merely to be silently near him: it means being actively with him. A meal would be incomplete without conversation.

The fact that the life of heaven is a meal God shares with man is promised symbolically in Holy Scripture in the reports of the meals Christ shared with his disciples. Every such meal is an allusion to the heavenly banquet. Thus on one occasion, he invited his disciples and the multitude of the people to a great supper. This led primarily to their bodily satisfaction, but physical satisfaction was not Christ's final—or even chief—aim here. If this had been the chief purpose of his action, the episode would not have meant very much in a world where millions were starving. Satisfaction on this occasion, however, signified something far bigger than it was itself: it was a parable of a future satisfaction. The bread which Christ offered his followers that evening was an image of a different bread, the real, genuine bread, which does not grow on earth, and does not fill in the earthly way, but which rather comes from heaven and is intended to give men eternal satisfaction. This bread of the future will appease all men's hunger, both the hunger of the stomach, and the hunger of the heart and spirit. The earth cannot bring forth the bread that can do this. Thus, in a world filled with the complaints of the hungry, man should not despair of final satisfaction, for Christ, in a symbolic action, kindled in him expectation of satisfaction in the future. What God will one day give him will be not mere sustenance but food in superfluity. God will distribute it lavishly: the baskets full of bread which remained over at that evening meal on the lake shore show that plenitude will come. In this present age, the Lord has given a pledge, a token, of this coming banquet in the Eucharist, which is a likeness of the eternal meal in heaven. The Eucharist is the herald of the heavenly meal. In the eucharistic meal, Christ gives his followers the food which will quiet their eternal hunger: he gives them himself, truth and love in bodily form. By eating the earthly Eucharist man is made ready for the heavenly meal. During the life of pilgrimage, the love of God is shown forth in a veiled manner in the Eucharist, but at the heavenly banquet the love and truth of God will be given unveiled to those who share in the meal, and will animate them for ever.

Thus, in the heavenly meal, the purpose of every meal on earth is fulfilled; the purpose of earthly eating is not merely the giving of bodily satisfaction, but union with God. According to the original concept of meals, God is the chief guest at every meal, and hence prayer should be part of eating on earth. Prayer at meals not only serves to ask for sustenance and give thanks for the earthly food received, but is also converse with the most important, although invisible, person at table. We cannot ignore our most important guest, but are bound to talk to him. And we must not grudge him the right to speak. Now, that which according to the original idea of eating takes place at every meal, attains its perfect form in the heavenly banquet, where the most important guest is plainly visible and shows himself unveiled to the other people at table with him. There, conversation proceeds openly, face to face.

Converse is proper to the heavenly meal: in it love and truth speak to man, not after the fashion of a conversation on earth, in words in which it may be possible to feel the splendour of truth and the warmth of love, but rather in God's giving himself—truth and love—to man. Hence it is possible to call this converse itself a kind of eating and drinking, for in it we shall be able to take into ourselves truth which will satisfy our minds, and love which will content our hearts. Thus the converse of heaven is an exchange with truth and love in person. What happens to the man who talks with personal truth and love? The mysteries of God and the world are revealed to him.

He is permitted to share in that converse of love which is conducted continuously between the Father and the Son. He is taken up into that exchange of life which is carried on between the Father and the Son. Because of his close union with Christ, he stands in a relationship to the Father which is at once similar and dissimilar to that enjoyed by the glorified Lord.

Just as the Father and the Son are bound together in the Holy Ghost—in that personalized flow of love which we call the Holy Spirit—so too that relationship between the Father and those made perfect, which is instituted through Christ, will be effected in the Holy Ghost. On that personalized stream of love which is the holy Ghost, those made perfect will be continually brought, as it were, before the face of the Father. The Spirit which the glorified Christ breathes into the blessed, lies, like an omnipotent bond, like a personalized atmosphere, about the heavenly Father and him who is made perfect. By this we can judge the intimacy and familiarity, power and intensity of this union. In the converse between the Father and the Son, everything in heaven and on earth is discussed. He who is made perfect can therefore learn from it the answers to all those questions about the problems of history and of his own life, which, during his life, he sought in vain. The Father explains to him in love everything he wants to know. He goes from one surprise to another. But his greatest delight comes, not through the enlightening of earthly darkness—great as his satisfaction at this may be—but in his experience of love itself. To be intimate with love itself—with that love which is at the same time truth—to receive it into a heart illuminated by the Spirit and to be able to contemplate God with a spirit glowing with love, will be the peak of blessedness for him.

Never again can he turn his gaze from love and truth. He is so full of them and governed by them, that he finds no pleasure in, and has no power to turn to things contrary to God. He is forever united to God. With the united power of his heart and mind he gives himself to truth and love. Of course, even he who is made perfect in heaven cannot enter fully into the converse between the Father and the Son. He has indeed been given a divine faculty of understanding, a divine faculty of hearing, greater than anything known on earth. But it is not sufficient to allow him to comprehend everything that is discussed in the converse conducted between the Father and the Son, in the Holy Ghost. He would have to be God to be able to do so. As God is a mystery even for him who is made perfect—a mystery he cannot penetrate—the converse carried on between the Father and the Son is also a mystery to him. Even though he has received divine vision and the divine faculty for love, he still cannot enter into all the profundity and breadth of the truth and love of God. Thus, even for those who have been made perfect, God remains finally incomprehensible, for all eternity.

We might then ask whether, if this is so, that last word is not tragedy's own. If God is ultimately and forever incomprehensible, does not the riddle of human life remain unsolved? Fears of this kind with respect to the irreducible incomprehensibility of God should not assail us, for he who is in heaven will receive every answer he is capable of assimilating from the converse he will conduct with God. God's truth and love will be given him in that measure in which he can accept them. As Augustine says, God will fill his capacity to the uttermost limit. Anyone who is so filled cannot yearn for further fulfilment. If God was to give himself to him more fully than he could stand, that would mean extra happiness for him, but would overstrain him fatally. If God were to explain to him more than he could understand, his mind and heart would not be more fully enlightened, but would be darkened. The overstraining which God required of him would destroy all his faculties. The degree in which he who is made perfect is united with God will depend on the measure of his earthly endeavours in that direction. It is different for each person. All gaze on one and the same figure, but everyone receives light and love from him in a measure suitable for him alone. We might compare it with a picture looked at by many people, or a symphony heard by a great crowd. All hear or see the same thing, but each sees or hears it according to the measure of his capacity to comprehend it.

And again, the mysterious nature of God affords him the opportunity to find ultimate fulfilment for one of his basic needs.

We mentioned it just now: the need to worship. This need does indeed find its fulfilment in Christ, but it will be completely and finally stilled only in the converse mediated by the glorified Christ with love itself. Because God is an impenetrable mystery, those who converse with him can look up to him with unreserved reverence. They have no need at all to fear that he whom they so honour will ever disappoint them. For it is intrinsically and essentially impossible for him to do so. The unreserved reverence with which they can look up to him we call adoration. The heavenly exchange of life between man and God, love and truth in person, is therefore a worshipping converse with truth and love. We might even call it the worship, glowing with love, of truth and love.

In this exchange of life, man finds the ultimate satisfaction of the hunger of his heart and mind. But he is not surfeited. He remains continually able to receive more truth and love. He is continuously both satisfied and yet receiving satisfaction. He possesses God whilst yet receiving him continually. There is a continuous flow of light and fire into his soul. We might ask whether this flow remains always the same, or whether it increases: whether those who are made perfect penetrate ever more profoundly into truth and love. This question is answered in different ways by different theologians. Most deny it. They explain their negative answer thus:

The fulness of the divine existence is completely simple, and is concentrated, as it were, on a single point. Thus those who can gaze on it, encompass it with a comprehensive gaze. In doing so they therefore see as much as they are capable of seeing.

But we could hold the opposite opinion: this is that those who are made perfect are ever more fully filled with truth and love. In their converse with love they continually learn new truths. They plunge ever deeper into the abyss of love and truth without ever reaching its bottom. They have enough, and yet, there, enough is never enough. Without being hungry, they can continually receive food. We might explain this state of affairs, in which the man is continually satisfied, and yet continually receiving more, by reference to an experience we can all share during our life on earth. The poet Conrad Ferdinand Meyer describes it thus:

Enough is not enough! Praised be the harvest!
There is no bough that lacks its fruit!
Many a bow bends low, all too heavy laden,
The apple falls hollowly to earth.

Enough is not enough! It laughs in the leaves!
The juicy peach beckons the parched mouth!
Drunken wasps buzz in circles
—Enough is not enough!—Around the grape.

Enough is not enough! The poet's spirit
Drinks deep at the well of pleasure;
Even the heart needs superfluity
Enough can never, nevermore suffice!

This eternal growing into truth and love, this eternal advance into heaven would be owed, not to man's endeavours, but to the grace of God alone. He reveals his truth and love ever more profoundly, and continually increases man's power of vision and love: those powers which are necessary for the reception of new worlds of light and life. Hence, he who is made perfect is led ever deeper into the infinity of God. This 'advance' is not accomplished in a continuous process, in a temporal flow, but according to the free pleasure of God, and is in no way merited. It can never come to an end because a creaturely being cannot measure infinity in all eternity —not in millions and billions of years.

Because heaven is a continual receiving, because it is continual reception of pure truth and love, it is obvious that heavenly life can never be tormented by boredom and satiety. This is true, whether heaven is a continual 'advance' or not. Boredom strikes man when he can receive no more and experience no more, because all possibilities are exhausted. We become bored with a person or a thing when we can feel nothing more with regard to him or it and we have the impression that it has nothing more to give us. This can never happen in the case of the life of heaven, for God's kingdom is inexhaustible. Man experiences personal love and truth as a blissful and inexhaustible treasure on which he can draw for ever. Any over-naive description of heaven might give rise to the fear that life there would prove boring, because of the continuity

272

of experiences which would last for hundreds and thousands of years. Such a fear is, in reality, completely out of place.

What Jakob Burckhardt said in the *Weltgeschichtlichen Betrachtungen* about the laws of temporal life do not apply here: 'Until the end there persists in man an urge for periodic and great changes, and whatever degree of average happiness is given him, he will one day begin to cry with Lamartine: *La France s'ennuie.*' When for instance Holy Scripture says that those made perfect cry continuously to God: 'Holy, holy, holy', it is saying parabolically that heaven is an everlasting and adoring converse with God. The groundlessness of such fears is made still more apparent if we think of heaven as an eternal advance. For then God explains to those made perfect in heaven, continually and with ever increasing clarity, the richness and splendour of his own life, and the glories of creation. He explains them in such a way that those who are in heaven can penetrate ever more deeply into the mystery of him. And his mystery can never be exhausted in eternity, for it is of inexhaustible richness. Just so, those in heaven will never grow tired, for their faculty of love and power of vision is inexhaustibly fresh and youthful.

At the same time, these considerations make it clear that the life of heaven is a life of the most intense activity. If we call it peace, we do not mean idleness and inactivity. The peace meant here is rather blessed activity without either weariness or ennervation. Heaven is not for the easy-going or slothful.

We call the life of heaven the reward of life on earth. What do we mean by reward? Is not such a definition of the life of heaven likely to arouse mistrust? We have been taught by Kant that any moral system that calls for good, not for the sake of good, but for the sake of a reward external to the good, is no true and genuine reality. What do we mean by a heavenly reward? Christ took the words of his age in order to pour into them, as into an earthen vessel, his heavenly promises. In order to rightly understand what we mean here by the word reward, we must first define and describe the reward itself. Christ promised those who hungered for justice satisfaction of their hunger. But with what will hunger for justice be satisfied? With justice. Those who care about justice will be given justice. In just the same way, those who

273

hunger for love will be given love. Earthly love does no more than keep love alive in its yearning for its ultimate and proper form. The perfect union which love desires will not be given it during our life of pilgrimage; but the prospect of it in the life after death is kept before it here. In just the same way, he who yearns for truth will be made a partaker of truth. During our earthly life, all our knowledge is superficial. But what is not attainable within earthly life, will be given to man in the life which he receives with death. To those who have concerned themselves with truth and love, God himself will give, after death, the fulness of truth and love. God will bring man's strivings to an end. He will crown with final success all those endeavours of man which cannot of themselves attain fulfilment. Man will receive as a gift from God what he could not accomplish by his own efforts. Without this prospect, the life of man would be a despairing thing: it would be a sisyphean task. He would continually have to strive for a goal he could never reach—which would, indeed, retreat further from him the more he strove towards it. For the more he longs for truth and love, the more widely and incomprehensibly opportunities for grasping them spread out before him. But when the time is come, God himself will give what the heart and soul long for but cannot attain. Then man will be able to do perfectly what he can never accomplish during his life on earth: he will be able to look and love as much as—indeed more than—he longed to do during time.

Heaven is, then, that state in which, according to Kant, perfect morality is to be found—in which assent is given to truth and love for their own sake. In the perfected man in heaven, truth and love attain to their true importance. Truth and love are welcomed in heaven not because they are in any way useful, or for the sake of expediency, but only because they are in themselves worthy of acceptance. In heaven, truth and love display absolute vitality, because they are worthy of existence. The powers contrary to them —the forces of lying and error, self-love and hatred—are exposed in heaven in all their weakness and helplessness.

Because God himself allays man's hunger for truth and love there, heaven is the fulfilment of everything in man that cries out for fulfilment, the perfecting of everything in man's nature. Thus, in heaven, man attains the life proper to him, in the fulness and perfection of its development. In heaven, man becomes himself —he acquires his full personality in being given the perfection of truth and love. For as long as he is earthbound he is not fully himself, is still *en route* to himself, as it were: his pilgrimage to truth and love is a pilgrimage to personal perfection. The perfected man in heaven is wholly himself and is fully conscious of himself, because God is with him. In God—in personalized truth and love— man possesses himself fully because his nature needs God. Man in heaven is thus really and truly man.

It is essential for the life of heaven that everyone who is made perfect should be united in the greatest intimacy not only with God, but also with those who are united with God. He sits down at the table of the heavenly banquet, not as an individual, but as one guest among many. Indeed, the individual will take part in the heavenly banquet only in so far as he is permitted to take his place at a table where many are already seated; he enters the choir of the perfect only by being taken into the community of the angels and saints.

In the heavenly companionship of the perfect, the relationships of earthly friendship and love find their fulfilment. During earthly life, impassable bounds are set on the relationships of human beings with one another. Even the most intimate friendship and love cannot surmount the wall which divides one person from another. This wall is personality itself. Personality is indeed man's highest treasure, but it cuts off every person from every other, isolating him in unconquerable loneliness. The individual's physical body is a token of the loneliness to which personality condemns every man. In the body, everyone is what he is, wholly and irreducibly an individual. Whilst the body is a bridge between one person and another, it is also an impenetrable wall, separating person from person. As a result of the fact that every individual is a prisoner within his own person, earthly love can never be more than an attempt at union: the outcome of earthly love is always in doubt. This has important consequences: it means not only that, by its very nature, earthly love is barred from attaining that intimacy which it desires, but also that it cannot reach that level of communion which is in keeping with its terrestrial nature. Man's love often fails to reach the level proper to it, and stops short of the given bounds, thus unjustifiably cutting itself off from others, so that it can make no further advance, and turns to love of self. Again, sometimes it tries to penetrate further into others than it should, so that its devotion becomes self-abandonment, and its object is driven to introversion, and hence to self-destruction. But those made perfect in heaven are not afflicted by any such restrictions. There, the ego is shaped simultaneously by love and reinforcement of personality in such a way that it can give itself unreservedly to others, without either losing itself, or becoming introverted. It is sufficiently well-balanced to be able to give itself to just that extent at which its self-possession will be preserved, and to retain possession of itself in such a way that it can simultaneously fully devote itself to another. It has thus a sure sense, which enables it to give itself fully whilst still retaining possession of itself. On the other hand, all other egos are so completely open to it that it can penetrate into them to the very limit beyond which lies self-destruction.

But bounds are set even on this most intimate and mighty of unions, for the ego does not so far blend with others as to entail its own diffusion. The ego keeps its individuality: the one remains the one and the other the other. Thus, even in the heavenly union, everyone in the last resort remains a mystery to everyone else. During earthly life, everyone is a continual mystery to the other, and this state of affairs cannot be altered through all eternity. But during our earthly pilgrimage one person can be a painful mystery to another: in heaven everyone is a blessed mystery to everyone else. Just as the perfect can look on the mystery of God, so too, they can look on the mystery of other people without being able to pierce it. This does not cause sorrow: on the contrary, happiness and bliss is found in the contemplation of the mystery of others. It is their joy to find that others, too, possess that greatest of all treasures—personality. The sacredness of that treasure ensures a flowering of love, and should it disappear, unhappiness alone would result. It is realized that it is only because others have individuality that they can enter into converse with them. God himself is the underlying reason why others are an unfathomable mystery. One person can never really succeed in exhausting the personality of another because the abyss of personality is fathomless, for it is God himself.

But although those who are in heaven are all united very intimately with one another, the unions between them are not all of the same intensity. Those who were united in love during their earthly lives, will also be united in a special way in heaven. As Hölderlin says, all divisions persist. The encounters between the perfect are therefore re-unions. Those so re-united find one another in that perfect state in which they have always longed to see one another, in that perfect bloom of life which they have always desired for one another, and in which they have always wanted to be united. They meet one another as they were meant to be, but can never be until they reach God. Just as the union of the perfect with God can never result in boredom or tiredness, so too the exchange of the perfect with one another can never give way to boredom and weariness. Those who are bound together in love converse together in such a way that satiety can never arise, for their love for one another is fed continuously by the inexhaustible love of God. The love and light which streams from one to another flows from the inexhaustible fount of God himself. The process is that described in Conrad Ferdinand Meyer's poem *Der römische Brunnen*:

> The jet rises, and falling
> Fills the marble basin
> Which, overfilled, overflows,
> Into a second beneath.
> The second becomes so full
> That bubbling, it gives
> A third its flood.
> As one, all take and give,
> And flow and rest. . . .

They live in the bliss of loving and being loved. In their blissful union with God, and their communion with one another, which is founded on God, they live, like a happy choir, in eternal youth.

Of course, until the end of the world, even they have to wait for their complete fulfilment in the resurrection of the body and the transformation of the world. But they wait with calm certitude for the moment when corporeal life, and with it the whole transformed earth, will be given them, and their joy can be full. For then joy will have reached that culmination which Christ promised his followers in his last discourse. On that occasion, he told them that he would give them a share in his joy, the joy of being loved by the Father, but that their joy would reach its perfection only in the age to come (John 15, 11). It will be attained when the blessed are given the new heaven and the new earth, and the glory of bodily life. God who lives in plenitude and beauty will transform the world, so that it flowers and glows with his own splendour. Everything man has to give up during the course of history, everything he has to abandon in death, God will return to him at that hour, filled with a new splendour, so that it may remain inalienably his forever. He will possess it forever because he will receive it continually from the hand of God. In heaven then, will be fulfilled what flashed out in Christ's miracles—in the miracle of the loaves, for example, or the stilling of the storm: namely, the world will serve man, its lord, perfectly.

Those who are so united with one another also remain in living communion with the faithful still on earth. For their love is given to all those who devote themselves to the love of God which fills their hearts. They continue to form part of the communion of those who are devoted to God, just like a multitude of brothers and sisters who have left home, but give their help in the bitter pilgrimage of life to those who have remained behind.

But in the choir of those already made perfect, one stands above all others: Mary, the mother of the Lord, about whom the Christian liturgy has recognized for centuries that even before the second coming of Christ, she has been given that corporeal perfection for which the others in heaven are still waiting. She is so ablaze with the love of God, the love of her Son, the Lord of mankind, that she encompasses the whole human race with her love, and gives them all the power of her prayer, for she is filled with longing that her Son's work may bear fruit in all men. It is a great consolation for the faithful to know that in the kingdom beyond death there glows for them a heart burning with God's own love.[1]

The brilliant choir of the blessed in the new heaven and on the new earth is set against a darker background. We must take a brief look at this. The way of life of those made perfect offers a

[1] Cf. P. Sträter, *Katholische Marienkunde*, vol. 2, 1948.

complete contrast to the life of complete imperfection—the life of hell.

In trying to explain the meaning of hell, we are again face to face with an impenetrable mystery. But if heaven is the way of life of complete union with God, then hell is the manner of life in which separation from God is final. To say what hell is, we must be able to say what God is, for only then can we really know what separation from God is, and what it means to men.

We can only fumble from a distance towards the mystery of hell. To experience hell is to experience man's self-glorification in its absolutely godless form, naked sin.

To go further than this, we must ask what sin is, and especially what mortal sin is. Generally speaking, we can say that mortal sin is self-will and self-glorification, arising either from weakness or obstinacy, leading by an act of free-will to opposition to God—that it is, therefore, absolute human autonomy in a sphere which is important as regards the establishment of the rule of God. In venial sin a man remains subject, but is slothful and negligent in his approach to God, but in mortal sin he chooses to shape and form his life independently of God. If at the moment of death a man holds fast to his godless self-glorying, he becomes obdurate in it forever, and it becomes impossible for him to turn again to God. His sin thus becomes an eternal sin, not because he constantly sins anew, but because he clings forever to his past sin. The main reason why he can never again repent is that God denies him the grace of repentance. Lacking it, he lacks the will to free himself from his godless self-glorying. He lives forever in the pleasure of absolute self-rule. It would be a false idea of the manner of life of hell, and of God himself, to think that he who is damned is in fact penitent, but that God rejects him: that he is led by thousands of years of torment to give in, but that God is too hard to give himself to him. The damned no longer wants to submit to God: it is his pleasure—we cannot call it joy—to stand apart from God's kingdom and shape his own life.

The price is a very high one. The damned live forever in everlasting imperfection and inner strife, for they can never reach that perfection in God which befits their nature. It may seem strange that separation from God should be so disastrously important for them. It is our experience that men can live apart from God without suffering much as a result. But earthly life provides no standard by which we can measure the life to come, for during his days on earth man cannot realize the unfathomable horror of separation from God through glorification of the world. He can hide from himself thoughts of the ultimate deprivation—loss of God—by recourse to the many consolations offered by the world. But such a flight into self-delusion is no longer possible for him when the glory of the things of this world is no more. He is then forced to recognize separation from God as the ultimate evil. He realizes that his whole existence is a cry for God, yet he can never again come to God. He lives in eternal hopelessness. It is difficult for us, living on earth, to form any idea of this condition, for although one hope after another collapses we continually find new ones. The condition of the damned, however, is such that, far from having this or that hope, they have lost all hope. Their lives are therefore completely meaningless to them, and yet they must bear them forever. The damned man cannot, as men can do on earth, escape torment by going to sleep or by committing suicide. Nor does he find any consolation in fellowship with the damned. The damned cannot share one another's fate, for they are not capable of love, and therefore cannot unite with one another in community.

If the process of cleansing in purgatory is connected with the material world, this is also and essentially even more true—indeed, true in a qualitatively different degree—in the case of the damned. The world to which, during his temporal life, he would not entrust himself, but which gave him the opportunity of building his life without God, impedes and fetters the man in hell. It hinders the free movement of his spirit—and, after the resurrection, will hinder that of his body, too.

Hell is therefore the state of icy loneliness, the state of absolute dumbness. And so it was described by Dante, for instance. The damned cannot live that form of life which alone is not empty: they are forbidden conversation. Hence, they live nihilistically —and yet they cannot die.

How is such a life possible? How, if he is love, can God permit it? Paradoxical as the answer may seem, there is no other we can give: God allows it because he is love. God's great concern is for human freedom; he values it so highly that, whatever the danger, he will under no circumstances prevent a man from doing what he chooses. He treats him as an adult, not like a machine. Anyone who maintains that God should preserve man from the danger of such a life as that of hell has a lower opinion of man than God himself. If his view were right, God would have to take man's greatness from him, for his greatness resides in his freedom. In respect for human independence—and hence ultimately for love—God will offer men no violence. He gives them the chance to choose what manner of life theirs shall ultimately be. He does not compel a man to accept the life of love and converse if he prefers the life of hate and loneliness, if he chooses the life of independence, and finds his eternal pleasure in it.

Of course, God also allows those who choose the life of self-glorification to realize what consequences must inevitably follow from such a choice. The love of God longs for universal salvation. But anyone who will not allow himself to be redeemed, because he will not allow himself to give himself to love, and in his pride will not bend to love, feels it to be a punishment. For him, redemption would seem to lead him against his own will to eternal destruction.

But although the life of hell is meaningless in itself, it yet plays its part in that purpose which has been the world's from the beginning: the establishment of the kingdom of God. Even among the damned, who have sought to withdraw from his rule, God is revealed as the Lord. It becomes apparent to them that although man has an uncanny knack of rebelling against God, he cannot live meaningfully apart from God. The fact that is demonstrated continually throughout the course of our lives on earth by our longing for God—the fact, namely, that separation from God means destruction and collapse, that rebellion against God is death to the world, and, on the other hand, that devotion to God is salvation for the world, is most clearly displayed in the life of the damned. Man cannot live without God, and thereby God's greatness is shown.

Terrible as hell's abyss is, it does not present an unavoidable danger to man. St. Paul, representing all men of good will, says: 'For I am sure that neither death, nor life, nor angels, nor principalities, nor powers, nor things present, nor things to come, nor might, nor height, nor depth, nor any other creature, shall be

281

able to separate us from the love of God which is in Jesus Christ our Lord' (Rom. 8, 38 f).

After this brief discussion of the abyss into which the ungodly fall, let us turn back to the perfect life led by those finally united with God. It will be given to man just as soon as he is cleansed from every trace of self-love and wholly governed by truth and love. It will attain its final form when Christ comes for the second time, to perfect his work.

The second coming of Christ will also bring into being that state of affairs towards which human history has been moving since its beginning, in the direction of which it made a great advance in the first coming. For then the goal will have been reached: God will be all in all. Then that day will dawn when night shall be no more because God, its Sun, will never set. It will be an eternal symphony of life, truth, love, joy and blessedness.

INDEX OF PROPER NAMES

SUBJECT INDEX